A Radiologic Atlas
of
ABUSE, TORTURE, TERRORISM, AND INFLICTED TRAUMA

A Radiologic Atlas
of
ABUSE, TORTURE, TERRORISM, AND INFLICTED TRAUMA

B.G. Brogdon, M.D.
Hermann Vogel, M.D.
John D. McDowell, D.D.S., M.S.

with contributions by
Richard Dirnhofer
Joel E. Lichtenstein
James M. Messmer
Gary S. Silverstein
Michael J. Thali
Peter Volk

CRC PRESS

Boca Raton   London   New York   Washington, D.C.

Library of Congress Cataloging-in-Publication Data

A radiologic atlas of abuse, torture, terrorism, and inflicted trauma / B.G. Brogdon,
Hermann Vogel, John D. McDowell; with contributions by Richard Dirnhofer ... [et al.] editors.
    p. cm.
  Includes bibliographical references and index.
  ISBN 0-8493-1533-6 (alk. paper)
  1. Forensic radiography—Atlases. 2. Wounds and injuries—Imaging—Atlases. 3.
Forensic sciences—Atlases. I. Brogdon, B.G. (Byron Gilliam) II. Vogel, H. (Hermann)
III. McDowell, John D.

RA1058.5 .R336 2003
617.1′0757—dc21   2002191168

Visit the CRC Press Web site at www.crcpress.com

Dedication

---

with enduring love to my precious Babs,
who meets all of life's challenges
with courage, grace, and unfailing good humor.

B.G.B.

to those who suffer,
to those who report,
to those who help.

H.V.

to my wife, Linda,
for her love, patience, and encouragement;
to my children, Michael, Joshua, Megan, and Marin,
for their understanding and support;
to my students, who make every day a new experience.

J.D. McD.

Preface

This book is about aggression, in its many forms, by people against the persons of others, ranging from the tiniest, most helpless infant to entire population groups. Man is the most indiscriminate animal in aggressive behavior, and the most innovative, his armamentarium ranging from the primitive fist to the most sophisticated instruments of destruction.

The results of aggression may be hideously obvious or may be entirely concealed from casual inspection, to be revealed only by exploration of the hidden recesses of the mind by psychiatric evaluation, or by exploration of the inner recesses of the body by the radiologic method.

The radiologic images documenting aggression may be suboptimal, often being acquired by inexpert persons under difficult, sometimes even surreptitious, conditions. Hence, we regret that some of the illustrations we present are not better, but we do not apologize for them. Most of the images presented are from the files of the editors, but these have been supplemented by the generosity of colleagues, both published and unpublished, who have shared their material with us and, consequently, with our readers. Whenever possible we have properly and gratefully acknowledged these contributions. Unfortunately, the origin of some of our images are lost to record and memory. For these oversights we do apologize while again expressing our gratitude.

Even when technically perfect, these pictures are not pretty. Our purpose here is not to celebrate the effects of aggression. Rather, it is our fondest hope that an atlas such as this will be impossible to accumulate in later decades of this century we now begin. If our images are seen as disturbing, repulsive, and vituperative against aggression in any form, then our efforts will have been amply rewarded. However, to eschew aggression is not to embrace pacifism. Indeed, the fight against aggression, whether individual or collective, is a worthy and noble cause for all.

B.G.B.

Acknowledgments

Already we have thanked in the Preface the generous donations of material from colleagues and have acknowledged them appropriately either in captions or on the Contributors page. We will again apologize to those donors no longer identifiable because of faulty records or, more often, faulty memory.

There are many others whose contributions are less tangible but no less significant. These are colleagues who have sparked, encouraged, and nurtured my interests in the field of forensic sciences. So many members of the American Academy of Forensic Sciences have strongly influenced and forwarded my efforts in this field that I dare not try to name them for fear of embarrassing omission. However, among those unsung supporters I must make an exception to mention John McDowell, one of my co-editors in this project. John has been a warm friend as well as a supportive colleague.

My other co-author, Hermann Vogel, and I met through our books on a common interest — the radiology of forensic problems, aggression, and violence. He has been delightful to work with and shares with all of us his exceptional, indeed unequalled, collection of radiologic material in this field.

We are enormously indebted to Tollef Tollefson, our departmental photographer, who has created the major portion of this picture book from an assortment of images in varied format, many of them suboptional in the original form.

Rose Jones has typed and retyped the manuscript from all contributors, and Michele Lockley, Vanessa Brown, Gerri Vance, and Thomie Brown have all pitched in when needed. I am thankful for their essential contribution.

Although I am in emeritus status, my department chairman, Dr. Steven K. Teplick, makes available office space and other facilities and personnel necessary to support my continued scholarly endeavors. Otherwise, an undertaking such as this would be impossible.

Lastly I am indebted to CRC Press for making this idea a reality. I particularly appreciate the confidence and support of Becky McEldowney, senior editor, and the forbearance and expertise of Sara Kreisman, manager, editorial project development.

B.G.B.

In the first place, I thank all those who gave me their material and asked me not to mention their names. They did this because they were afraid of repercussions and sanctions. Since my material was collected during some 20 years and I received images, comments, and support from many colleagues, a selection is unavoidable. I apologize to those who contributed but who are not mentioned.

I thank, in Mexico, Dr. Gonzales-Morantes, head of the x-ray department, and Dr. Pineiro, the former dean of the medical faculty, as well as president, of the Universidad Autonoma de Nuevo Leon (UANL) in Monterrey; in Peru, Dr. Flores, Dr. Villanueva-Meyer (former president of Peruvian Radiological Society), Dr. Hidalgo, and Professor Ballon-Medina; in Columbia, Dr. Varon, Dr. Rotlewickz, Dr. Rivera, Dr. Reina, Dr. Prado, Dr. Diazgranados, Dr. Perez, and especially Dr. Borrero; in Thailand, Dr. Perkanan and Professor Notasut; in China, Professor Bai Run-Xian (chief of radiology in the Tianjin Cancer Hospital), Professor Sun, Dr. Liu Pei-Fan, Dr. Xi-Xhan Hao, and Wand Young-Uman; in South Africa, Dr. Tobias (Hilbroh Hospital in Johannesburg), Professor Altini, Professor Evans, Professor Lownie, Dr. Classens, and Dr. Toysz (School of Dentistry of the University of Witwatersrand); in Zimbabwe, Professor Levy and Mrs. Kaupny in the Perirenatwa Hospital, Harare; in Tansania, Dr. Ndosi and Dr. Llweno of the Muhimbili Hospital, Dar es Salaam; in Egypt, Dr. Dekan, Professor Rizh, Professor Hanssanein, Dr. Ramadan, and Dr. Mahmoud El Sheikh, faculty of medicine in Alexandria; in Algiers, Dr. Yaher (vice president of the Algiers Society of Radiology), Professor Hatani, and Professor Hamad.

In Germany, I thank the German diplomatic service for helping me, especially my former classmate, Herr Starnitzky, Dr. Hinrichsen, Herr BoudréëGröger, former German ambassador to Vietnam, and Herr Vollbrecht from the Goethe Institute. I am also grateful to my academic teacher, Professor Büchelerand, my colleagues, Dr. von Wechmar, Dr. Pleser, and Dr. Brinckmann. For their support, I would also like to thank Mr. Lohmann, Mr. Becker, Dr. Mellmann, and Professor Bohme, medical director of the General Hospital Hamburg, Ochsenzoll; Mrs. Khan and Mrs. Weber, my secretaries; and my colleague, Dr. Bartelt, of St. Georg Hospital in Hamburg, who undertook the difficult task of correcting my English manuscript and translating difficult passages. I am obliged and thankful to Amnesty International, which took charge of me during my travels and created an exhibition that has been shown to the nonmedical public in Paris, Vienna, Berlin, Hamburg, and 15 other places in cooperation with Mr. Henning, director of the German Röetgenmuseum, and his co-worker, Mr. Bush. I thank them all for their interest and support.

In Hamburg, I thank Professor Püschel, director of the Institute of Forensic Medicine of the University of Hamburg, and Dr. Hayek of the Children Hospital, Wilhelmstift. I also acknowledge Dr. Niestroj and Dr. Oswald of General Hospital St. George, Dr. Szieslack of General Hospital Barmbeck, and Professor Heller of University Kiel for their cooperation and contributions.

I got insights in torture by visiting the Rehabilitation Center for Torture Victims (RCT or AVRE) in several countries. I admire and thank my colleagues and their collaborators for their contributions, especially Dr. Genefke and Dr. Rasmussen from RCT in Copenhagen; Dr. Jaffe from AVRE in Paris; Dr. Veli Lök from Izmir, Turkey; Dr. Hinshilwood from London; Professor Jakobsson from Stockholm; and Dr. Graesner from Berlin. This also holds true for Dr. Quincke and Dr. Mason from the World Health Organization in Geneva.

The radiology of victims of the war in former Yugoslavia was presented to me in Zagreb by Professor Montani, Professor Simunic, Dr. Skrbic, Dr. Fattorini, Dr. Cop, and Dr. Bumci; in Belgrad, Professor Lisanin, Professor Kamenica, Dr. Nikolic, Dr. Pervulou, Dr. Lucac Stevan, Dr. Elakovic, Professor Tadic, Dr. Roganovic, and Dr. Slobodan; the radiology of poison gas effects was analyzed by my co-workers and I in Recklinghausen, Germany, with Professor Firusian and with Dr. Sohrabpour, Teheran, Iran. I am thankful and obliged to each of them.

The radiology of terrorism was shown to me in Northern Ireland by Dr. Laird, Dr. Brown, Mr. Hood, M.D., Dr. Lavery, Dr. McKienstry, and Dr. Thompson, and, in Israel, by Dr. Donchin and Professor Barsiv, Hadassah University Hospital, Jerusalem. I admire their work and thank them.

In France, Professor Fauré and Professor Menantheau allowed me to use their cases; Dr. Hasebrouqc helped me greatly; and Professor Cabanis, secretary of the Societé d' Imagerie Médico-Légale, encouraged me to continue. Lots of thanks to them.

In general, the figures of the book come from radiographs and slides that I photographed all over the world. These photographs were evaluated by my colleagues and myself in Hamburg, frequently in the form of medical dissertations, especially those made by Dr. Bergunde, Dr. Forquignon, Dr. Hartmann, Dr. Hushahn, Dr. Jung, Dr. Kintzel, Dr. Okkovat, Dr. Olrogge, and Dr. Lotz. I thank them for contributing.

H.V.

I acknowledge my mentors during my residency and fellowship at the University of Texas Health Sciences Center, Dr. Ole Langland and Bob Langlais, for assisting me with cases during my early career in oral and maxillofacial radiology. I also acknowledge the instruction and case experience that came through the exceptional teaching of Dr. Vincent J.M. Di Maio at the Bexar County (Texas) Medical Examiner's Office. Special appreciation goes to my colleagues at the University of Colorado Health Sciences Center, Dr. Eric Miller (director, general practice residency) and Dr. Mike Savage (chair, oral and maxillofacial surgery) for their ongoing assistance with our many domestic violence cases.

J.D. McD.

Editors

Gil Brogdon, M.D., grew up on an Arkansas farm unsullied by electric lights or indoor plumbing. He attended the state university, earning two baccalaureate degrees. In 1952, he received his M.D. from the University of Arkansas School of Medicine where he was later named a Distinguished Alumnus. His radiological training, which began in Arkansas, was completed at the Bowman-Gray College of Medicine from where he later received a Distinguished Achievement Award. He was certified by the American Board of Radiology in 1956.

After serving as a Regular Officer in the U.S. Air Force, Dr. Brogdon began a 43-year academic career, which has included appointment as radiologist-in-charge of diagnostic radiology at Johns Hopkins and as professor and chairman of the departments of radiology at the University of New Mexico and the University of South Alabama.

Dr. Brogdon is past president and life member of the Southern Radiological Conference, past president and gold medalist of both the Association of University Radiologists and the American College of Radiology.

He also has been awarded the Gold Medal of the American Roentgen Ray Society, the Schinz Medal of the Swiss Society of Medical Radiology, the Medal of Honor of Leopold-Franzens University of Innsbruck, the Medal of the International Skeletal Society, and the Austrian Cross of Honor for Science and Art, First Class.

Dr. Brogdon's interest and experience in forensic radiology spans almost four decades. He has received the Hunt Award and the Distinguished Fellow Award and Medal from the American Academy of Forensic Sciences. He serves on the editorial board of the *Journal of Forensic Sciences* and is a member of the board of trustees of the Forensic Sciences Foundation.

Dr. Brogdon is the author or co-author of 280 publications including the 1998 classic, *Forensic Radiology*, published by CRC Press.

Hermann Vogel, M.D., born July 7, 1942, grew up in Hamburg, Germany. As a student, he excelled in natural sciences as well as modern and classical languages. He went on to the medical school at the University of Hamburg, Germany, and received a scholarship from the French government to Montpellier, the second oldest medical school in Europe. He also studied law in Hamburg and Heidelberg. After receiving his degree in medicine, he served in the German Navy and then worked in Sweden in the department of anesthesia and dialysis, General Hospital of Vanersborg. He started his university career in the radiological clinic of the University of Hamburg, where

in 1972 he qualified as a specialist and became Privat Dozent (*habilitation and venia legendi*). In 1973, he became vice director of the radiological clinic of the University of Hamburg, and in 1978, professor of the faculty of medicine. In the same year he also became head of the x-ray department of Ochsenzoll Hospital, Hamburg, one of the academic and teaching hospitals of the University of Hamburg. In 1998, he was appointed the head of the Albers-Schönberg-Institut, the x-ray department of St. Georg Hospital, Hamburg, also one of the academic and teaching hospitals of the University of Hamburg, famous for its contributions to the development of radiology and for the pioneers of x-ray applications.

In 1982, he was visiting professor at the UANL, Monterey, Mexico, where he started to collect x-ray pathology typical for developing countries, which led to his works on x-ray diagnostics of violence (war, torture, crime). Each year, he visits one to three third world countries in search of typical and extraordinary pathology.

Dr. Vogel has published more than 250 articles in German, as well as English, French, Spanish, Japanese, and Arabic. He has authored 18 books and 1 leaflet collection. By invitation he has given lectures and postgraduate courses in more than 30 countries such as Japan, Vietnam, Peru, Columbia, Serbia, and Bosnia. His scientific interest is in radiation protection, postoperative radiology, radiology of tropical diseases, and x-ray diagnostics of violence. He is a member of the working group for the new x-ray legislation in Germany, vice-chairman of the working group for the radiation protection at the NAR/DIN in Germany, and a member of the directory of the Societe Medico-Legale d'Imagerie in Paris. He has been invited as an expert to the hearings of the European Union and the German authorities. Furthermore, he coordinates research with physicists from DESY (the German electron synchrotron) and mineralogists from the University of Hamburg, investigating pearls and precious stones and projects for diminishing the radiation exposure, both of which have led to patents and were honored with prizes. His work has resulted in cooperation with Amnesty International. As a member of different human rights groups, he was in Chad, Africa, to investigate the crimes of the former government. In addition, an exhibition of his collection of x-rays, called, "X-ray Diagnostic of Violence" for the nonmedical public was created, which was shown in more than 20 places such as Paris, Berlin, Amsterdam, and Vienna.

Dr. Vogel is married to a radiologist and has four children.

John D. McDowell, D.D.S., M.S., is an associate professor in the department of diagnostic and biological sciences at the University of Colorado School of Dentistry. He is a graduate of Brigham Young University, Provo, UT, earning a B.S. in zoology in 1970. He received his D.D.S. in 1974 from Loyola University of Chicago School of Dentistry. Dr. McDowell has completed a residency in diagnostic sciences and a fellowship in geriatric dentistry at the University of Texas Health Sciences Center in San Antonio. He has also received a masters degree from the Graduate School of Biomedical Sciences from the University of Texas where his thesis compared the radiographic features of facial fractures in battered women and female victims of motor vehicle accidents.

Dr. McDowell presently serves as the director of oral medicine and forensic sciences and chairman, division of oral diagnosis, medicine and radiology. He serves as chairman of the University of Colorado Health Sciences Center Faculty Assembly (Schools of Medicine, Dentistry, Nursing, Pharmacy, and the Graduate School) and serves as secretary of the system-wide University of Colorado Faculty Council. He has been selected one of the initial participants in the Emerging Leaders program for the University of Colorado.

He has received multiple awards recognizing his teaching skills. He has been named the University of Colorado School of Dentistry Professor of the Year and has received the Chancellor's Award for Teaching Excellence. Additionally, he is a four-time recipient of the Outstanding Didactic Instructor award from the School of Dentistry.

Dr. McDowell is a board-certified forensic odontologist serving as a consultant to various forensic organizations. He is a trustee of the Forensic Sciences Foundation and the past president of both the American Academy of Forensic Sciences and the American Society of Forensic Odontology. He additionally serves on the board of directors and as co-chairman of the Sciences and Math Education Committee and former co-chairman of the Ethics Committee for the Council of Scientific Societies Presidents, an organization representing over 1.5 million American scientists.

In addition to his busy forensic consulting practice, Dr. McDowell has an oral medicine practice at the University of Colorado with primary emphasis on oral manifestations of systemic disease and the infections and tumors associated with HIV/AIDS. He is the dental representative for the Mountain/Plains AIDS Education and Training Center in Denver, and a former dental representative to the National AIDS ETC in Washington, DC.

He served 2 years on active duty for the U.S. Army. He is a colonel in the U.S. Army Reserves having served twice as commander of dental units. He presently serves as the Command Dental Surgeon for the 96th Regional Support Command.

Dr. McDowell has authored multiple publications in the professional literature describing the diagnosis and treatment of the domestic violence victim. He is a reviewer for the *Journal of the American Dental Association* and is a member of the editorial board of the *American Journal of Forensic Medicine and Pathology.*

Contributors

B.G. Brogdon, M.D.
University Distinguished Professor Emeritus of Radiology
University of South Alabama College of Medicine
Mobile, Alabama

Richard Dirnhofer, M.D.
Professor and Director
Institute of Forensic Medicine
University of Berne
Berne, Switzerland

Joel E. Lichtenstein, M.D.
Professor and Director, Gastrointestinal Radiology
University of Washington School of Medicine
Seattle, Washington

John D. McDowell, D.D.S., M.S.
Chair, Oral Diagnosis, Oral Medicine and Oral Radiology
Director, Oral Medicine and Forensic Sciences
University of Colorado School of Dentistry
Denver, Colorado

James M. Messmer, M.D., M.Ed.
Professor of Radiology, Virginia Commonwealth
  University
Consultant, Chief Medical Examiner's Office
Richmond, Virginia

Gary S. Silverstein, M.D.
Formerly Chief Forensic Radiologist
Suffolk County, New York
Radiology Affiliates of Central New Jersey
Upper Holland, Pennsylvania

Michael J. Thali, M.D.
Attending Physician and Research Fellow
Institute for Forensic Medicine
University of Berne
Berne, Switzerland

Hermann Vogel, M.D.
Professor and Chairman
Department of Diagnostic Radiology
Albers-Schoenberg Institute
St. Georg Hospital
Hamburg, Germany

Peter Volk, M.D.
Professor and Director
Institute of Diagnostic Radiology
University of Berne
Berne, Switzerland

Table of Contents

Section I

Abuse

Abuse may be defined as an improper action leading to physical injury. But abuse perhaps rests not as much on definition as on conceptualization. The concept of abuse is inextricably entangled in history, religion, and culture. Therefore, it is variable across the expanse of time, geography, and social evolution.

From biblical times through the Industrial Revolution the power of the parent, or his surrogate, was absolute and unquestioned. The child could be abandoned, enslaved, mutilated, worked to death, or cut in half. The notion of abuse or cruelty to children was slow aborning, and its prevention tied to regulations pertaining to more valuable livestock. The annual meetings of the Mobile [Alabama] Society for the Prevention of Cruelty to Animals and Children were regularly reported in the local newspaper, *The Mobile Register*. A 1902 article lauds the passing of the horse-drawn streetcar, "one of the most prolific sources of cruel treatment of horse and mule." The plight of children was not mentioned.

Even now there is no universal agreement upon what constitutes abuse of a child. Unfortunately, extreme examples are tolerated in some parts of our world. Genital mutilation, purdah, or deformation of body parts is considered unacceptably cruel in some societies, but desirable or obligatory in other cultures or religions.

Abuse of spouses or intimate partners is a modern concept of limited range. Such partners still may be stoned or burned to death in some countries. In relatively modern times, a husband legally could beat his wife in Alabama—as long as he used a rod no thicker than his thumb.

The widespread tradition of veneration of elders now is eroded by a spate of granny-bashing.

In the United States, civil or political abuse, excessive force, brutality, or cruel and unusual punishment is constitutionally prohibited. In other jurisdictions, it may be considered a justifiable procedure for apprehension, interrogation, incarceration, punishment, or ensuring civil obedience.

This section will illustrate the radiologic manifestations of actions generally accepted as abusive. It must be recognized that many types of abuse are not revealed by the radiologic method.

B.G.B.

1 Child Abuse

B.G. Brogdon, M.D. and Hermann Vogel, M.D.

HISTORICAL PERSPECTIVE

Arguably, radiology's largest contribution to the forensic sciences is its role in the public awakening to, and recognition of, intentional physical abuse of infants and children by those responsible for their protection and care. It is a sad commentary on earlier attitudes concerning children that this breakthrough came half a century after all other applications of radiology to forensics had been predicted or accomplished.

John Caffey, M.D. (Figure 1.1), a pediatrician turned self-taught radiologist at Babies Hospital of New York City, reported in 1946[1] the rather puzzling association of peculiar skeletal lesions with subdural hematoma in infants and children with no history of trauma (Figure 1.2). He described metaphyseal fragmentation (Figure 1.3), *involucrum* formation (Figure 1.4), and multiple fractures in different stages of healing (Figure 1.5). Later, Caffey[2] described traumatic bowing of metaphyses (Figure 1.6), metaphyseal cupping (Figure 1.7), and *ectopic* ossification centers (Figure 1.8). Caffy and colleagues in other venues came to appreciate the contribution of history, physical examination, laboratory tests, and biopsy to understanding the radiologic findings. They then evolved the final criterion: injury inappropriate to the history, circumstance, age, or stage of development of the involved child.[3–7]

SKELETAL INJURIES

Although head trauma is the leading cause of death and physical child abuse,[8] it is injury to the skeleton that most often brings the abused child to medical and civic attention.

METAPHYSEAL INJURY

The metaphyseal injury of child abuse is virtually pathognomonic. It is a transverse fracture across the extreme end of the metaphysis, separating a disc of bone from the primary spongiosa of the metaphysis and the zone of provisional calcification of the physis or growth plate. Variation in position and projection may cause the fracture to appear as a straight line (Figure 1.8B) rarely, more frequently as the well-known *corner* fracture (Figures 1.3 and 1.9), sometimes as the so-called *bucket handle* fracture (Figure 1.10),

FIGURE 1.1 John Caffey, M.D., the father of pediatric radiology and first to describe the radiologic manifestations of child abuse. (From the Archives of the American College of Radiology. With permission.)

and occasionally, as an ellipse (Figure 1.11). *Bowing* may result from associated vascular injury and interference with growth[9] or from a torus (greenstick) fracture of the metaphysis (Figure 1.7).

PERIOSTEAL NEW BONE

The loosely attached periosteum of infants and children is easily separated by twisting and pulling with subsequent subperiosteal bleeding. The resultant hematoma eventually calcifies (Figures 1.4 and 1.12). A concomitant fracture is not necessary.

DIAPHYSEAL FRACTURES

Oblique or spiral long bone fractures are found in only 5 to 15% of suspected child abuse,[10,11] but are highly suggestive of the diagnosis, especially if the child is nonambulatory (Figure 1.13). Transverse diaphyseal fractures have a high specificity for abuse in the nonambulatory child and are a fairly common finding (Figure 1.14). Spiral fractures usually are due to twisting and torsion forces. Transverse fractures are more likely due to grabbing and swinging forces that snap the bone cleanly.

DISLOCATION

Dislocation of joints and epiphyseal separation and dislocation are rare in child abuse and usually associated with massive trauma. Subluxation of the hip can result from the collection of blood, sterile effusion, or pus within the joint capsule (Figure 1.15).

RIB FRACTURES

Although probably more common in child abuse than long bone fractures,[11] rib fractures may easily be missed on radiographs, especially when fresh (Figure 1.16). Because they can not be immobilized, rib fractures usually heal with abundant callus and become quite obvious as time lapses (Figure 1.17). This allows ballpark aging of rib fractures (Figure 1.18). Nuclear radiology studies (bone scans) are highly sensitive to fractures.[12,13] Unfortunately, bone scans require considerably more time than radiography and are not always immediately available (Figure 1.19). Posterior rib fractures (Figure 1.20) are thought to be caused by grasping the child with an anterior compression of the chest and are particularly suggestive of child abuse. Force applied from front to back may cause lateral rib fractures (Figure 1.21).

HANDS AND FEET

Rarely, fractures of the distal phalanges are caused by a closing door; otherwise, fractures in the hands and feet are highly suspicious of abuse (Figure 1.8C).

SCAPULA

Acromial fractures are highly suggestive of abuse (Figure 1.22) but must not be confused with an ununited apophysis. Other scapular fractures are even more rare.

THE SPINE

Vertebral fractures or subluxations are extremely rare. Unless associated with massive and multiple trauma, possible abuse should be investigated (Figure 1.23).

FACIAL AND MANDIBULAR FRACTURES

The facial bones of a child are less prominent and more protected by soft tissue, especially fat, than those of adults.

Fractures from any cause are rarely described. However, facial battering is fairly common in abused children; it may be that fractures remain undetected. The rapid biomechanical changes occurring in the mandible during the first few years of life may make it particularly susceptible to injury (Figure 1.24).[14] Battered children with mandibular-facial injuries usually will have other incriminating findings.

SKULL FRACTURES

Simple linear skull fractures can occur from accidental trauma and may not have associated clinical (neurological) findings. However, even simple fractures should raise suspicion if there are other skeletal, visceral, or cutaneous lesions (burns, bruises) or neurological findings (Figure 1.25). Compound or depressed skull fractures significantly raise the level of suspicion (Figures 1.26 to 1.28).

INTRACRANIAL INJURIES

Intracranial injury, with or without skull fracture, frequently is associated with inflicted trauma. Subdural hemorrhage or hematoma (Figures 1.2 and 1.29), subarachnoid hemorrhage, intracerebral and intracerebellar hemorrhage, massive edema (brain swelling), or combinations can be found (Figures 1.30 to 1.33). Very careful attention must be paid to the history of the causative incident and the presence of other findings. Early referral of nonfatal cases for computed tomography (CT) or magnetic resonance imaging (MRI) is recommended.

SHAKEN BABY SYNDROME

In shaken baby syndrome intracranial bleeding and brain edema of massive proportions may cause spreading of cranial sutures without associated fracture or external bruising (Figures 1.34 and 1.35). However, the head may encounter direct injury in the course of a shaking episode.

VISCERAL TRAUMA

Blows to the abdomen of infants and children can cause severe injury to abdominal organs, particularly the duodenum (Figures 1.36 and 1.37). The liver, pancreas, and biliary tract (Figures 1.38 to 1.40) may be injured as they are compressed against the spine. Traumatic perforation of the bowel is less common (Figure 1.41). Foreign bodies may be maliciously introduced into the gastrointestinal (GI) tract or respiratory tract with harmful intent (Figure 1.42).[15] The spleen and urinary tract usually are spared.

MULTIPLE INJURIES AND SEQUENTIAL INJURIES

Multiple fractures, fractures in various stages of healing, or combination injuries absent of a consistent history of appropriate trauma are highly specific for child abuse (Figures 1.43 and 1.44).[2,10]

PRENATAL ABUSE

Transplacental transmission of preventable and treatable disease can be considered as prenatal abuse. Examples would include congenital syphilis (Figure 1.45) and rubella (German measles) (Figure 1.46). A similar consideration could apply to fetal blighting by maternal indulgence in alcohol or drugs (Figure 1.47).

ABUSE RELATED TO RELIGION AND CULTURE

An example of this type of abuse would be the female Bedouin from the Negev Desert who lives in poverty in a society where she must cover her whole body. She therefore becomes vitamin D deficient. Since she is low in the hierarchy she is fed a deficient diet of leftovers. This results in rickets in both mother and child (Figure 1.48). The same findings are seen in women who live in Purdah in India.

Purposeful deformity of an infant was seen in the Imperial Chinese tradition of the bound foot in upper class females. The forefoot was forcibly bent against the heel with deformity of the metatarsals and antrophy of the toes. This produced the fashionable *lotus foot* much admired as a thing of beauty as well as a symbol of wealth (Figure 1.49).

PITFALLS IN THE DIAGNOSIS OF CHILD ABUSE

PHYSIOLOGIC PERIOSTEAL CALCIFICATION OF THE NEWBORN

A single thin line of periosteal calcification can exist normally in healthy infants up to 4 months of age. It is bilateral, symmetrical, and unilamellar. It is not diagnostic of child abuse (Figure 1.50).

COMMON INJURIES

Certain fractures are relatively common at certain ages and levels of activities. The common fracture of childbirth is that of the clavicle (Figure 1.51) and is not suggestive of abuse. It is worthwhile to point out that ribs of normal newborns are virtually never fractured during parturition. As already shown, intrapartum manipulation can cause traumatic lesions of the skeleton.

The *toddler fracture* is well known as a common result of the somewhat uncoordinated, often pigeon-toed, effort of locomotion by children in this age group (Figure 1.52). It is not an indication of abuse. However, in the nonambulatory child (Figure 1.13b) it waves a red flag of warning.

Similarly, the supracondylar fracture of the humerus in slightly older and more active children is the most common fracture of falls on the outstretched arm (Figure 1.53).

CONFUSING BONE LESIONS OF NONTRAUMATIC ORIGIN

A number of disease processes may simulate or resemble to some extent the bony injuries due to intentional trauma.[17,18] They will be familiar to most physicians specializing in the diseases of children but may be confusing to others. Osteogenesis imperfecta is the darling of defense attorneys in cases of child abuse (Figure 1.54). Other entities would include:

1. Congenital syphilis (Figure 1.45)
2. Ricketic conditions (Figure 1.55)
3. Caffey's disease (Figure 1.56)
4. Leukemia (Figure 1.57)
5. Menkes' syndrome (kinky hair disease) (Figure 1.58)
6. Vitamin A intoxication (Figure 1.59)
7. Scurvy (Figure 1.60)
8. Osteomyelitis (Figure 1.61)
9. Congenital indifference to pain (very rare) (Figure 1.62)
10. Dilantin® therapy (Figure 1.63)*
11. Normal variants (Figure 1.64)

INTRAPARTUM TRAUMA

Intrapartum trauma may be confused with abuse if not recognized early. Fractures of the extremities during childbirth have been shown. Ping-pong ball fractures of the skull were fairly common in the days of forceps deliveries, but are rarely seen now (Figure 1.65). Intrapartum version of fetal position may cause skeletal injuries (Figure 1.66).

---

* Parke-Davis, 201 Tabor Road, Morris Plains, New Jersey, 07950.

REFERENCES

1. Caffey, J., Multiple fractures in long bones of children suffering from chronic subdural hematoma, *Am. J. Roentgenol.*, 56, 163, 1946.
2. Caffey, J., Some traumatic lesions in growing bones other than fractures and dislocations clinical and radiological features, The MacKenzie Davidson Memorial Lecture, *Br. J. Radiol.*, 30, 225, 1957.
3. Caffey, J., Significance of the history in the diagnosis of traumatic injury to children, Howland Aware Address, *J. Pediatr.*, 68, 1008, 1965.
4. Silverman, F.N., The roentgen manifestations of skeletal trauma, *Am. J. Roentgenol.*, 69, 413, 1953.
5. Kempe, C.H., Silverman, F.N., Steele, B.F., Droegemueller, W., and Silver, H.K., The battered child syndrome, *JAMA*, 181, 105, 1962.
6. Kempe, C.H., Pediatric implications of the battered baby syndrome, Windermere Lecture, *Arch. Dis. Child.*, 46, 28, 1971.
7. Elmer, E., *Children in Jeopardy*, University of Pittsburgh Press, Pittsburgh, 1967.
8. Reece, R.M., *Child Abuse: Medical Diagnosis and Management*, Lea & Febiger, Philadelphia, 1994, chap. 1.
9. Kleinman, P.K., *Diagnostic Imaging of Child Abuse*, William & Wilkins, Baltimore, 1987, chap. 2.
10. Hilton, S.V.W., Differentiating the accidentally injured from the physically abused child, in *Practical Pediatric Radiology*, Hilton, S.V.W. and Edwards, D.K., III, Eds., W.B. Saunders, Philadelphia, 1994, chap. 14.
11. Kleinman, P.K., Marler, S.C., Jr., Richmond, J.M., and Blackbourne, B.D., Inflicted skeletal injury: a postmortem radiologic-histopathologic study in 31 infants, *Am. J. Roentgenol.*, 165, 647, 1995.
12. Sty, J.R. and Starsbuk, R.J., The role of bone scintigraphy in the evaluation of the suspected abused child, *Radiology*, 146, 369, 1983.
13. Sty, J.R., Radiological Imaging Applications in Forensic Medicine, workshop at the Annual Meeting of the American Academy of Forensic Science, New Orleans, Feb. 14, 1994.
14. Kroman, A.M., Symes, S.A., Smith, O'B.C., Love, J.C., Mincer, H.N., and Lemmon, J.W., The hidden truth: mandibular condyle fractures in child abuse, in *Proc. Am. Acad. Forensic Sci.*, Colorado Springs, CO, 2002, 250.
15. Nolte, K.B., Esophageal foreign bodies in child abuse, *Am. J. Forensic Med. Path.*, 14, 323, 1993.
16. Shopfner, C.F., Periosteal bone growth in normal infants: a preliminary report, *Am. J. Roentgenol.*, 97, 154, 1966.
17. Brill, P.W. and Winchester, P., Differential diagnosis of child abuse, in *Diagnostic Imaging in Child Abuse*, Kleinman, P. K., Ed., William & Wilkins, Baltimore, 1987, chap. 11.
18. Brogdon, B.G., *Forensic Radiology*, CRC Press, Boca Raton, FL, 1998, chap. 15.
19. Wesenberg, R.L., Gwinn, J.L., and Barnes, G.R., Radiologic findings in kinky-hair syndrome, *Radiology*, 92, 500, 1069.
20. Caffey, J. and Madell, S.H., Ossisification of the pubic bones at birth, *Radiology*, 67, 436, 1956.

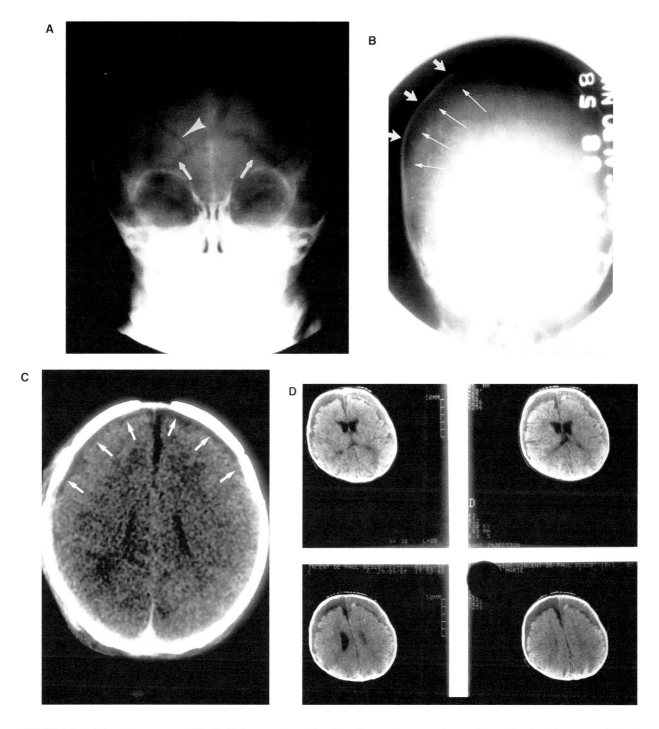

FIGURE 1.2 Subdural hematoma. **(A)** Skull fracture (arrowhead) and spread sutures (arrows) associated with acute subdural hematoma. **(B)** Angiographic demonstration of acute subdural hematoma as the dark space between the bony calvaria and the vascularized cerebral cortex (arrows). **(C)** Subdural hematoma around frontal lobe (arrows) on unenhanced CT. **(D)** Bilateral subdural hematoma extending into the interhemispheric space (unenhanced CT).

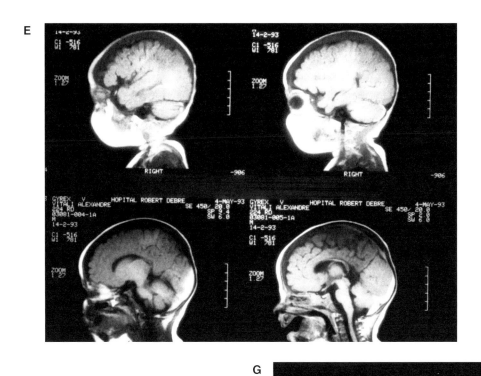

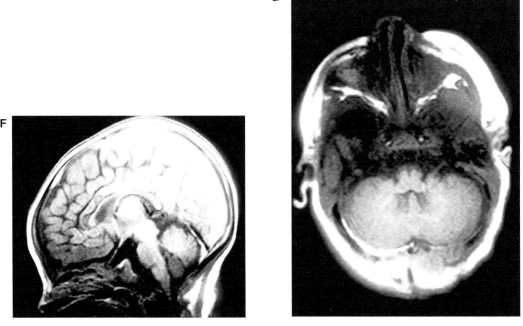

FIGURE 1.2 (Continued) Subdural hematoma. **(E)** Low signal subdural hematoma separating cerebrum from calvaria (MRI). **(F** and **G)** Subdural blood around the cerebellum and temporal, frontal, and occipital lobes (MRI).

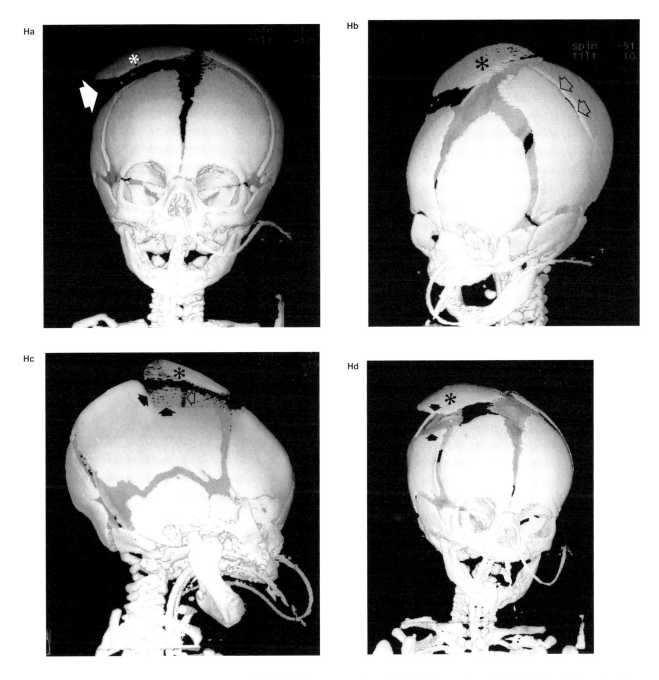

FIGURE 1.2 (Continued) Subdural hematoma. **(Ha-Hd)** 3-0 reconstruction of skull with massive subdural raising right parietal flap (asterisk), transverse right parietal fracture (arrow), vertical left parietal fracture (open arrows), and spread sutures.

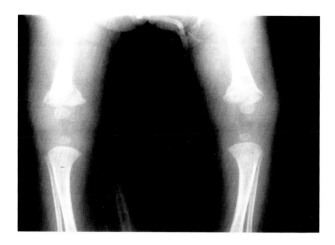

FIGURE 1.3 Metaphyseal fragmentation presenting as bilateral corner fractures.

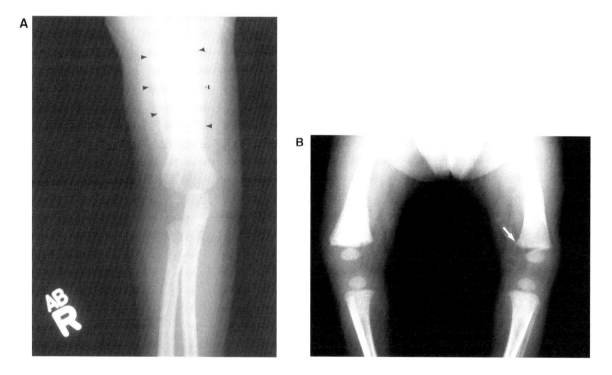

FIGURE 1.4 **(A)** Calcified subperiosteal hematoma surrounding the humeral shaft. Caffey called this involucrum. **(B)** Small corner fracture of left (arrow), involucrum on right.

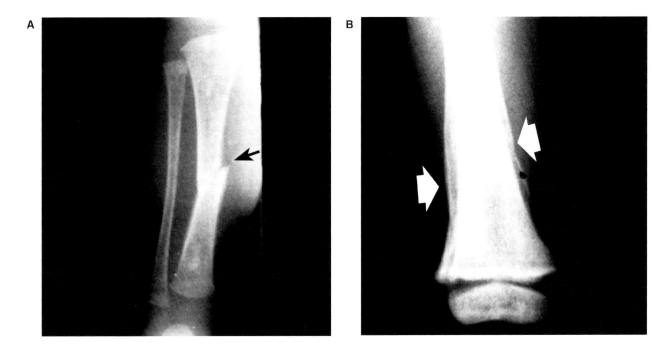

FIGURE 1.5 (A) Fresh transverse diaphyseal fracture of tibia (arrow). (B) Old periosteal new bone around distal femur from earlier trauma (arrows).

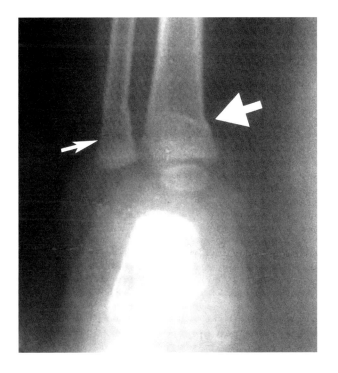

FIGURE 1.6 Example of what Caffey called traumatic bowing, greenstick fractures of the metaphyses (arrows).

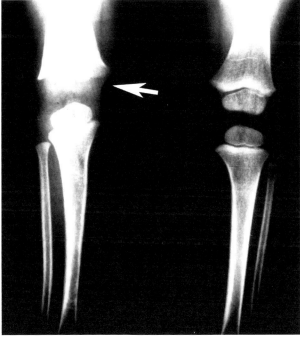

FIGURE 1.7 Metaphyseal cupping due to traumatic disturbance of the growth plate.

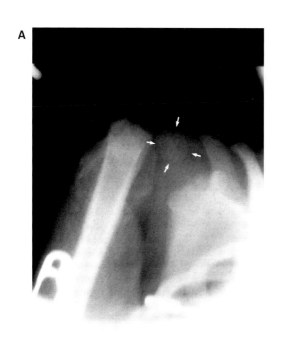

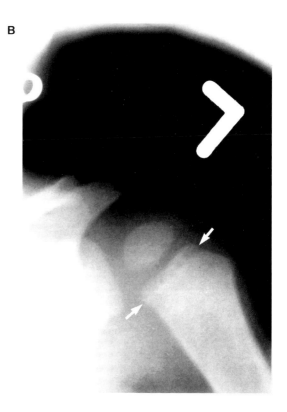

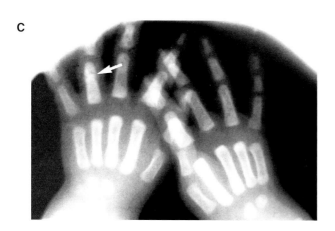

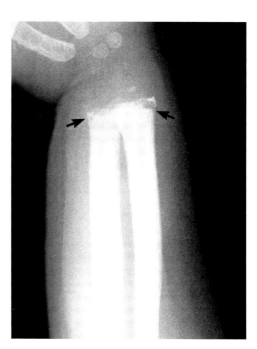

FIGURE 1.8 (**A**) Epiphyseal separation and dislocation at the proximal right humerus, Caffey's "ectopic" ossification centers. (**B**) Same child had transverse fracture of left proximal humeral metaphysis and (**C**) healing fracture of a proximal phalanx.

FIGURE 1.9 Typical corner fractures.

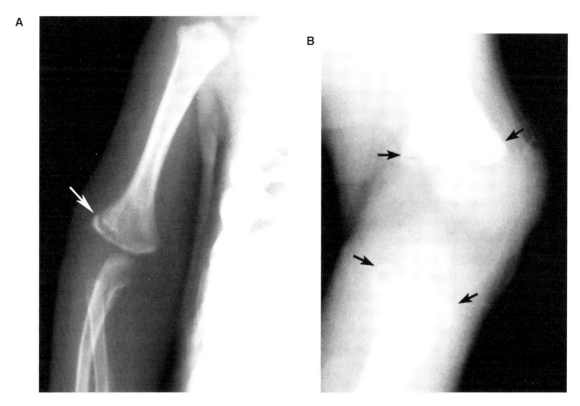

FIGURE 1.10 **(A and B)** Typical bucket-handle metaphyseal fractures of the distal humeri. **(B)** Corner fractures of the proximal tibia.

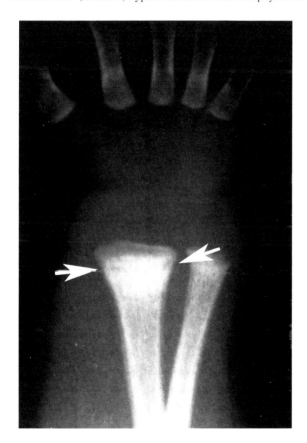

FIGURE 1.11 Disc-like or elliptical appearance of metaphyseal fracture (arrows).

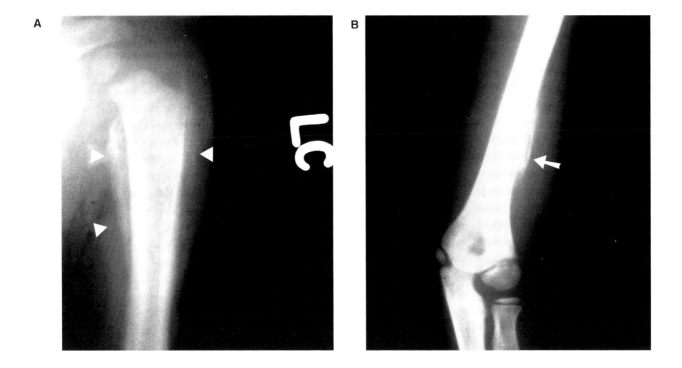

FIGURE 1.12 (**A**) Calcifying subperiosteal hematoma without fracture due to separation of periosteum from bone by twisting or pulling. (**B**) Localized calcified hematoma from direct blow.

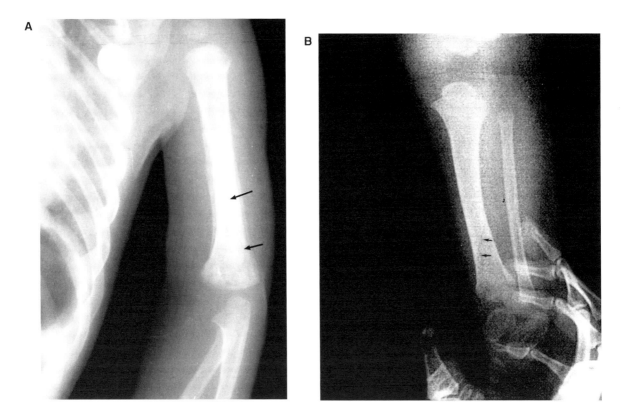

FIGURE 1.13 (**A**) Healing spiral fracture of the humeral diaphysis with associated calcifying subperiosteal hematoma. (**B**) Fresh, undisplaced spiral fracture of the tibia in a nonambulatory infant, highly suggestive of abuse.

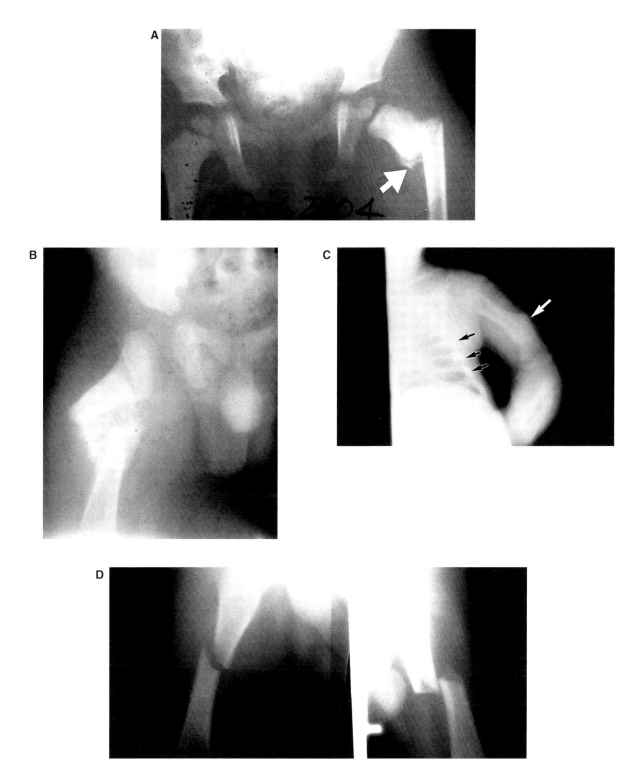

FIGURE 1.14 **(A)** Displaced transverse fracture of the proximal femur in a nonwalking child. **(B)** Healing displaced transverse fracture of the femur in a 4-month-old abused infant. **(C)** An almost completely healed transverse fracture of the humeral diaphysis with residual angulation (large arrow). There are lateral rib fractures as well (small arrows). **(D)** Bilateral transverse femoral fractures in a nonwalking abused child.

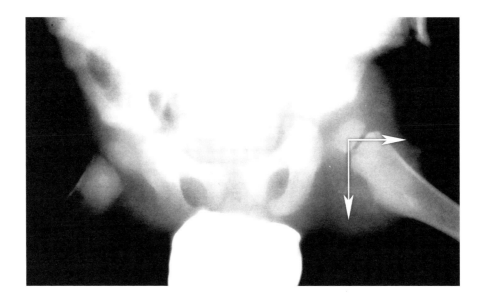

FIGURE 1.15 Subluxation of the left capital femoral epiphysis due to intracapsular blood or effusion in a child with massive trauma elsewhere (probably swung by this extremity). Compare with normal right hip.

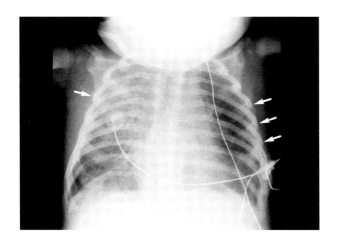

FIGURE 1.16 Fresh, minimally displaced lateral rib fractures are difficult to see, child sent home. (Courtesy of Dr. Damien Grattan-Smith.)

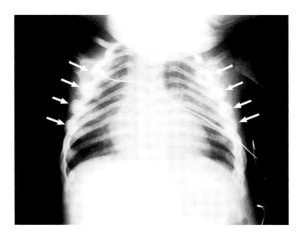

FIGURE 1.17 Same child as in previous figure returns with large hazy callus formation around healing fractures. (Courtesy of Dr. Damien Grattan-Smith.)

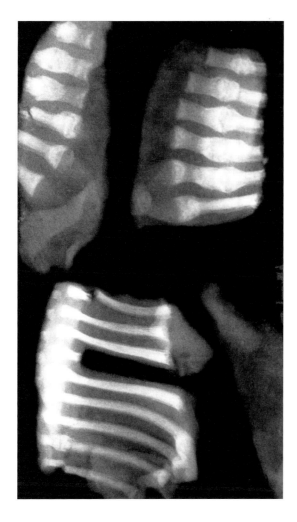

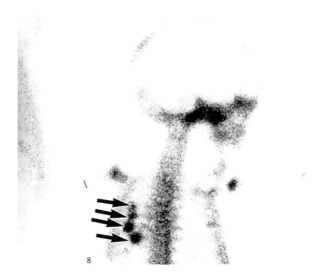

FIGURE 1.19 Nuclear bone scan reveals multiple rib fractures (arrows) not yet visible on radiographs. Note the normal high uptake at the growth plates in the humeri; bilateral symmetrical metaphyseal injuries would be difficult to appreciate. Here the baby is slightly rotated so the uptake is slightly asymmetrical at the shoulders. (Courtesy of Dr. Damien Grattan-Smith.)

FIGURE 1.18 Rib sections removed at autopsy show multiple rib fractures ranging in age from fresh (0 to 7 days) to some that are 4 to 6 weeks or more posttrauma and essentially healed. (Courtesy of Dr. W.U. Spitz.) (From Brogdon, B.G., Forensic aspects of radiology, in *Medicolegal Investigation of Death*, 4th ed., Spitz, W.U., Ed., C.C. Thomas, Springfield, IL, chap. XXI. With permission.)

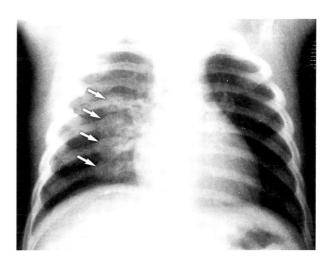

FIGURE 1.20 Typical healed posterior rib fractures.

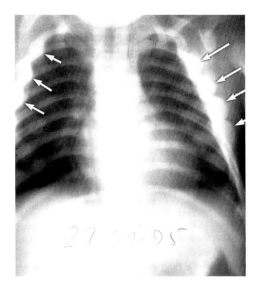

FIGURE 1.21 Typical healed lateral rib fractures.

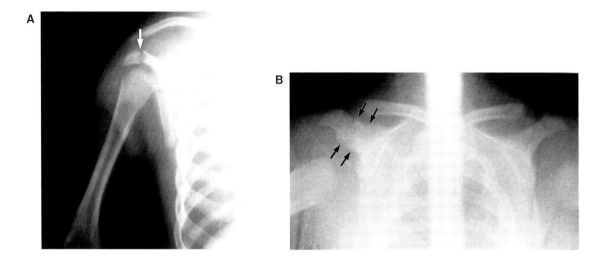

FIGURE 1.22 (A) Acute fracture of the acromion, highly suggestive of abuse. **(B)** Healed acromial fracture on the right.

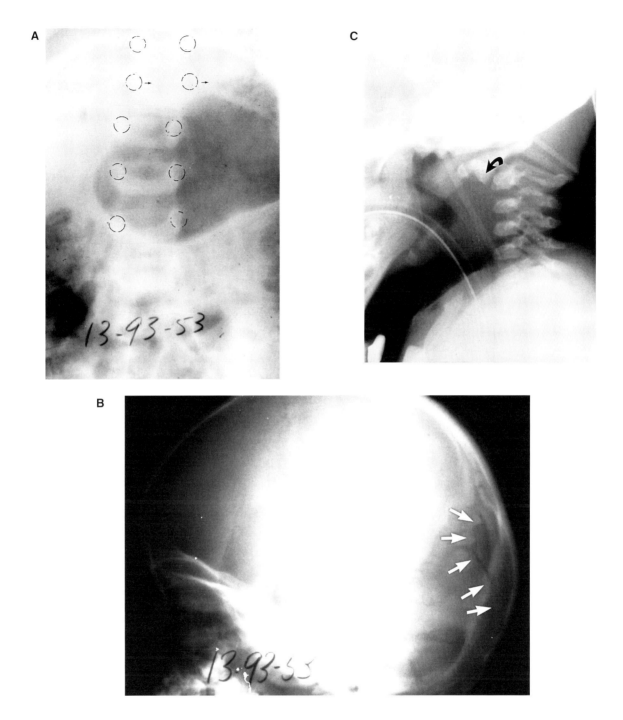

FIGURE 1.23 (**A**) Lateral dislocation of the T-12 on L-1. The pedicles are outlined to emphasize the lateral displacement. This 2-year-old was brought because she "couldn't pass her water." (**B**) She also had a skull fracture. She had been slammed against a wall. (**C**) Another infant hit in the back of the head with a blunt weapon, producing a separation of the odontoid process from the body of C-2 and anterior subluxation of C-1.

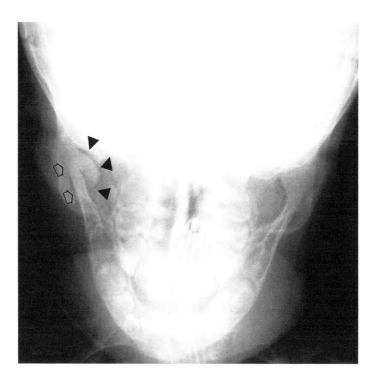

FIGURE 1.24 Fractured right mandibular neck (arrows) with dislocated mandibular head (arrowheads). (Courtesy of A.M. Kroman and Dr. S. A. Symes.)

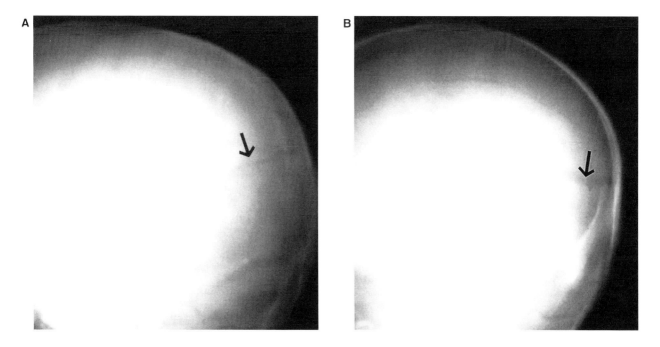

FIGURE 1.25 (A and B) Simple parietal skull fracture.

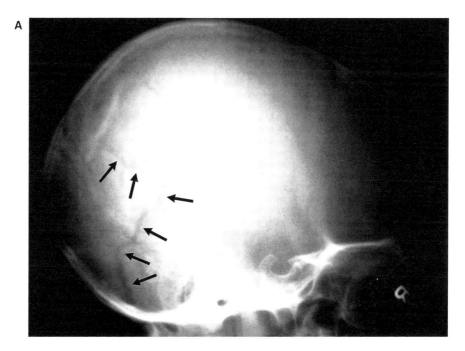

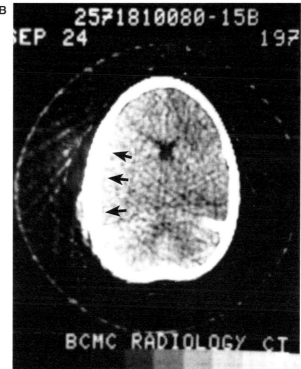

FIGURE 1.26 **(A)** Compound skull fracture (arrows) with **(B)** associated subdural hematoma (arrows).

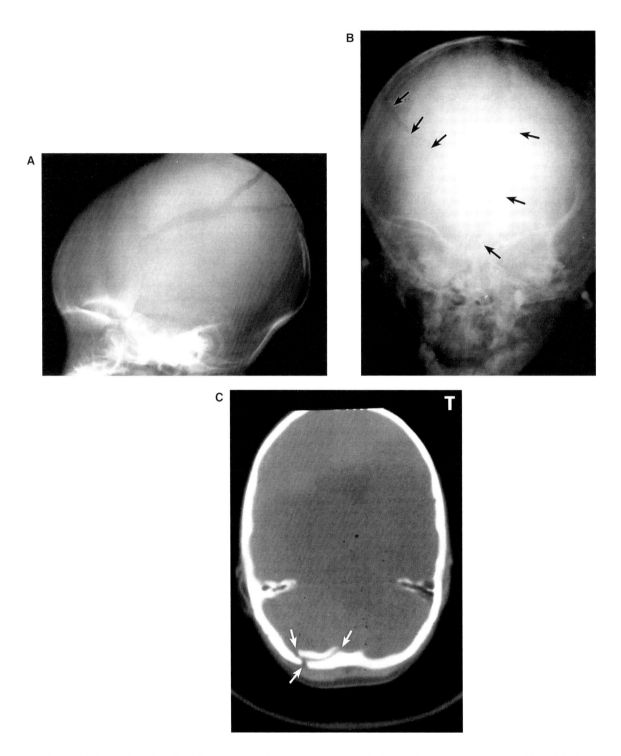

FIGURE 1.27 (**A**) Complex skull fracture. This is the same child with the rib fractures in Figures 1.16 and 1.17. (Courtesy of Dr. Damien Grattan-Smith.) (**B and C**) Another child with complex (black arrows) and depressed (white arrows) skull fractures. (The boyfriend claimed he had accidentally hit the child's head against the door-frame while carrying her from room to room.)

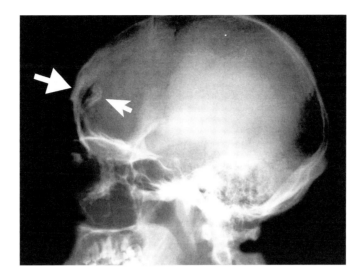

FIGURE 1.28 Depressed frontal fracture.

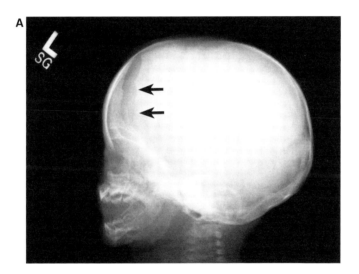

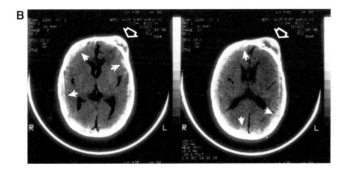

FIGURE 1.29 This 3-month-old reportedly slipped from her mother's hands in the bath and suffered a simple frontal fracture under a large hematoma. She was stable with no neurological symptoms and was sent home. She was returned to another hospital one month later. **(A)** The frontal fracture is widened (arrows). **(B)** There is a partially calcified subgaleal hematoma (open arrows), fresh subdural blood (arrowheads), and cerebral edema. (Courtesy of Dr. W.U. Spitz.)

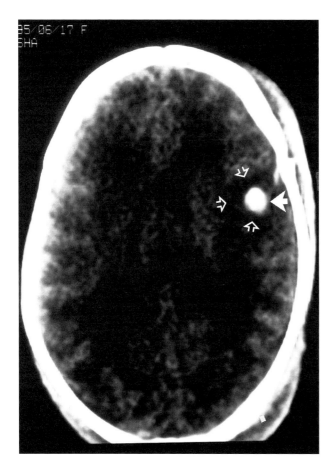

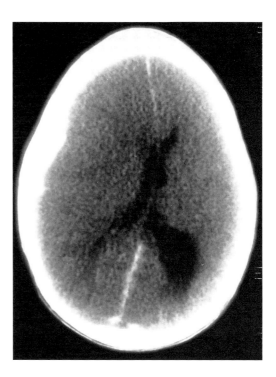

FIGURE 1.31 Unenhanced CT shows blood in interhemispheric fissure, scattered subarachmoid hemorrhages.

FIGURE 1.30 Hemorrhagic contusion (arrow) with surrounding edema (open arrows) on unenhanced CT.

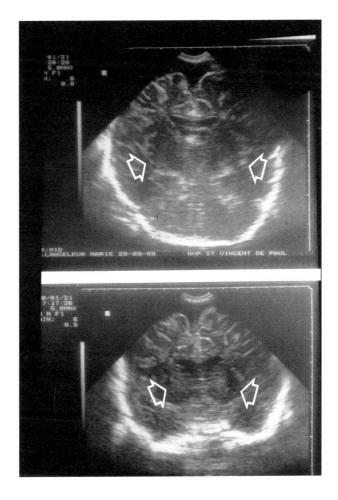

FIGURE 1.32 Intraventricular blood demonstrated by transfontanellar sonography.

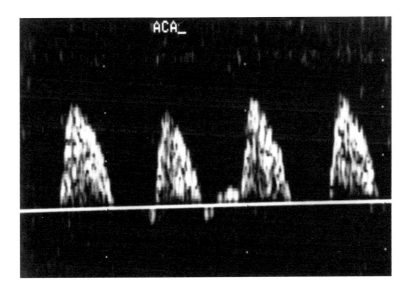

FIGURE 1.33 Evidence of increased intracerebral pressure by Doppler ultrasonography; the diastolic pressure is below the zero line.

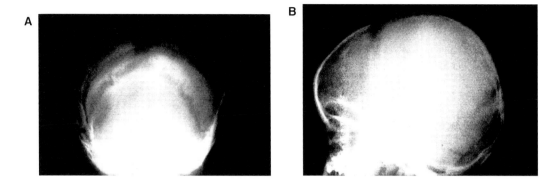

FIGURE 1.34 Shaken baby syndrome. No fractures but marked widening of all cranial sutures due to subdural hematoma and cerebral edema.

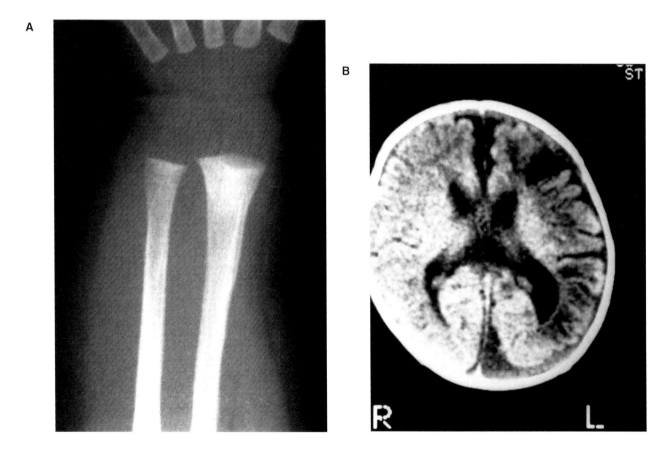

FIGURE 1.35 Shaken baby, 2 months old. (**A**) Healing distal radial and ulnar metaphyseal fractures with maturing subperiosteal hemorrhages. (**B**) Posttraumatic cerebral atrophy.

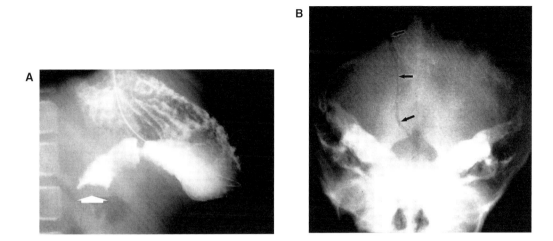

FIGURE 1.36 (A) Intramural hematoma obstructing the second portion of the duodenum (broad arrow) shown on GI series. The impression or pad sign on the greater curvature of the gastric antrum suggests pancreatic edema or hemorrhage. (B) This child also had an occipital skull fracture (arrows).

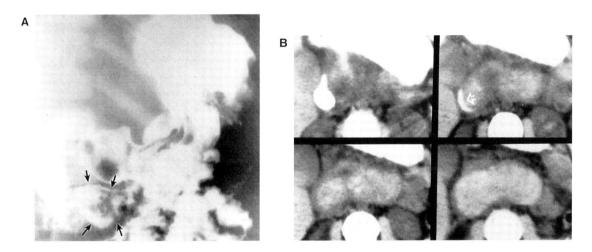

FIGURE 1.37 (A) GI series shows widening and incomplete filling of the third portion of the duodenum due to intramural hematoma. (B) CT scan shows mottled densities of blood and contrast material in the duodenum. A remaining narrow channel (open arrow) permits a small flow of contrast medium. (From Hughes, J.J. and Brogdon, B.G., *J. Comput. Tomogr.*, 10, 231, 1986. With permission.)

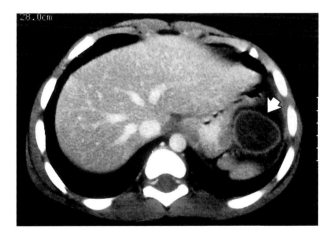

FIGURE 1.38 Enhanced CT shows pseudocyst in the tail of the pancreas (arrow) from abusive trauma to the abdomen. (Courtesy of Dr. Damien Grattan-Smith.)

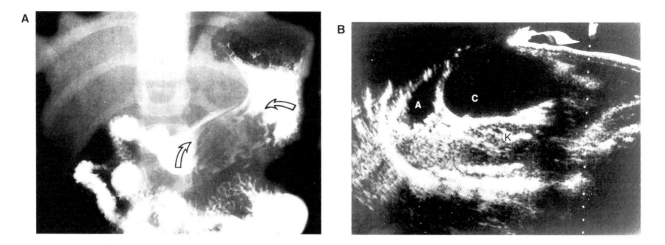

FIGURE 1.39 **(A)** GI series shows pad sign on greater curvature of stomach (curved arrows) from pancreatic pseudocyst. **(B)** Ultra-sonography displays this as an anechoic mass **(C)** anterior to the left kidney (K) and ascites (A). (From Kleinman, P.K., Raptopoulos, V.D., and Brill, P.W., *Radiology*, 14, 393, 1981. With permission.)

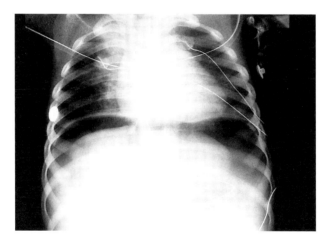

FIGURE 1.40 Free intraperitoneal air collected beneath the diaphragm due to traumatic rupture of the stomach. (Courtesy of Dr. Damien Grattan-Smith.)

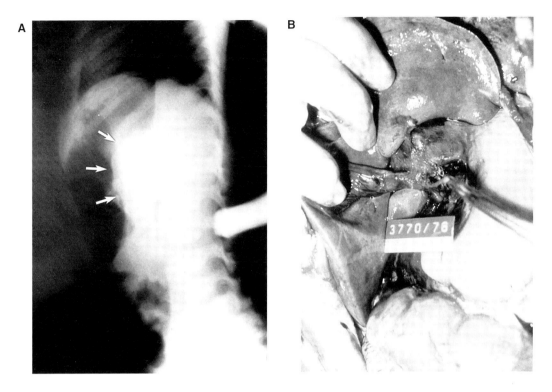

FIGURE 1.41 **(A)** A dying battered baby was brought to the emergency department. Cross-table lateral view of the abdomen showed a large retroperitoneal mass (arrows). This proved to be due to a collection of blood and fluid resulting from **(B)** lacerations of the liver and pancreas and transection of the bile duct. The weapon was the fist of the father's new girlfriend.

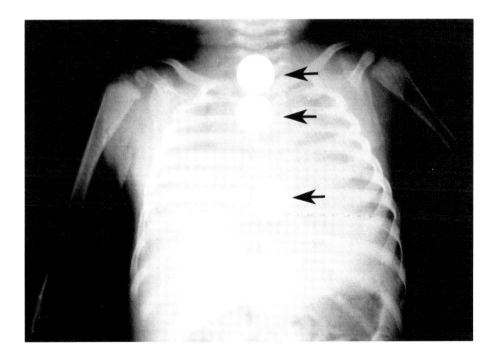

FIGURE 1.42 This baby was brought in dead. Examination showed three coins lodged in the esophagus in typical *en face* presentation. This same infant had been brought in earlier with seven coins in the esophagus, which were at that time considered accidental, now signed out as homicide. (Courtesy of Dr. Kurt Nolte.) (From Nolte, K.B., *Am. J. Forensic Med. Path.*, 14, 323, 1993. With permission.)

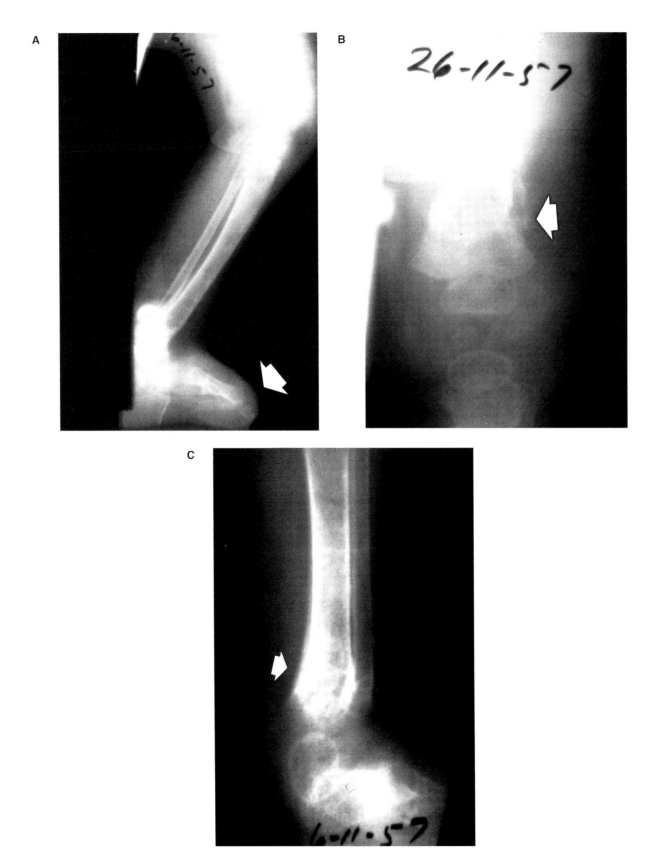

FIGURE 1.43 This 11-month-old female was brought in from a hippie commune with 30% burns. **(A)** The toes had been burned off of a foot. After the burns were treated multiple underlying fractures were found including **(B)** the distal femur and **(C)** the ankle on the same extremity as the destroyed toes.

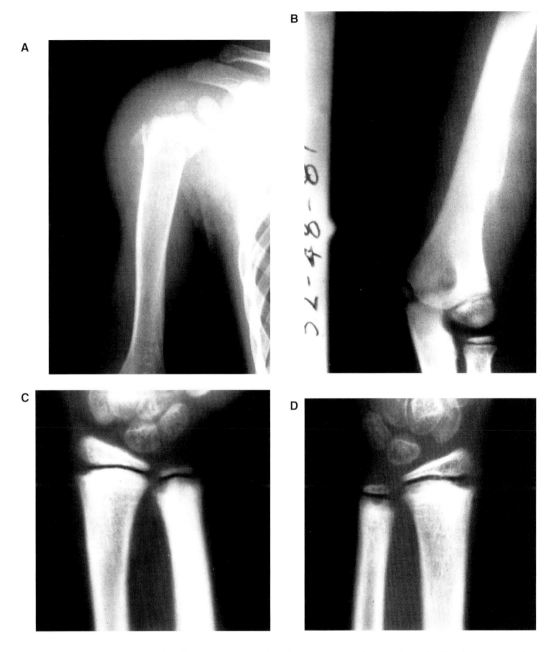

FIGURE 1.44 This 7-year-old girl said her father beats her when he gets drunk. Survey showed: **(A)** old fracture of the proximal humerus with residual deformity; **(B)** myositis ossificans in left arm; **(C and D)** bilateral epiphyseal injuries to the distal radius and ulna.

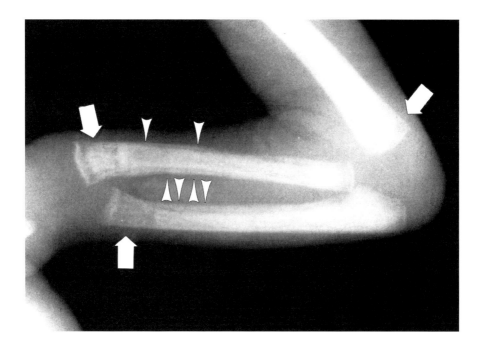

FIGURE 1.45 Congenital syphilis in a newborn. Characterized by destructive metaphyseal lesions (arrows) and periostitis (arrowheads).

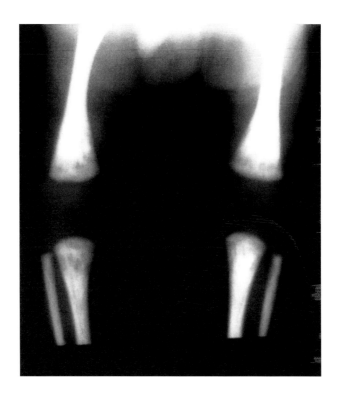

FIGURE 1.46 Intrauterine rubella (German measles) infection producing linear radiolucencies in the metaphyses. This has been described as the celery stalk appearance. It is not exclusive to rubella. Some other intrauterine infections will have a similar appearance.

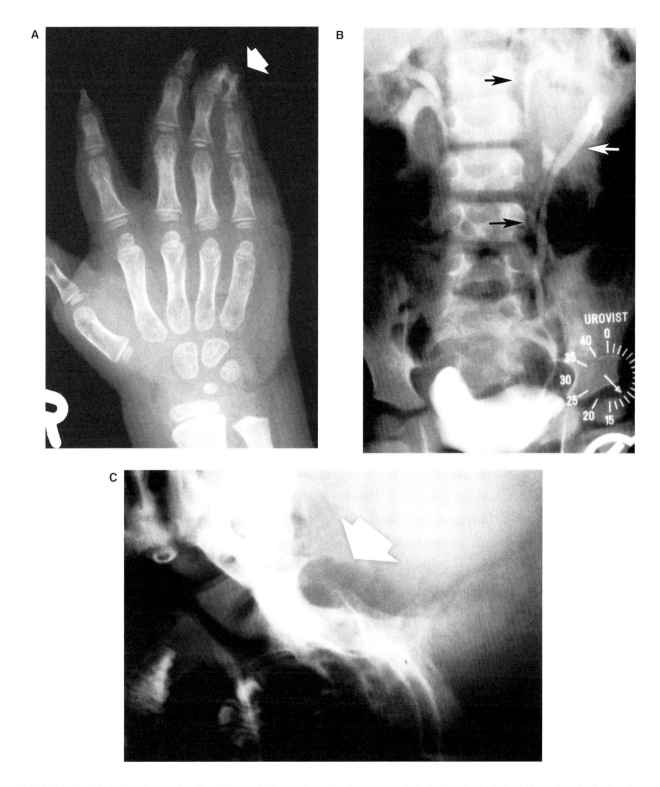

FIGURE 1.47 Alcohol embryopathy. Conditions which may be related to maternal alcohol intake include: **(A)** syndactyly, both soft tissue and bony (arrow); **(B)** duplication of the kidney and ureter (arrow); **(C)** craniopharyngioma (arrow) producing enlargement of the sella turcica and erosion of the dorsum sella.

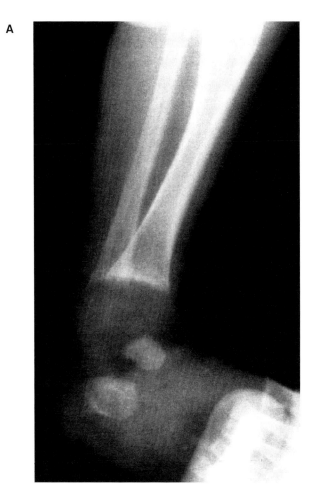

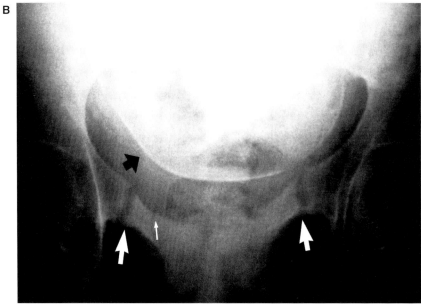

FIGURE 1.48 (**A**) Congenital rickets in a Beduin infant. Note the malacic bone with loss of cortico-medullary distinction and the widened, frayed metaphysis with no zone of provisional calcification. (**B**) Pregnant Beduin female with insufficiency fractures in both superior pubic rami (large arrows). The bones are profoundly osteomalacic (small white arrow). The fetal skull is thin and poorly mineralized (black arrows).

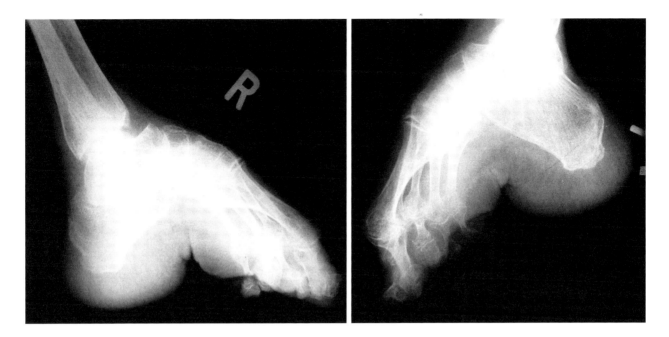

FIGURE 1.49 Lotus foot deformity in an octogenarian Chinese woman whose feet were bound as a child.

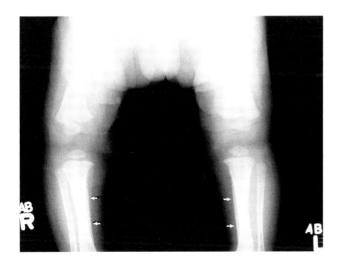

FIGURE 1.50 Physiologic periosteal elevation and calcification in a 4-month-old male. Note the symmetry and the single thin lamina of subperiosteal calcification.

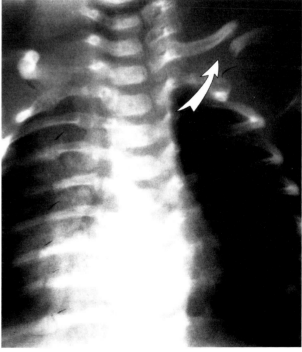

FIGURE 1.51 Fracture of the clavicle sustained at childbirth.

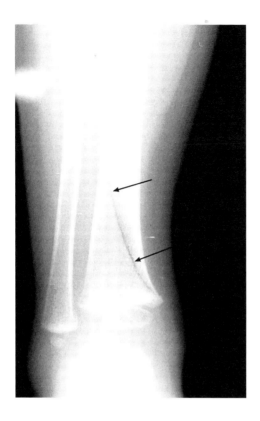

FIGURE 1.52 Toddler fracture in a normal 20-month-old boy.

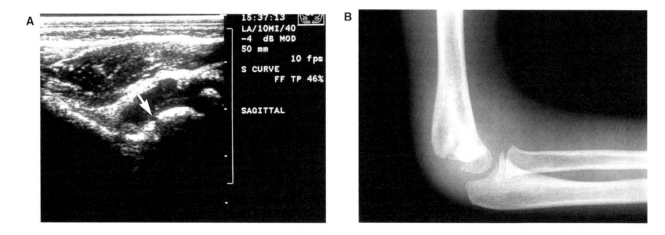

FIGURE 1.53 Supracondylar fracture of the humerus. (**A**) Demonstrated in the emergency department by ultrasonography (arrow). (**B**) Confirmatory radiograph.

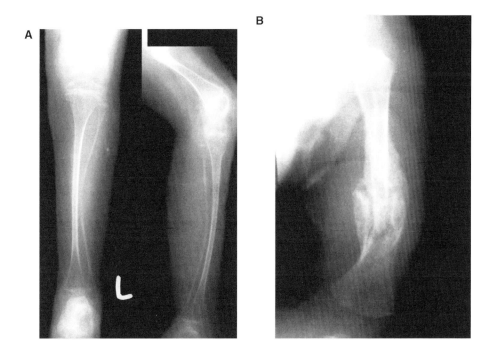

FIGURE 1.54 Osteogenesis imperfecta, characterized by: **(A)** thin gracile osteoporotic bones deformed by healed fractures; **(B)** acute fractures heal with superabundant callus.

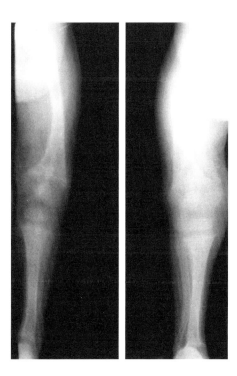

FIGURE 1.55 Rickets. Softened, osteomalacic bone with bending fractures, periosteal reaction, widened and frayed metaphysis with no zone of provisional calcification.

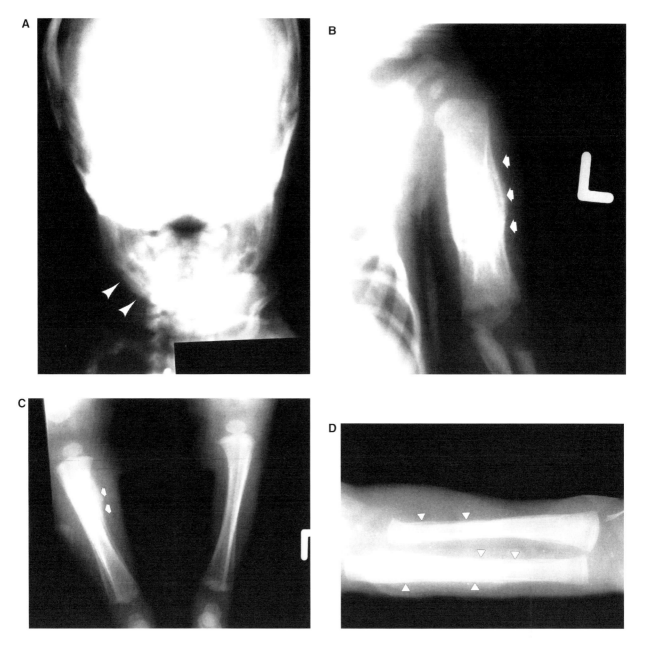

FIGURE 1.56 Caffey's disease. Abundant periosteal calcific reaction involving: **(A)** the mandible; **(B)** the left humerus; **(C)** the right tibia; **(D)** radius and ulna.

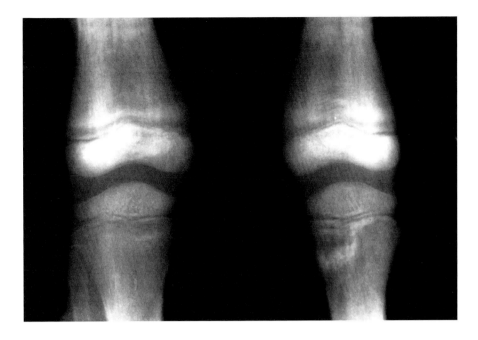

FIGURE 1.57 Leukemia involving bones in children is characterized by rarefaction just beneath the zone of provisional calcification and periostitis.

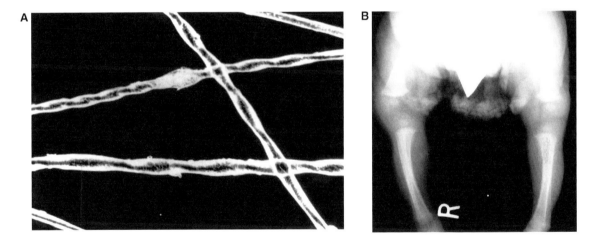

FIGURE 1.58 Menkes disease (kinky hair syndrome). A degenerative disease with mental and motor retardation, clonic seizures and (**A**) peculiar kinky hair. (**B**) They may show rachetic-like bony changes related to copper deficiency.[19]

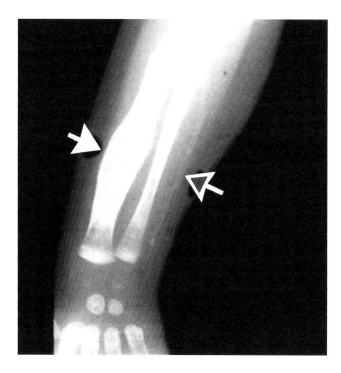

FIGURE 1.59 Vitamin A intoxication can cause a periosteal reaction (white arrows). This patient also had excessive vitamin D medication causing the vascular calcification (black and white arrow).

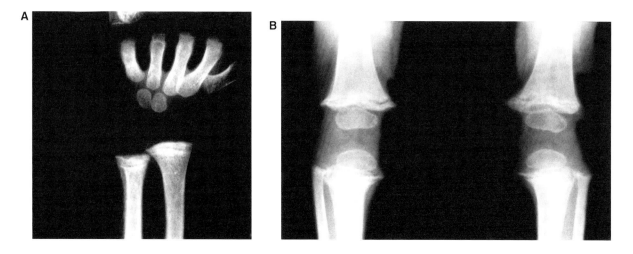

FIGURE 1.60 Scurvy. **(A)** Upper extremity with osteoporotic bone, beak-like metaphyseal corners and other metaphyseal changes giving the appearance of a double zone of provisional calcification. Subperiosteal bleeding produces a calcified periosteal elevation. **(B)** Similar changes at the knee plus the typical ring-like secondary epiphysis.

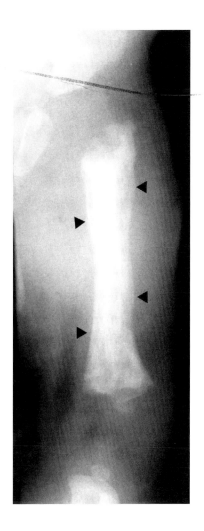

FIGURE 1.61 Osteomyelitis with involucrum (arrowheads) surrounding the deformed and partially destroyed bone.

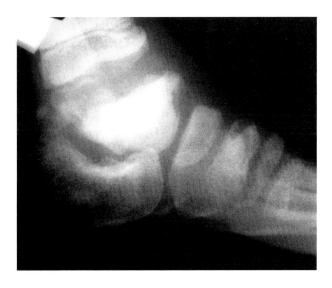

FIGURE 1.62 Congenital insensitivity to pain (cause unknown) can result in osteomyelitis, fractures, and charcot joints as in this 7-year-old.

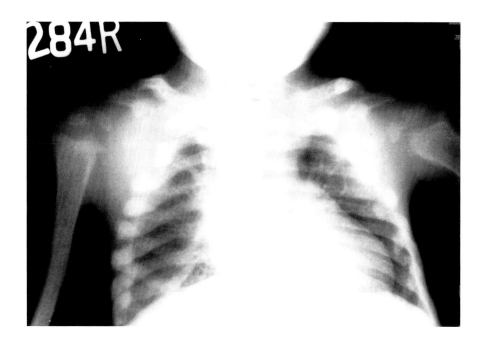

FIGURE 1.63 Dilantin® (phenytoin sodium) interferes with hydroxylation of vitamin D and long-term high doses can produce rickets in children.

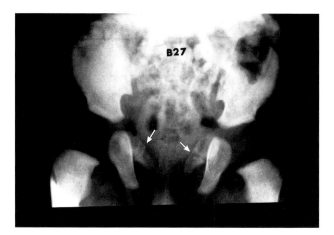

FIGURE 1.64 Normal variant. In fewer than 2% of children there is more than one ossification center for the pubis on one or both sides. The appearance can be mistaken for a fracture.[20]

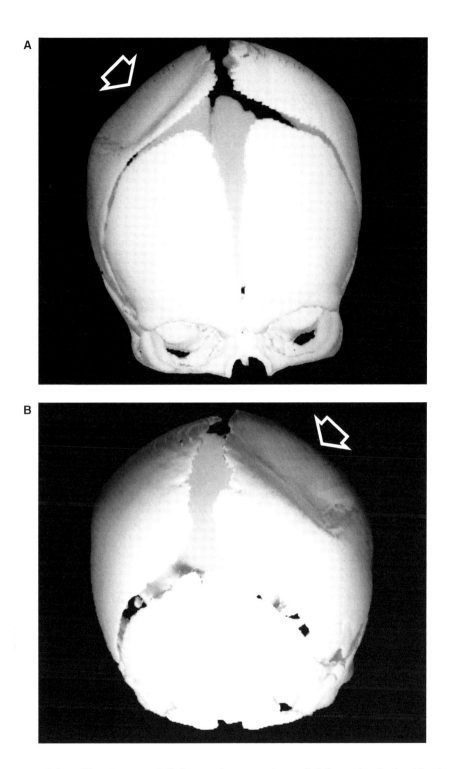

FIGURE 1.65 Intrapartum injury. The ping-pong ball fracture is a smooth rounded depression in the thin elastic newborn skull without a fracture line. Frequently seen after forceps extraction when they were common. This newborn's head was already in the birth canal when a cesarean section was begun. The obstetrician pushed it back from below into the uterus. **(A)** Right parietal ping-pong fracture in frontal view. **(B)** Occipital view, 3-D CT reconstruction.

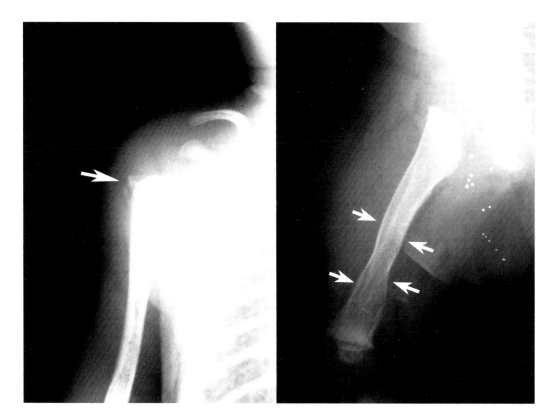

FIGURE 1.66 This baby had an intrauterine conversion from a transverse lie, suffering fractures in the process. (The white dots are film artifacts.)

2 Abuse of Intimate Partners

John D. McDowell, D.D.S., M.S. and B.G. Brogdon, M.D.

Although psychological and sexual abuse are substantial problems, this discussion is limited to the physical abuse of intimate partners that may be demonstrable by the radiologic method. Such violence in marriage, cohabitation, or dating is primarily directed toward the female partner. Abuse is the most common etiology for trauma in women, exceeding motor vehicle accidents, muggings, and rapes combined.[1,2] Population-based estimates show that battered women may be more numerous than battered children.[3,4]

The term *battered women* was first introduced in 1974,[5] and again the concept of spousal abuse is a relatively modern one. Wife beating was both legally and socially acceptable until relatively recent times, being explicitly written into the laws of the church and state.[6,7] Changing mores have led to the inclusion of cohabiting and dating couples under the umbrella term of *intimate partners*.

Unlike the case of battered children, the principal targets of assault on women are the head, neck, and face. The most common causes of facial injury in women are domestic violence and automobile accidents. Somewhat distinctive patterns emerge from evaluations of these two mechanisms of injury.[8] Massive and multiple injuries to the facial bones and mandible (Figure 2.1), such as the LeFort fractures, and worse, are seen in accident victims. Battered women, on the other hand, show mostly fractures of the mandibular body or angle and the contralateral mandibular ramus (Figures 2.2 to 2.4). Of course, other mandibular and facial fractures (nasal, orbital, zygomatico-facial), fractures of the teeth, and dislocations are seen in battered women (Figures 2.5 to 2.13). Defensive injuries (fending fractures) of the hand and forearm are also evident (Figures 2.14 and 2.15).

Blows to the body are less common and rarely produce fractures or other injuries diagnosed radiologically. Rib fractures, for instance, are rarely seen. Only occasionally can nonskeletal injuries be identified (Figure 2.16).

The female victim who is pregnant is an exception to the generalizations cited above. In this case, the breast and abdomen are common targets. In the latter case, the term *prenatal child abuse* has been applied. An increased rate of abortion and premature births reportedly has been found in women who show a positive history of physical abuse.[6,9–11]

The term *premarital abuse* describing physical violence associated with dating and courtship was first used only 20 years ago. The term was a result of a survey that reported 22% of respondents had been victims of premarital violence or had been violent toward a premarital partner.[12,13]

A major problem in diagnosing and surveying physical violence to partners is the woman's reluctance to admit to the victimization or to seek help. Delay in seeking help may be an important indication of violence between partners. The majority of intimate partner victims sustaining intentional trauma delay seeking medical attention for 24 hours or more, while the vast majority of motor accident victims seek medical attention on the day of the incident.[8,14]

The physical abuse of males by female partners is much less common and more difficult to investigate because of the male's reluctance to seeking help or admit to the causation of his injuries. Further, since the female is generally smaller and weaker than her male partner, she is less likely to inflict serious injury in her attempts at battering. Consequently, she may resort to an equalizer. These episodes can show up in subsequent chapters (i.e., Chapters 18 and 21). One unusual example is shown here (Figure 2.17).

Of course, intimate partner abuse can, and does, escalate beyond mere battering, with serious, even fatal, results (Figure 2.18).

REFERENCES

1. Stark, E. and Flitcraft, A., Spouse Abuse in Surgeon General's Workshop on Violence and Public Health: Source Book, Centers for Disease Control, Leesburg, VA, 1985, p. SA1.
2. Drossman, D.A., Leserman, J., Nachman, G., Li, Z.M., Gluck, H., Toomey, T.C., and Mitchell, C., Sexual and physical abuse in women with functional or organic gastrointestinal disorders, *Ann. Int. Med.*, 113, 828, 1990.
3. Dewsbury, A.R., Battered wives, Family violence seen in general practice, *R.R. Soc. Health*, 95, 290, 1975.
4. Collier, J., When you suspect your patient is a battered wife, *RN*, 50, 22, 1987.
5. Pizzey, E., *Scream Quietly or the Neighbors Will Hear*, R. Enslow, Short Hills, NJ, 1977.
6. Hilberman, E., Overview: "the wife-beater's wife" reconsidered, *Am. J. Psychiatr.*, 137, 1336, 1980.
7. Walker, L.E., *The Battered Woman Syndrome*, Springer-Verlag, New York, 1984.
8. McDowell, J.D., A Comparison of Facial Fractures in Women Victims of Motor Vehicle Accidents and Battered Women, published thesis, University of Texas Graduate School of Biomedical Sciences, San Antonio, 1993.
9. Schei, B. and Bakketeig, L., Gynaecological impact of sexual and physical abuse by spouse: a study of a random sample of Norwegian women, *Br. J. Obstet. Gynaecol.*, 96, 1379, 1989.
10. Sampselle, C.M., The role of nursing in preventing violence against women, *J. Obstet. Gynecol. Neonatal Nursing*, 20, 481, 1991.
11. Bewley, C. and Gibbs, A., Violence in pregnancy, *Midwifery*, 7, 107, 1991.
12. Berrios, D.C. and Grady, D., Domestic violence: risk factors and outcomes, *West. J. Med.*, 155, 133, 1991.
13. Cate, R.M., Henton, J.M., Koval, J., Chistopher, F.S., and Lloyd S., Premarital abuse: a social psychological perspective, *J. Fam. Issues*, 3, 79, 1982.
14. Brogdon, B.G., *Forensic Radiology*, CRC Press, Boca Raton, FL, 1998, chap. 16.

CREDIT

From Brogdon, B.G., *Forensic Radiology*, CRC Press, Boca Raton, FL, 1998. With permission. Figures 2.2, 2.9A, 2.10, 2.16.

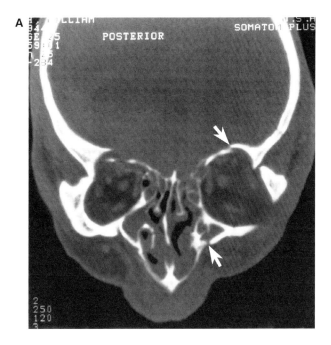

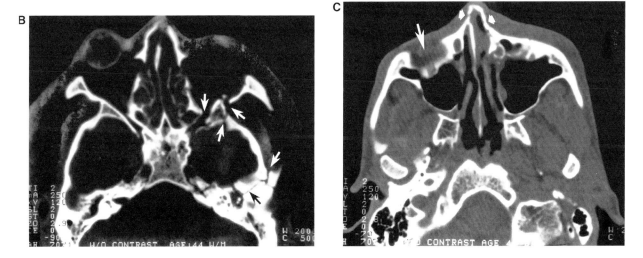

FIGURE 2.1 (A–F) Examples of massive injuries to the nasal bones, maxilla, mandible, orbits, and base of skull from automobile accidents as shown by computed tomography examination. Note how in several cases the paranasal sinuses and nasal passages are filled with blood.

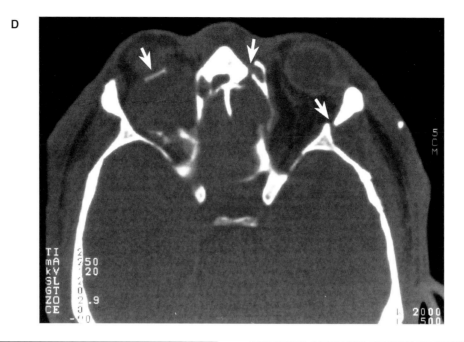

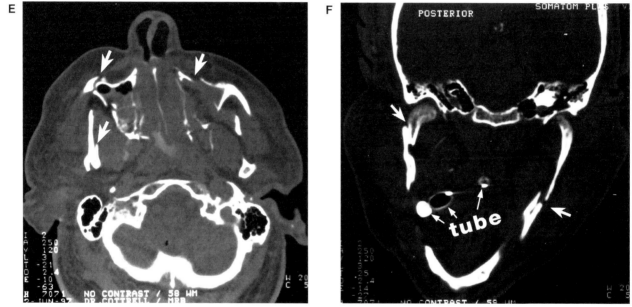

FIGURE 2.1 (Continued) Examples of massive injuries to the nasal bones, maxilla, mandible, orbits, and base of skull from automobile accidents as shown by computed tomography examination. Note how in several cases the paranasal sinuses and nasal passages are filled with blood.

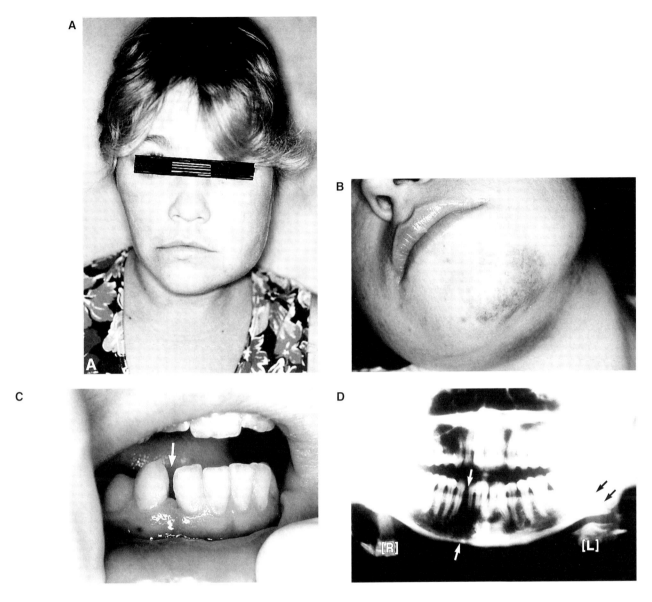

FIGURE 2.2 (A) This 43-year-old woman was beaten with her husband's fist. She has massive swelling over the left jaw. (B) Bruises and abrasions to the chin. (C) There is separation of the teeth indicating a fracture. (D) Panoramic examination shows fractures to the left mandibular angle (black arrows) and the right mentalis (white arrows).

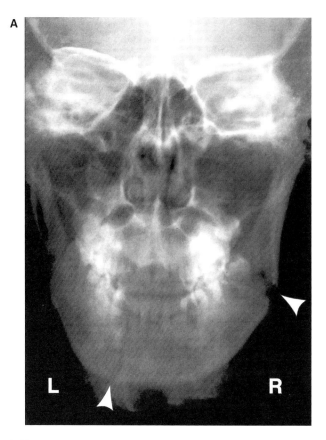

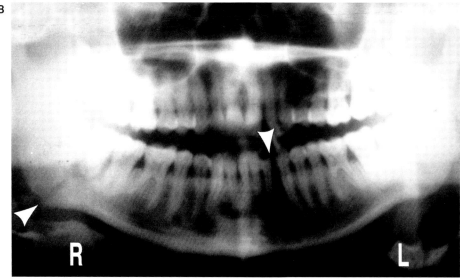

FIGURE 2.3 Typical battering fractures in a 53-year-old female. **(A)** Frontal radiographies of the mandible show a right angular fracture (arrowheads) and, faintly, a left mental fracture (arrow). **(B)** Panoramic view shows the angle fracture and separation of the left mandibular lateral incisor and canine (arrows).

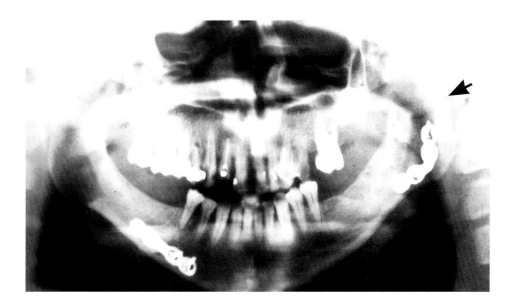

FIGURE 2.4 This 51-year-old female presented after a recent battering. Examination revealed old metallic fixation devices stabilizing typical battering fractures from a previous episode. There is a new fracture of the left mandibular neck.

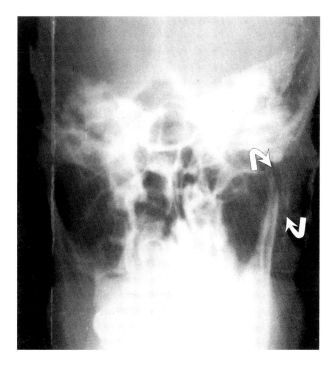

FIGURE 2.5 Oblique fracture of the left mandibular neck in a battered woman.

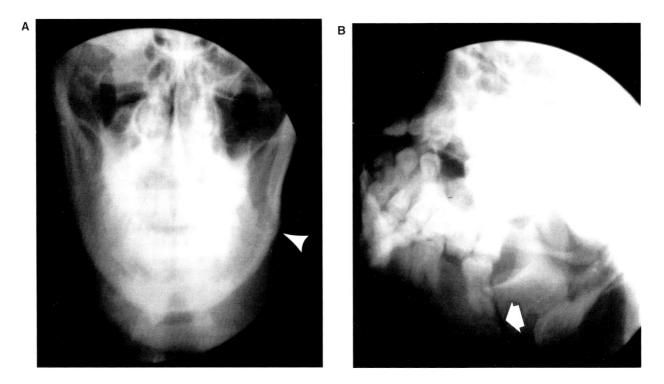

FIGURE 2.6 Typical mandibular angle fracture through the socket of the third molar. **(A)** Frontal view. **(B)** Oblique view.

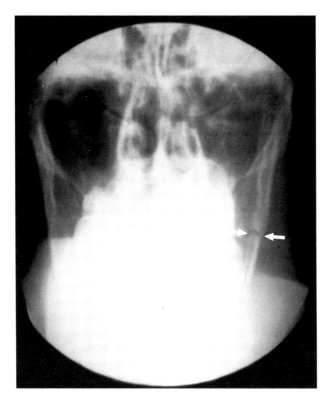

FIGURE 2.7 Fracture of the left mandibular body.

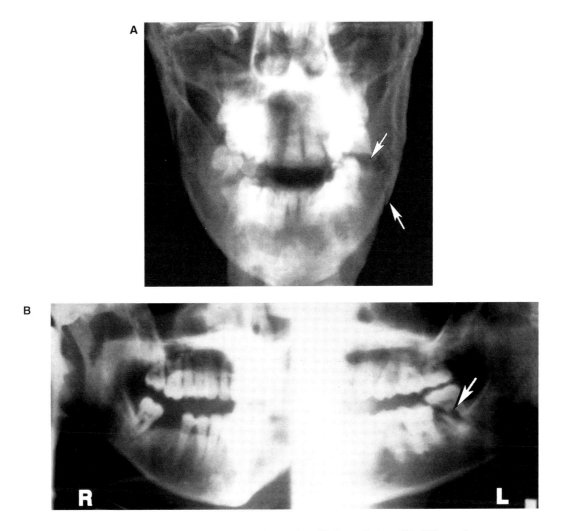

FIGURE 2.8 Left mandibular angle fracture with fractured third molar. **(A)** Frontal view. **(B)** Oblique views.

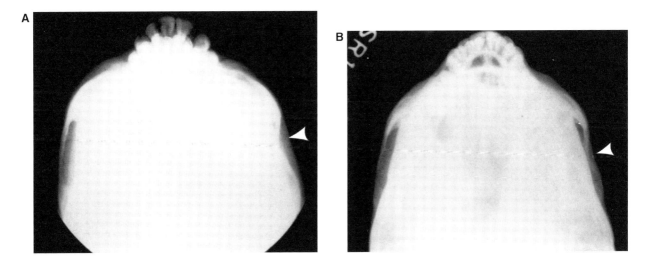

FIGURE 2.9 (A and B) Almost identical depressed fractures of the zygomatic arch in two battered women.

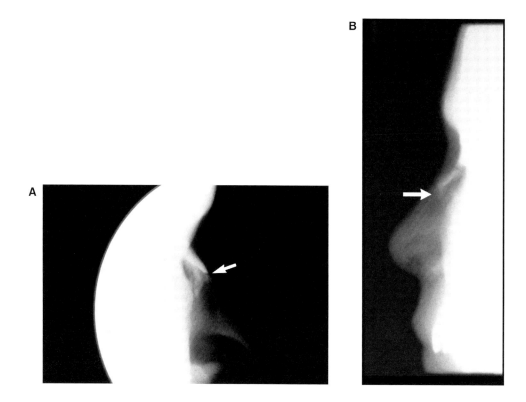

FIGURE 2.10 (A and B) Almost identical fractures of the nose of two women from battering.

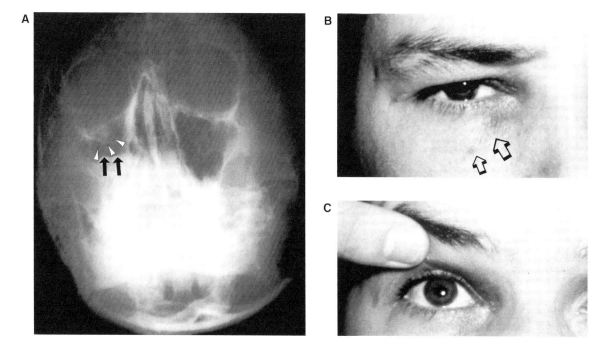

FIGURE 2.11 Blowout fracture of the orbital floor from being struck with a fist. **(A)** Water's view shows herniation of soft tissues from the orbit into the right maxillary sinus (white arrowheads) and an air-fluid level indicating fresh blood in the maxillary sinus (black open arrows). **(B)** Photograph of victim showing narrowing of the palpebral fissure from swelling. Note ecchymosis (subcutaneous blood) beneath the eye (arrows) due to bleeding from the orbital floor fracture. **(C)** Loss of upward-outward gaze on the right due to herniation of extraocular muscle into the floor fracture. The victim has diplopia (double-vision) as a result.

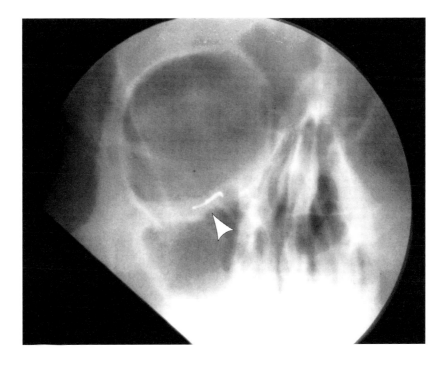

FIGURE 2.12 Metallic fixation and stabilization of an orbital floor fracture (arrow).

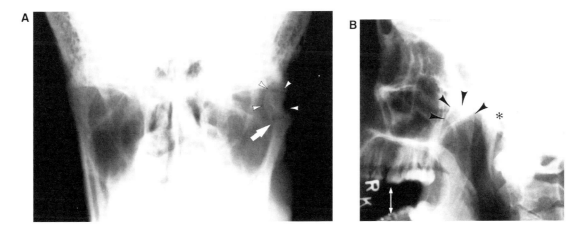

FIGURE 2.13 **(A)** Fracture of the mandibular neck (arrow) with dislocation of the mandibular head (arrowheads). **(B)** The anterior dislocation of the head (arrowheads) out of the mandibular fossa (asterisk) prevents closure of the jaw. It is locked open (arrows).

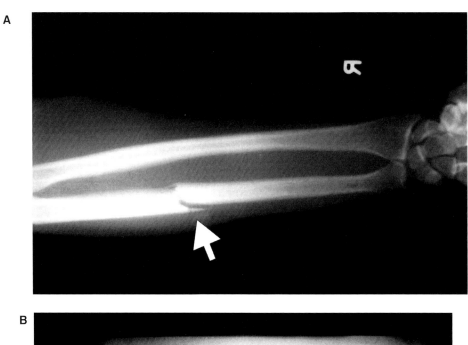

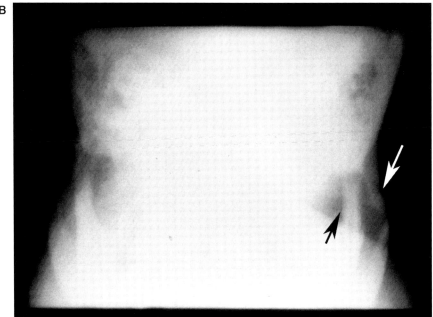

FIGURE 2.14 (A) Typical defensive injury, fending fracture (arrow) of the ulna in a woman who suffered (B) a fracture of the mandibular neck (white arrow) overriding the ascending ramus (black arrow).

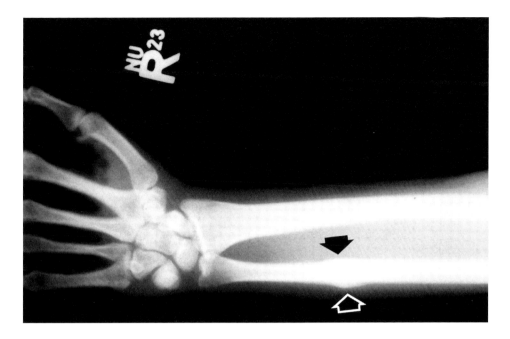

FIGURE 2.15 This woman who came in with fresh contusions from a recent beating was found to have a healed fending fracture (arrow), no longer symptomatic, from a previous episode of battering.

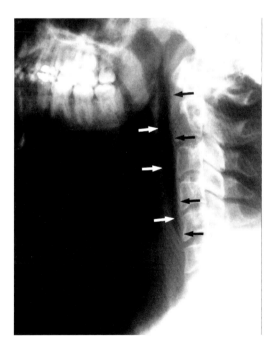

FIGURE 2.16 This young woman was hit in the throat by her boyfriend, sustaining a rupture of the larynx with subsequent dissection of air into the paravertebral space (arrows).

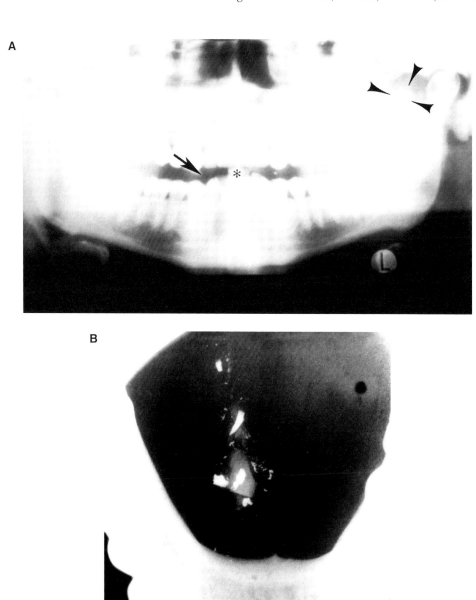

FIGURE 2.17 This young male abuser was shot from a distance of 10 to 12 feet with a Saturday Night Special in the hands of his regular victim. (**A**) The nonlethal bullet entered the mouth, sheering the right lateral mandibular incisor (arrow) and coming to rest in the left oropharynx of the abuser (arrowheads). (**B**) A subsequent dental examination (occlusal film) shows tooth flakes and bullet fragments embedded in the tongue. One of the largest fragments can be seen between the teeth in (**A**) and is marked with an asterisk.

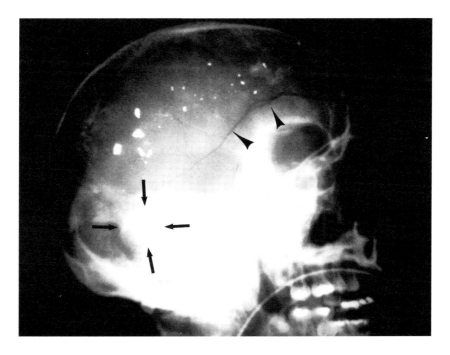

FIGURE 2.18 Fatal partner dispute. A male abuser shot his girlfriend twice, once through the mouth and then through the posterior parental area. The first bullet, little deformed (arrows), is almost hidden by the overlying petrous bone. The second bullet fragmented upon striking the skull, revealing its track. Either gunshot wound would have been fatal. Note the skull fracture (arrowheads) associated with the second wound of entry and massive sudden increase in intracranial pressure.

3 Abuse of the Aged

B.G. Brogdon, M.D. and John D. McDowell, D.D.S., M.S.

INTRODUCTION

Violent domestic abuse is an intergenerational learned behavior.[1] Abused children become abusive parents or intimate partners. Abused mothers are likely to have abused children. Partners abuse each other and that activity has no age limit. Grown-up children may abuse elderly parents. So the cycle continues viciously.

Almost 30 years after Caffey's first paper on abused children, Burston introduced the concept of elder abuse in his letter to the *British Medical Journal* on granny-battering. It was treated as a new phenomenon, but it was not. Elder abuse simply had been largely unremarked and ignored as a societal problem. Actually, it is almost as common as child abuse and, as aging of the population continues, may soon exceed it. Statistical studies on elder abuse are suspect because it is estimated that only one in five cases is reported to the authorities.[2–6]

Domestic abuse has been prevalent in Western society with a strong American predilection. As many as 50% of all American families have experienced some sort of inter-family violence.[7–10] Despite the fear of nursing homes, most elderly victims suffer physical abuse from family members rather than nonrelated caregivers.[5] Now we are learning that the problem extends beyond the Western world, being reported in Eastern cultures famous for filial piety and veneration of elders.[11]

RADIOLOGIC EVIDENCE

The actual act of physical violence can range widely from a push or shake, grabbing or shoving, thrown objects, slaps, blows with the fist, to kicks or bites.[3,5] Consequently, diagnosis by radiologic examination is difficult. The patterns of injury have similarities to those seen in both children and intimate partners. Maxillo-facial injuries (Figures 3.1 to 3.4) and long bone fractures predominate. The latter may represent either defensive injuries or the results of grabbing, twisting, squeezing, or physical restraint (Figures 3.5 and 3.6).

Senile osteoporosis exacerbates the diagnostic problem since fractures may result from relatively minor forces or even ordinary handling (Figure 3.7).

Abuse of the elderly is difficult to prove. The victim may be unable to relate the circumstance of the injury. If able, the victim may be reluctant to implicate the perpetrator (usually a caregiver). The victim may be afraid of being sent to a nursing home if currently residing independently or with family. Conversely, if already in a nursing home the victim is afraid that a complaint may bring about expulsion. The caregiver or perpetrator is unlikely to volunteer a confession. This "fox in the henhouse" dilemma can lead to tragic results (Figure 3.8).

REFERENCES

1. Brogdon, B.G., *Forensic Radiology*, CRC Press, Boca Raton, FL, 1998, chap. 16.

2. Burston, G.R., Granny-beating, *Br. Med. J.*, 3, 592, 1975.

3. Wolf, R.S., Elder abuse: ten years later, *J. Am. Geriatr. Soc.*, 36, 758, 1988.

4. American Medical Association, Council on scientific affairs report: elder abuse and neglect, *JAMA*, 257, 966, 1987.

5. Pillemer, K. and Finkelhor, D., The prevalence of elder abuse: a random sample survey, *Gerontologist*, 28, 51, 1988.

6. Lett, J.E., Abuse of the elderly, *J. Fla. Med. Assn.*, 82, 675, 1995.

7. Staus, M.A., Gelles, R.J., and Steinmetz, S.K., *Behind Closed Doors: Violence in the American Family*, Sage Publications, Newbury Park, CA, 1988.

8. Hilberman, E., Overview: "the wife-beater's wife" reconsidered, *Am. J. Psychiatr.*, 137, 1336, 1980.

9. Gelles, R., *The Violent Home: A Study of Physical Aggression Between Husbands and Wives*, Sage Publications, Beverly Hills, CA, 1974.

10. Dobash, R.E. and Dobash, R.P., The case of wife beating, *J. Fam. Issues*, 2, 439, 1981.

11. Yan, E., Tang, C.S-K., and Yeung, D., No safe haven: a review of elder abuse in Chinese families, *Trauma, Violence and Abuse*, 3, 167, 2002.

CREDIT

From Brogdon, B.G., *Forensic Radiology*, CRC Press, Boca Raton, FL, 1998. With permission. Figures 3.1, 3.5, 3.7.

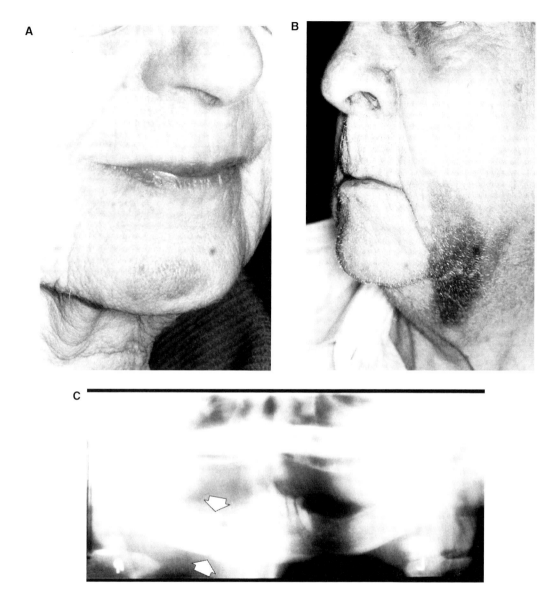

FIGURE 3.1 Battered elder woman. **(A)** Shows a bruise on the right jaw at the site of a mental fracture. **(B)** Shows a large hematoma draining down from a left mandibular angle fracture. The flattened left cheek prominence suggests a possible left zygomatic or malar fracture, but this was not investigated. **(C)** Panoramic view defines the right mental fracture well (arrow). The left mandibular angle fracture was demonstrated on another film (not shown).

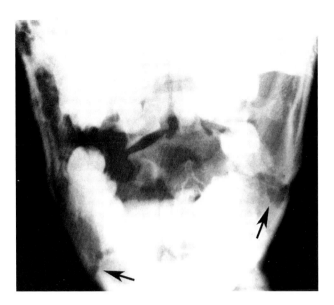

FIGURE 3.2 Typical mandibular fractures (arrows) in a battered elderly man.

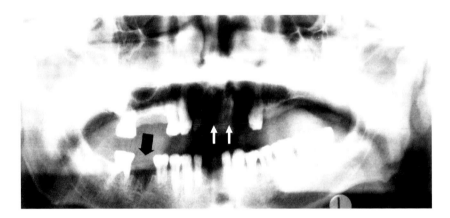

FIGURE 3.3 This 67-year-old woman was assaulted by her adult son. Her maxillary incisors were avulsed (small arrows) and her right mandibular first molar also was avulsed (arrow) in an unusual location for avulsion from a blow.

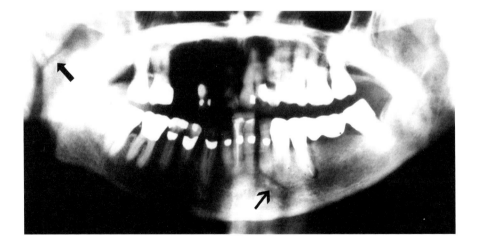

FIGURE 3.4 The woman, 64, was beaten by her husband. Examination shows fresh fractures of the right mandibular neck (arrow) and of the left mentalis with extension through the root of the lateral incisor (broad arrow).

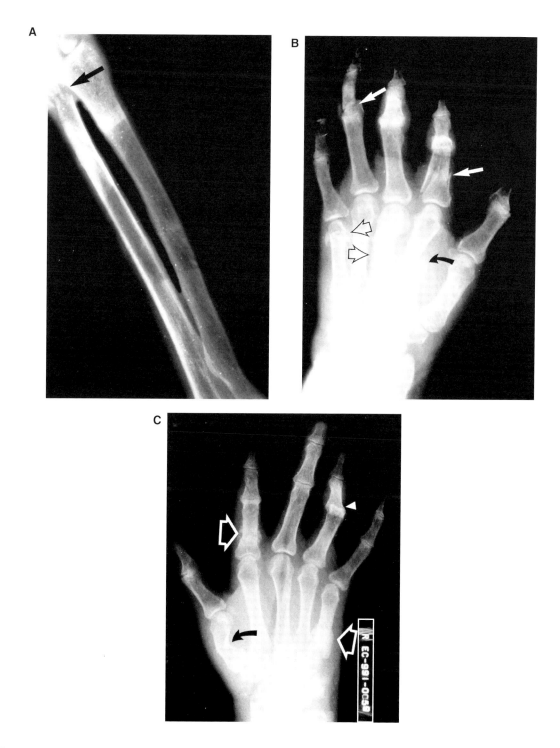

FIGURE 3.5 This octogenarian female was bedfast. Injuries inappropriate to her level of activity and multiple injuring in various stages of healing were signs of abuse. **(A)** Forearm with marked osteoporosis and with a displaced comminuted fending fracture of the distal ulna at the edge of the picture (arrow). **(B and C)** Both hands show new fractures (arrows), healing fractures (open arrows), and healed fractures (curved arrows) with residual deformity and dislocation (triangle). The fending fractures of the ulna are again seen (open curved arrow) in **(C)**. (Courtesy of Dr. M.G.F. Gilliland.)

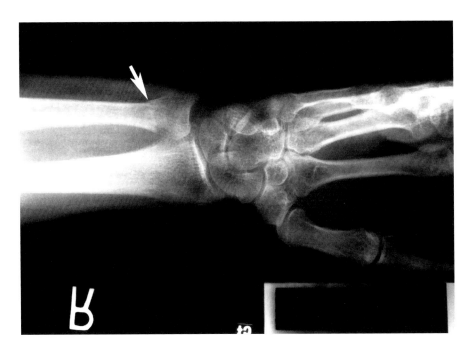

FIGURE 3.6 Minimal displaced fractures of the distal end of the ulna in an elderly nursing home patient. Is it a fending fracture, a twisting or restraint injury, or simply a result of extreme osteoporosis and normal handling? (From Brogdon, B.G., Forensic aspects of radiology, in *Medicolegal Investigation of Death*, 4th ed., Spitz, W.U., Ed., C.C. Thomas, Springfield, IL, chap. XXI. With permission.)

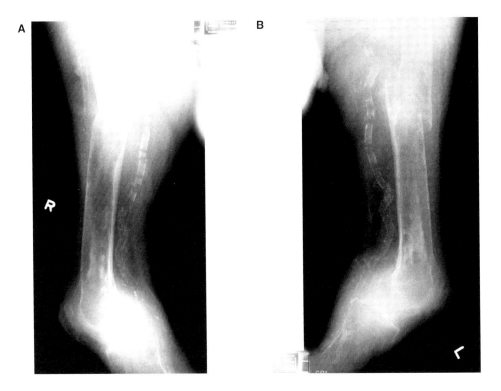

FIGURE 3.7 This obese elderly male diabetic had kidney failure, profound osteoporosis, and bilateral below-the-knee amputations. He was quite difficult to lift or move. His lower extremity stumps necessarily were used as handles, but were unable to take the strain. **(A)** The right femur was fractured while being cared for at home. **(B)** The left femur was fractured while being lifted for transport to the hospital by trained EMS personnel. Impression: no abuse. (Courtesy of Dr. J.C.U. Downs.)

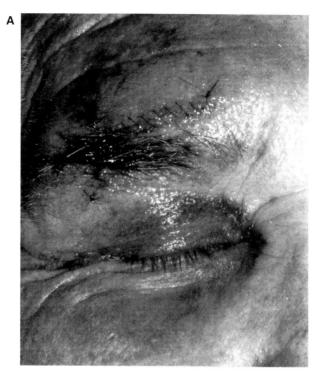

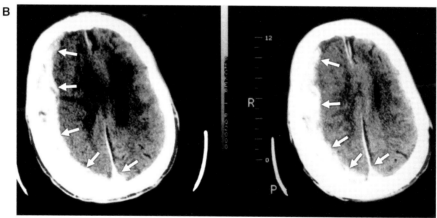

FIGURE 3.8 This elderly man with dementia was taken from the nursing home where he was domiciled to the hospital. **(A)** He had scrapes and bruises about the forehead and one eye and a split lip. His attendant suggests that the patient either fell down or against something while walking or had fallen out of bed. The patient was treated and released back to the nursing home. **(B)** Two days later, he was returned to the hospital with massive subdural hematoma (arrows) that proved fatal. The attendant abruptly left town. Investigation revealed that the victim was not ambulatory and that his mattress was already on the floor to prevent his falling out of bed! (From Brogdon, B.G., Forensic aspects of radiology, in *Medicolegal Investigation of Death*, 4th ed., Spitz, W.U., Ed., C.C. Thomas, Springfield, IL, chap. XXI. With permission.)

4 Self-Abuse

Hermann Vogel, M.D. and B.G. Brogdon, M.D.

We are concerned here with the sometimes unfathomable things people do to themselves, thus becoming both perpetrator and victim. They may be driven to these actions by cultural pressures, religious beliefs, psychological impulses, or sexual urgencies. Sometimes people harm themselves unintentionally as the result of negligence, occupation, or addiction.[1,2]

SELF-ABUSE BY PRESSURES OF CULTURE, RELIGION, OR FASHION

DRESS CODES

Harmful effects of vitamin D deprivation and nutritional deprivation as a result of religion- related dress codes and social hierarchy have already been illustrated (Figure 1.48).

NECK RINGS

Neck rings, still applied to young women in certain African tribes, are well-known and have been illustrated in *National Geographic* and cigarette advertisements. They deform the neck, pectoral girdle, mandible, and base of the skull. The neck muscles atrophy to the extent that the woman could not live without the supporting rings (Figure 4.1).

BODY PIERCING

NIPPLE RINGS

Rings placed in and about the nipple or areola area have been associated with abscess formation (Figure 4.2).

TONGUE PIERCING

Tongue piercing increases the risk of infection with hepatitis and inflammatory complications during dental treatment. Injuries to the teeth can be sustained from the metallic devices (Figure 4.3). Rings in other locations have some risk of infections. For instance, rings in the labia and clitoris may increase the risk of AIDS, hepatitis, and sexually transmitted diseases.

PRESSURE FOR FERTILITY

"In N'djamena, the capital of Chad, I (H.V.) visited the one municipal hospital. Upon learning I was a radiologist, I was asked to help. Having agreed, I was confronted with a pile of some 80 hysterosalpingograms that had been made by the technicians without direction or supervision. Nobody in the hospital could read the radiographs; no medical consequence occurred, and any risk of the procedure was ignored. I asked for background information and learned that in Africa the woman is under enormous pressure to be fertile. If she does not conceive, she must expect societal sanctions. If she cannot get pregnant, she tries to postpone recognition of her failure as long as possible. This is the reason hysterosalpingograms are performed in such large numbers, despite the fact that neither evaluation nor treatment is available" (Figure 4.4).

SEXUAL ENHANCEMENT

BREAST AUGMENTATION IMPLANTS

Potential complications from breast implants have been widely discussed in the lay press. There are a number of implantable devices now in use with different radiologic appearances. One example is shown (Figure 4.5).

PENILE IMPLANTS

Several forms of penile implants have been devised. All carry some risk of harmful effect. A device that allows intermittent erection of the penis is shown (Figure 4.6).

SELF-HARM IN THE COURSE OF CRIMINAL ACTIVITY

THEFT OF FUEL

Inhalation hydrocarbon pneumonia is a risk of stealing fuel by the process of siphoning where the liquid can be either aspirated or swallowed. There is a high incidence of pneumatocele formation in hydrocarbon pneumonia (Figure 4.7).

BODY-PACKING

The body-packer or "mule" transports illegal drugs in the alimentary canal. More will be said about this in Section VII. A body-packer is at great risk if any of the drug packets rupture (Figure 4.8). Other complications include obstruction and impaction.

SELF-ABUSE BY DRUG ADDICTION

COCAINE SNIFFING

Habitual, long-term sniffing has been associated with destruction of the nasal septum (Figure 4.9), rhinitis, and sinusitis (Figure 4.10).

ARTERIAL DAMAGE DUE TO INJECTION

Arterial injection of heroin by error can cause arterial occlusion. The example shown is of a young user who erroneously injected heroin in the brachial artery with subsequent necrosis of the distal fingers (Figure 4.11). Repeated insults of multiple injections can cause occlusion of even large arteries. Numerous needle punctures can cause aneurysm formation as well.

BROKEN NEEDLES

Repetitious and inexpert injections can cause needle breakage with the fragment left inside the body (Figure 4.12).

HARMFUL ADULTERANTS

Nonnarcotic powders and crystals are used to cut or adulterate narcotics. Some are harmful. Talcum powder used to cut heroin is one of the worst offenders (Figure 4.13).[3]

INGESTION/INSERTION OF FOREIGN MATERIAL IN THE BODY

Some individuals seem driven by psychological urges to ingest unreasonable foreign material. These are usually manufactured devices. Ingested paper clips, razor blades, mechanical pencils, and assorted hardware are frequently encountered. Unless the objects are too long to make turns in the bowel, most will make their way through the alimentary canal and will eventually be expelled from the rectum. There are certain places in the alimentary tract where foreign bodies are most likely to hang up. These are, in order:

1. The level of the insertion of the cricopharyngeus and the esophagus
2. The esophagus where it crosses over the left mainstem bronchus
3. The gastroesophageal junction
4. The pylorus
5. The junction of the second and third portions of the duodenum
6. The ligament of Treitz
7. The ileo-cecal valve
8. The splenic flexure and the sigmoid flexure

Swallowed foreign bodies will not be appreciated radiographically unless metallic or made of certain radio-dense plastics (Figures 4.14 to 4.19). Visualization of radiopaque poison in the stomach has been reported.[2]

RECTAL INSERTION OF FOREIGN BODIES

Foreign bodies are placed in the rectum for sexual gratification or occasionally as a sexual punishment. Foreign bodies are also inserted in the vagina but rarely come to radiologic attention, since they are easily removed. Unfortunately, foreign objects inserted in the rectum are not easily retrievable and come to medical (and radiologic) attention. The range of objects one may find in the rectum is mind-boggling.[4] A few examples are shown (Figure 4.20).

URETHRAL INSERTION

Insertion of foreign objects into the urethra occurs in both sexes, but we have seen it more commonly in males. Sexual gratification seems to be the goal in most instances (Figure 4.21).

SKIN PIERCING

We have repeatedly seen a young man who has a penchant for inserting wires under his skin. These are usually paper clips that he has straightened out. They have been rather widely distributed on the right side of his upper body (he is left-handed). On at least one occasion, presumably unintentional intravascular insertion was made (Figure 4.22).

SUICIDE

Suicide can be called the most sincere and the ultimate form of self-abuse. In the United States the gun is the most preferred method (Figure 4.23). Hanging is the next preference (Figure 4.24). The use of a blade is fairly common (4.25). Immolation by fire, drowning, asphyxiation, inhalation, and poisoning are all methods that have their adherents. The automobile is often suspected as a weapon of self-destruction. Some methods of suicide are suggested by the profession or occupation of the perpetrator or victim (Figure 4.26). A most unusual suicide by pneumatic hammer has been reported by De Letter and Piette (Figure 4.27).[5]

REFERENCES

1. Vogel, H., *Gewalt in Röntgenbild*, ecomed verlagsgesellschaft mbH, Landsberg/Lech, 1997, chap. 8.
2. Brogdon, B. G., *Forensic Radiology*, CRC Press, Boca Raton, FL, 1998, chap. 3.
3. Feigin, D., Talc: understanding its manifestations in the chest, *Am. J. Roentgenol.*, 146, 295, 1986.
4. Burch, D.B. and Starling, J.R., Rectal foreign bodies: case reports and a comprehensive review of the world's literature, *Surgery*, 100, 512, 1986.
5. De Letter, E.A. and Piette, M.H., An unusual case of suicide by means of a pneumatic hammer, *J. Forensic Sci.*, 46, 962, 2001.

CREDITS

From Brogdon, B.G., *Forensic Radiology*, CRC Press, Boca Raton, FL, 1998. With permission.
Figures 4.8, 4.20A, 4.20B, 4.22, 4.24.

From Vogel, H., *Gewalt in Röntgenbild*, ecomed verlagsgesellschaft mbH, Landsberg/Lech, 1997. With permission.
Figures 4.7, 4.11, 4.12, 4.20C, 4.20D, 4.20I, 4.21, 4.23, 4.26.

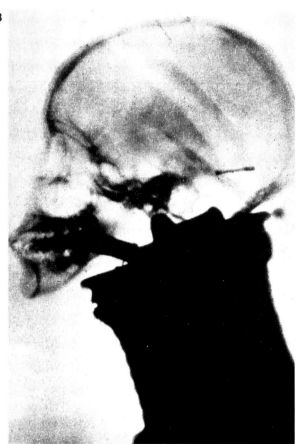

FIGURE 4.1 (A) Anthropologists from the German Röentgenmuseum (probably in the late 1920s or early 1930s) used portable x-ray equipment to examine a young African woman in neck rings. (B) Positive print of the negative x-ray image obtained. (Courtesy of the German Röentgenmuseum.)

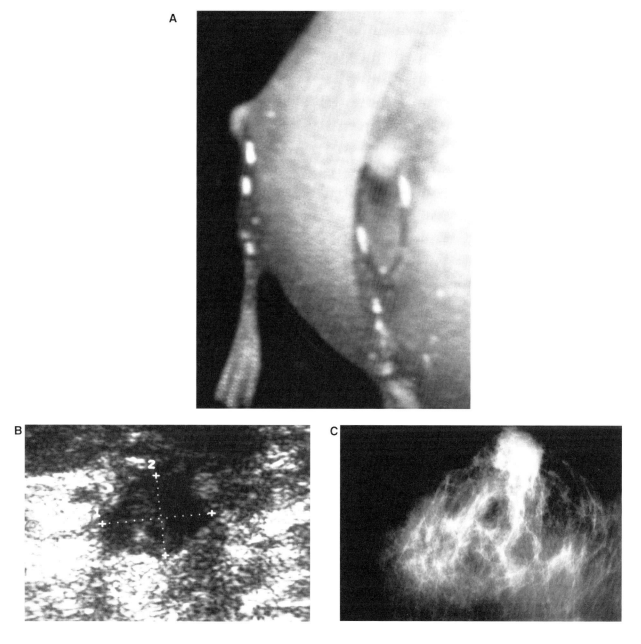

FIGURE 4.2 **(A)** Photograph of nipple rings with tassels. **(B)** Ultrasound examination showing subareolar abscess. **(C)** Mammogram showing abscess.

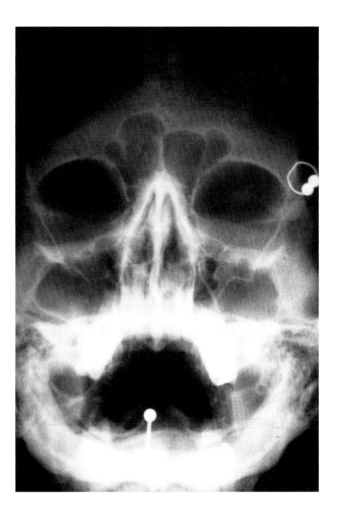

FIGURE 4.3 Young woman with a dumbbell-shaped metallic insert in the tongue and a ring in the left eyebrow.

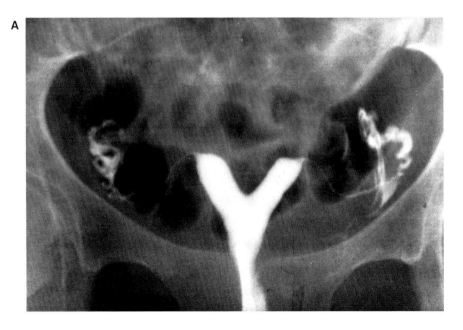

FIGURE 4.4 Hysterosalpingograms showing: **(A)** bicornuate uterus.

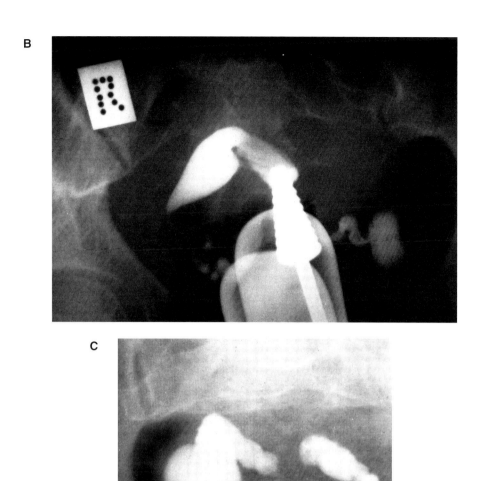

FIGURE 4.4 (Continued) Hysterosalpingograms showing: **(B)** unicornuate uterus; **(C)** bilateral hydrosalpinx secondary to tubal obstruction.

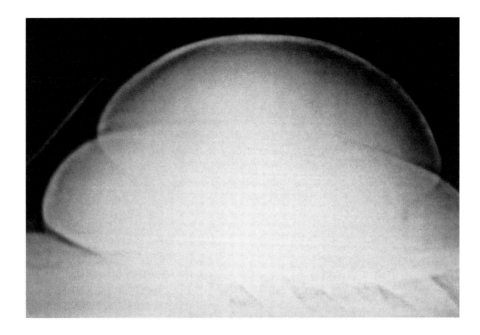

FIGURE 4.5 Breast implant for augmentation.

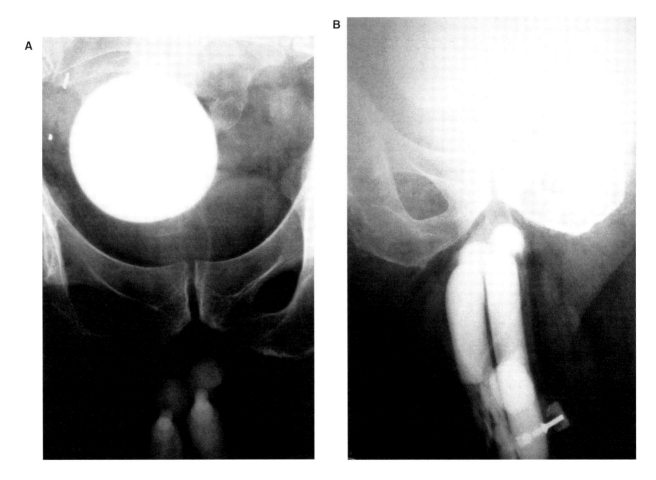

FIGURE 4.6 (**A**) Compressible balloon-type reservoir implanted just above the symphysis can be compressed to fill (**B**) the penile implants, thus provoking erection. The fluid in this hydraulic system is made radio-opaque with an iodine solution.

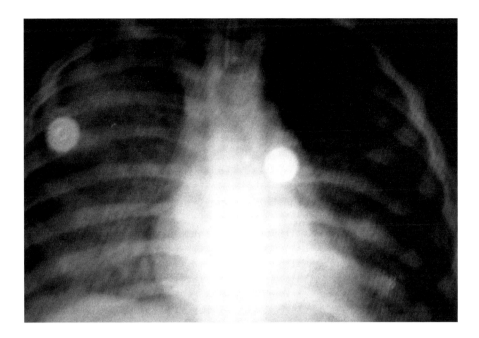

FIGURE 4.7 Frontal chest film showing aspiration pneumonia in the right lower lobe from hydrocarbon aspiration. The round densities are electrocardiogram leads.

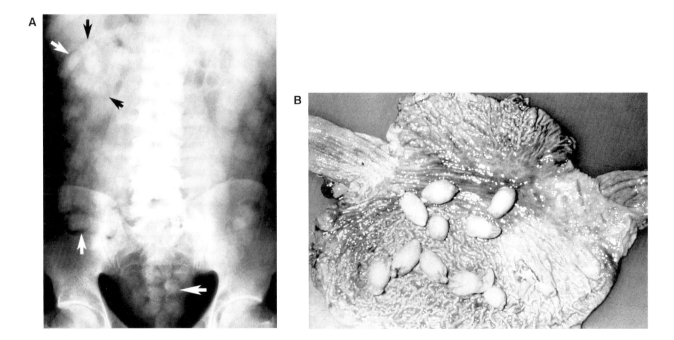

FIGURE 4.8 **(A)** Abdominal radiograph of a body-packer who has swallowed multiple packets of narcotics that have been wrapped in condoms. Visualization of the slightly hyperdense packets is enhanced by halos of entrapped gas or air within the layers of latex. (Courtesy of Dr. Richard N. Aizupuru.) **(B)** Latex covered narcotics packages are shown in the open stomach of a body-packer who died of an overdose when one of the packages broke. (Courtesy of Dr. James M. Messmer.)

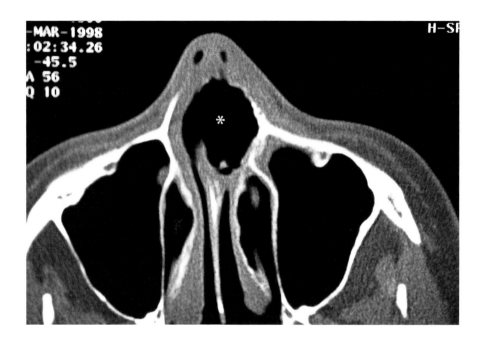

FIGURE 4.9 Computed tomography examination in the coronal plane of the nasal cavity and ethmoid and maxillary sinuses shows absence of the nasal septum (asterisk).

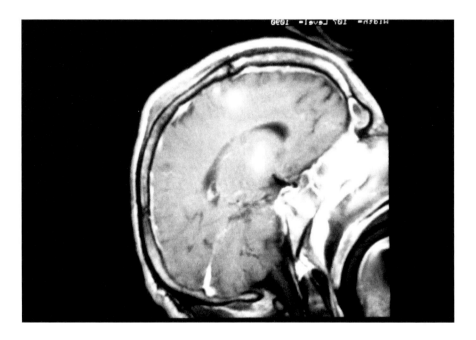

FIGURE 4.10 Sagittal magnetic resonance imaging shows high signal in the ethmoid and the sphenoid sinuses from cocaine rhinitis and sinusitis.

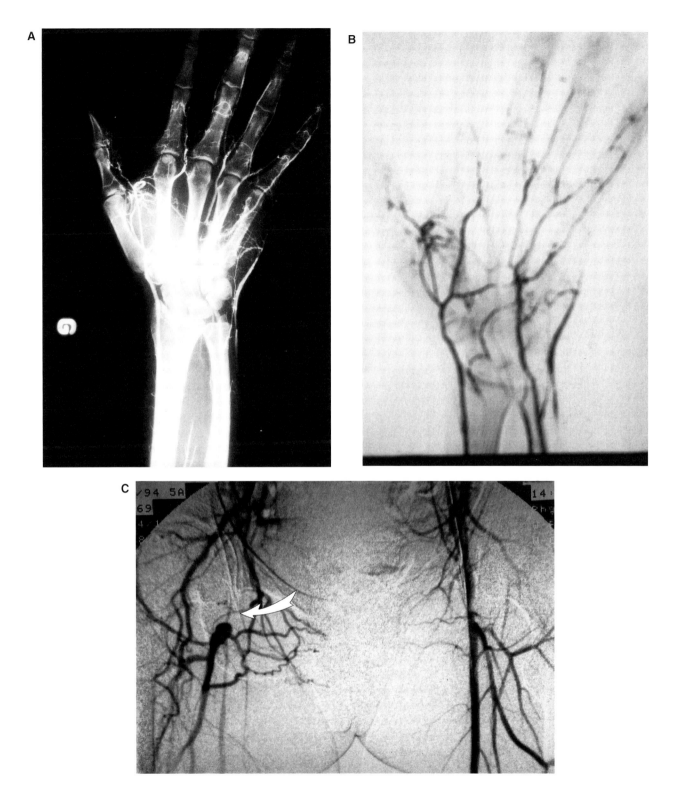

FIGURE 4.11 Occlusions in the small arteries of the hand with loss of profusion to large portions of the fingers due to injection of heroin into the brachial artery as shown by: **(A)** conventional arteriography; **(B)** digital subtraction angiography. **(C)** Femoral artery occlusion secondary to false aneurism (due to multiple injections) and failed bypass.

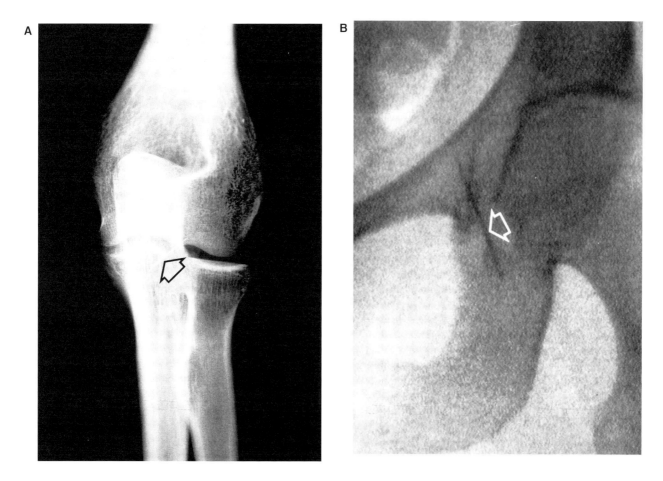

FIGURE 4.12 Broken needle fragments (arrows) in: **(A)** the left antecubital fossa; **(B)** the left inguinal region.

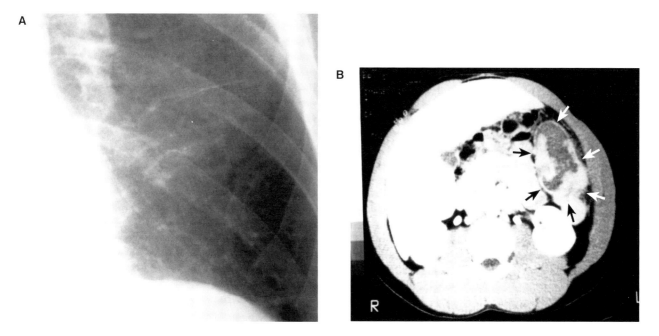

FIGURE 4.13 **(A)** Pulmonary talcosis from intravenous injection of heroin cut with talcum powder. Note the fine linear strands of fibrosis in the left lung base. There are also tiny punctate densities representing the talc deposits. **(B)** Concomitant splenic abscess (arrows) from contaminated needle or injected material.

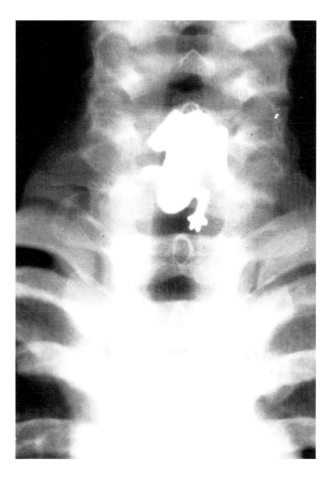

FIGURE 4.14 "A frog in the throat": broken metallic ornament lodged at the junction of the cricopharyangeus and esophagus.

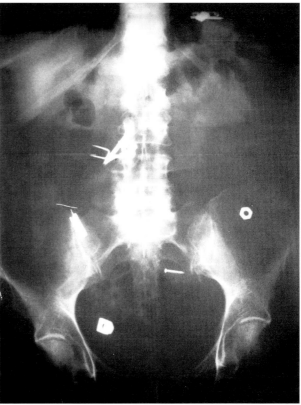

FIGURE 4.15 This woman on furlough from a mental institution trailed her husband through a hardware store as if she were at a cafeteria, sampling the buffet as she went along. (Courtesy of Dr. Joseph Sullivan.)

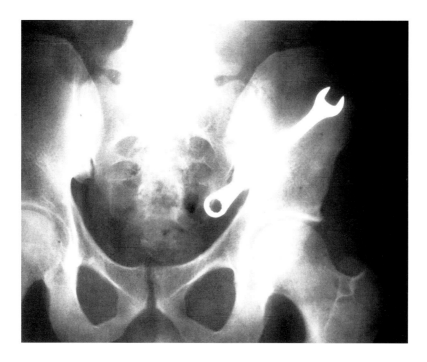

FIGURE 4.16 Ingested wrench lodged at the junction of descending and sigmoid portions of the colon. (Courtesy of Dr. Joseph Sullivan.)

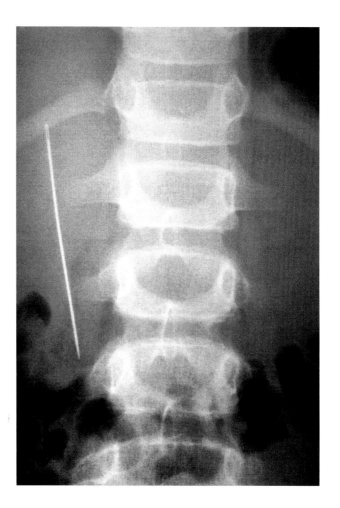

FIGURE 4.17 Sewing needle overlying the right upper abdomen. It later proved to be outside the bowel. It probably perforated the duodenum, being too long to negotiate the duodenum C-loop.

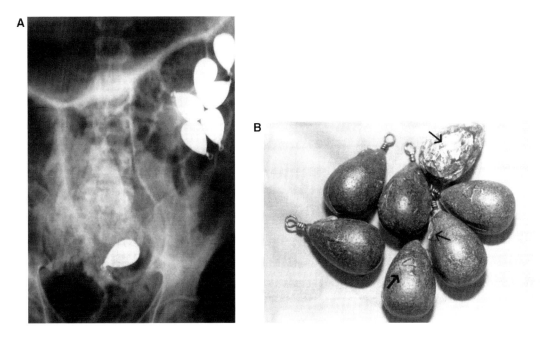

FIGURE 4.18 This man apparently decided he had a dietary deficiency of lead, so he swallowed seven lead fishing sinkers. This was a fatal decision. (A) Shows that one sinker has escaped the stomach where the remaining six reside. (B) Post-autopsy photograph shows corrosive changes (arrows) from stomach acid, allowing absorption and lead poisoning. (Courtesy of Dr. David Sipes.) (From Brogdon, B.G., Forensic aspects of radiology, in *Medicolegal Investigation of Death,* 4th ed., Spitz, W.U., Ed., C.C. Thomas, Springfield IL, chap. XXI. With permission.)

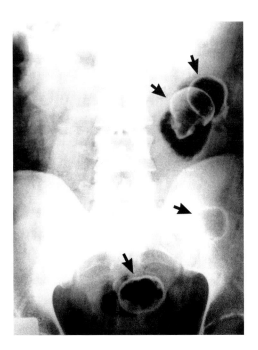

FIGURE 4.19 "Kenophilia?" This young man collects Ken dolls (Ken is Barbie's boyfriend, perhaps intimate partner). The collector likes to pull the plastic heads off his dolls and swallow them (arrows). Later, he would retrieve the heads, clean them, and recycle them.

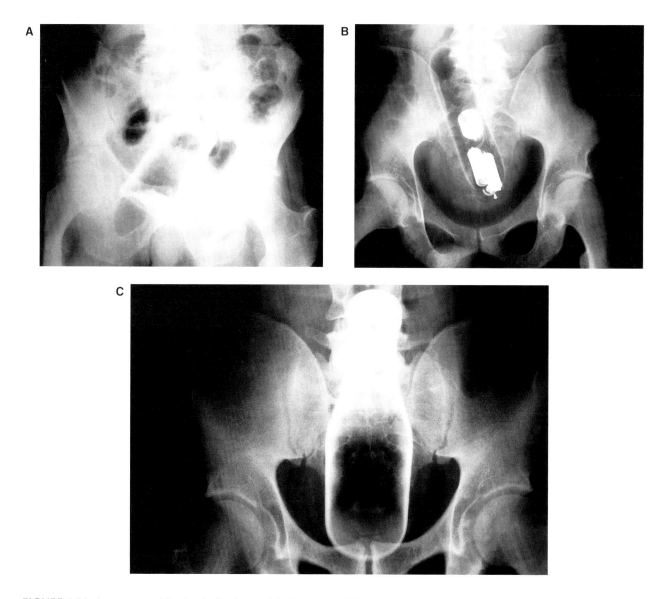

FIGURE 4.20 A spectrum of foreign bodies inserted in the rectum. **(A)** Water glass. **(B)** Plastic vibrator. **(C)** Bottle in the rectum, right side up.

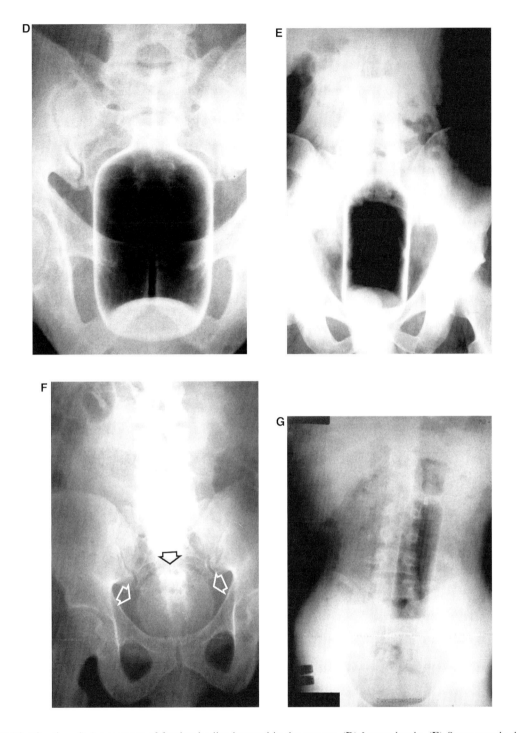

FIGURE 4.20 (Continued) A spectrum of foreign bodies inserted in the rectum. **(D)** Larger bottle. **(E)** Some people think a "Lone Star longneck" is a collector's item. **(F)** Baseball in the rectum. (Courtesy of Dr. Todd Stanley.) **(G)** This man was surprised to find he had a can of butane lighter fuel in his rectum on the morning after his 40th birthday party. (Courtesy of Dr. Jennifer George.).

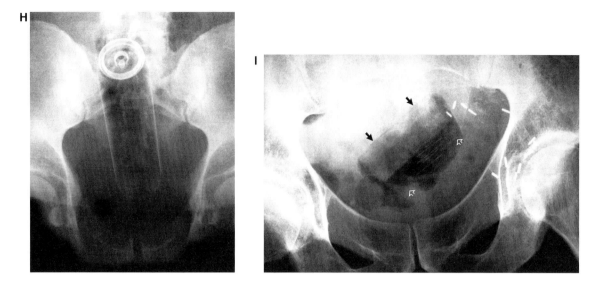

FIGURE 4.20 (Continued) A spectrum of foreign bodies inserted in the rectum. **(H)** This man claimed he slipped in the shower and impaled himself on an aerosol can of hair spray. (Courtesy of Dr. Peter Petruzzi.) **(I)** This thief rolled his wad of paper money in plastic wrap and deposited it in his rectum for safekeeping.

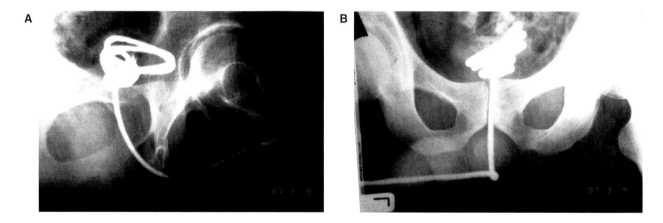

FIGURE 4.21 **(A and B)** Two males with insulated wires threaded through the penis and the bladder where they are coiled so that they cannot be withdrawn. The wire in **(A)** actually seems to have a knot in it (arrow).

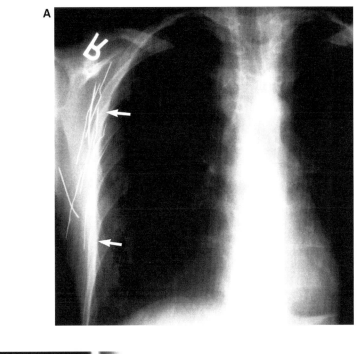

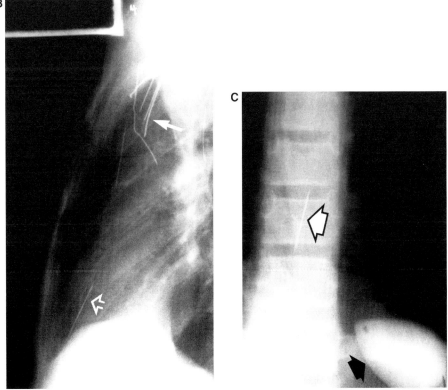

FIGURE 4.22 (**A**) Disturbed young man who inserts wires (arrows) under his skin. (**B** and **C**) A wire in the right ventricle (open arrows) obviously was inserted into a vein, probably by mistake. He also swallows foreign objects (black arrow).

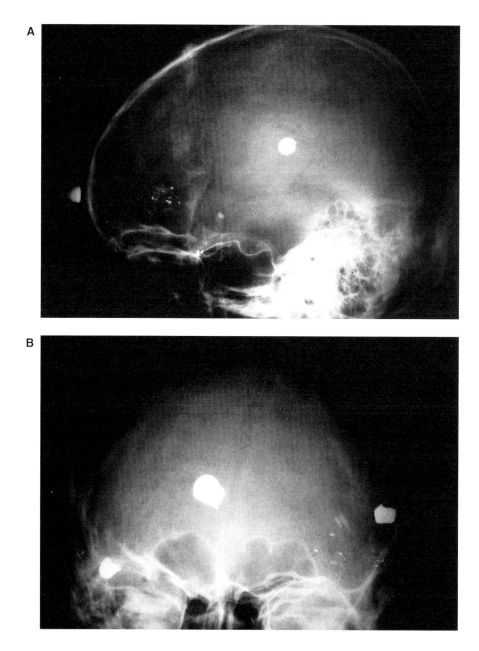

FIGURE 4.23 (**A** and **B**) Attempted suicide with three gunshots to the head.

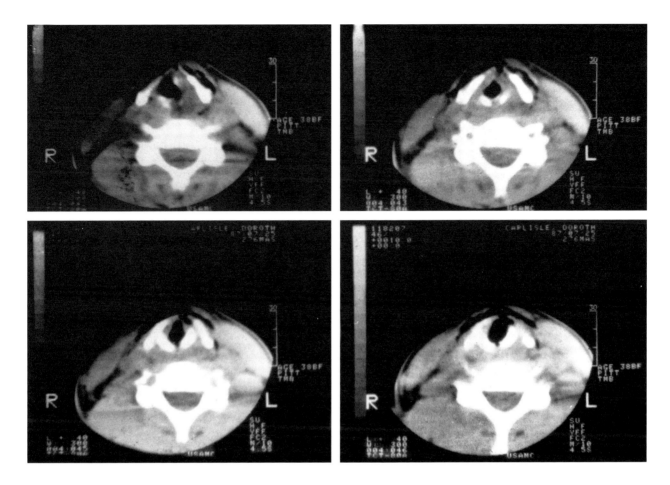

FIGURE 4.24 Attempted suicide by hanging that resulted in fracture of the larynx and extravasation of air into the soft tissues of the neck (computed tomography examination).

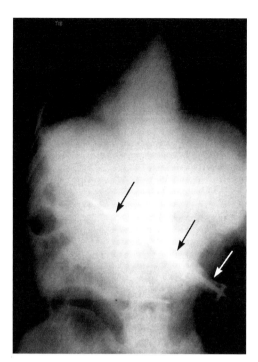

FIGURE 4.25 This patient successfully committed hari-kari. The body was brought to the morgue with the knife (arrows) still in the abdomen. (Courtesy of Dr. Leroy Riddick.) (From Brogdon, B.G., Forensic aspects of radiology, in *Medicolegal Investigation of Death*, 4th ed., Spitz, W.U., Ed., C.C. Thomas, Springfield, IL, chap. XXI. With permission.)

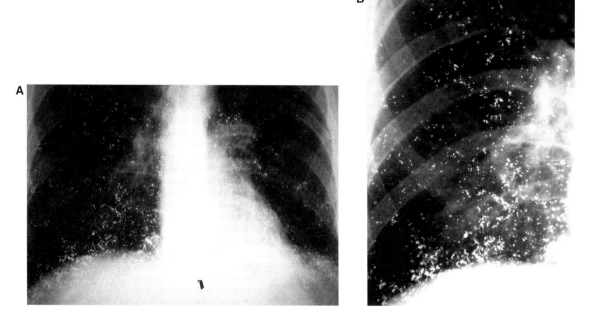

FIGURE 4.26 This nurse committed suicide by intravenous injection of liquid mercury. (**A**) Shows the distribution of mercury particles throughout the lungs. (**B**) Close-up view of the right lung.

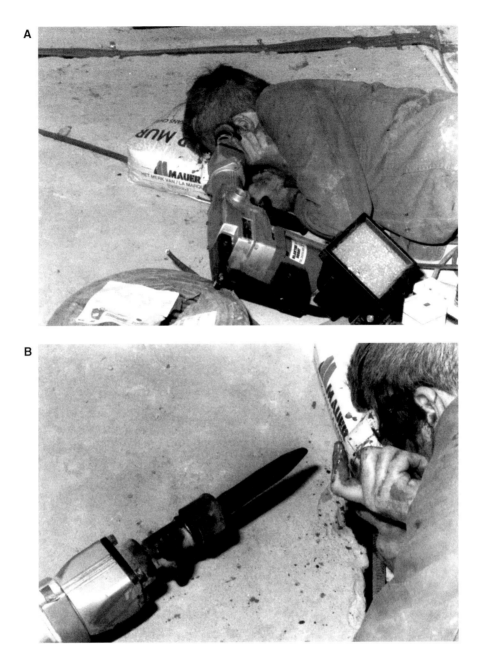

FIGURE 4.27 (**A**) Man found dead at a construction site holding a pneumatic hammer. (**B**) The hammer bit (13 cm × 15 mm) that was driven into the head produced. (Courtesy of Drs. E.A. De Letter and M.H.A. Piette.) (A and D: Copyright ASTM International. With permission.)

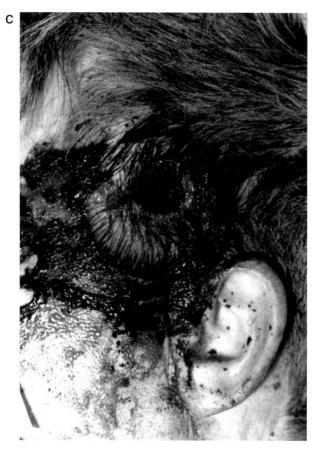

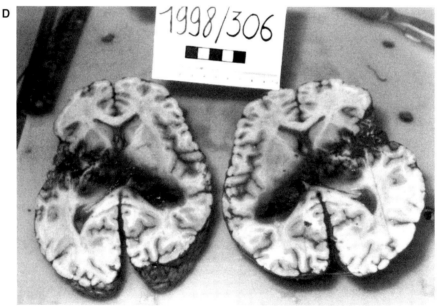

FIGURE 4.27 (Continued) **(C)** A massive temporal wound; **(D)** a track 11 cm × 15 mm extending from the left temporal to the right parieto-occipital lobe. (Courtesy of Drs. E.A. De Letter and M.H.A. Piette.) (A and D: Copyright ASTM International. With permission.)

5 Civil/Political Abuse

B.G. Brogdon, M.D.

INTRODUCTION

We who live in the United States enjoy constitutional protection against civil and political abuse. There are instances of abuse of power and authority in terms of excessive force employed against a person in the course of law enforcement activities. It is believed that most of these unfortunate episodes are the result of inexperience, fear, inadequate training, overzealousness, uncontrolled impulse, or occasionally, actual malignity. The injured party can turn to the courts for recourse. Often, the issue is not entirely clear; the precise chain of events is arguable. The radiologic evaluation of the injuries sustained may help clarify the event for the trier of fact.

Four example cases are presented below:

CASE 1

A 69-year-old man with Alzheimer's disease lived at home with his wife and was able to take care of most of his personal needs. One afternoon he wandered off to a nearby convenience store where he just hung around—not buying, not conversing, just there. A clerk apparently tired of his presence and called the police. Subsequent events were captured by a surveillance camera.

A large policeman came up behind the man and without warning, grasped him from behind and swung his feet off the floor. Turning to the right, the patrolman crashed the old man to the floor on his right front, landing with his full body weight on top—a classic takedown maneuver (Figure 5.1). The old man was handcuffed and led outside to the patrol car where he required help to get his legs inside and complained of his right shoulder. The patrolman's partner recognized the old man, and he was taken home without offer of medical evaluation or assistance. He was placed sitting on a couch in a den. Several hours later, his wife found him on the floor, unconscious and incontinent. He was taken to the hospital.

Multiple radiographs and computed tomography (CT) studies were required to disclose the full extent of his injuries (Figure 5.2) which included multiple fractures and a liver injury. He was discharged after a long hospitalization to a nursing home where he is totally incapacitated, incoherent, incontinent, and unaware of his surroundings.

His wife sued the city for Fourth Amendment violation and other charges. The city settled the case in favor of the plaintiff without trial.

CASE 2

A police officer was called to a darkened house for a domestic disturbance. He entered the house with verbal warnings and his six-cell flashlight held in approved position at his right shoulder. A small man tried to run past the officer and out of the house. There was some sort of altercation, and the man fell to the floor, paralyzed from the shoulders down.

Radiologic investigation revealed a most unusual, possibly unique, isolated fracture of the posterior arch of the fifth cervical vertebra (Figure 5.3). The vertebrae above and below were unaffected. CT examination, not shown, revealed severe focal soft tissue injury posterior to the fracture. Again, the spinous process and lamina of C-5 were shown to be driven into the neural canal, severely compressing the spinal cord and sparing the vertebrae above and below. These findings suggest a direct blow to the posterior neck by a very firm object with a relatively narrow leading edge. Even if the neck was flexed, the space between the unharmed spinous processes of C-4 and C-6 would not have been more than 1.5 to 2.0 cm.

The policeman claimed the man must have sustained his injury upon falling to the floor or perhaps against the door jamb or a firm part of the officer's accoutrements. The victim claimed he was struck with the flashlight and filed suit against the policeman and the city.

The case never went before a grand jury. It was dismissed by summary judgment for lack of witnesses, and that decision was upheld on appeal.

CASE 3

A teenaged male was stopped for a traffic violation. He was given a field sobriety test and was told that he had failed. The youth fell to his knees, begging the officer not to arrest him. At this point the story diverged.

The officer said the youth attacked him, forcing the officer to his back on the ground, and tried to take the officer's weapon from its holster. The officer kicked his assailant away, and when attacked again, fired twice up through his legs at the youth's chest (Figure 5.4).

The teenager claimed the patrolman shot him while he was down and trying to get away from a terrifying situation. He was taken to the hospital. Photographs revealed two round holes—one atop the left shoulder and the other high on the left back—and a ragged wound in the left axilla.

A forensic expert from the patrol officer's same agency testified that the victim's T-shirt clearly showed that there were two entrance holes in the chest and axilla and one exit hole in the back.

Radiologic review showed that one bullet had entered high posterior on the left shoulder and exited through the axilla (Figure 5.5). The second bullet entered high on the left back and came to rest against the descending aorta (Figure 5.6). CT confirmed this (Figure 5.7). Clearly the young man was shot in the back from above and could not have been attacking the officer as claimed. A Fourth Amendment excessive force case was filed in federal court on behalf of the teenaged driver. The jury found in favor of the plaintiff.

CASE 4

Police were informed that a young male scofflaw with a lot of traffic warrants out against him might be found at his girlfriend's house. Their appearance at the door frightened the young man, who may have been on drugs. He ran through the kitchen (picking up a small knife) and downstairs, going through a laundry room and into the furnace room. There he cut his wrists superficially. Four officers stationed themselves in the laundry room (Figure 5.8A). Patrolman Able was on the stairs; Sergeant Baker was at the foot of the stairs, bracing his weapon on the handrail; Patrolman Charlie was on the back wall facing the door to the furnace room; and Patrolman Delta was to his right. Each had a different weapon and each weapon had a different load.

They called out to the fugitive, who came into view holding the knife in his right hand and dripping blood. A host of shouted, confusing orders was followed by four gunshots spaced within a two second interval. Baker fired twice, Charlie (who had a shotgun) did not fire. The other two officers each fired once. The police officers stated they had been attacked by the man with the knife.

The victim had two entrance wounds very close together on his left side, another in the left lower back, and one high and posterior on the left shoulder. There was one exit wound on the right front lower chest at about the nipple line.

One bullet found on the floor was from Baker's weapon. Three bullets were inside the body (Figure 5.9). Of those, the first was removed from the right lower abdomen anteriorly and came from Delta's weapon. The second was lodged in the lower spine (Figure 5.10). The last bullet (Figure 5.11) was lodged low in the soft tissues of the chest near the midline (arrow). The track of the bullet found on the floor was shown by CT examination (Figure 5.12).

Evaluation of radiologic finding with respect to firing position, entrance and exit wounds, trajectories, and internal bullet paths and location (Figure 5.8) revealed the sequence of events. Instead of attacking, the victim whirled to his right to reenter the furnace room. This sudden movement apparently precipitated the gunfire against his left side and back. Baker and Delta fired at about the same time (Figure 5.8B). Their entrance wounds nearly coincided, but the paths diverged. Baker's round lodged in the spine, while Delta's round lodged in the lower abdomen and was removed at surgery. As the victim turned further to his right (Figure 5.8C), Baker's second round entered the left back and exited the right chest anteriorly. Only Able, who was on the stairs (Figure 5.8D), could have fired the round that traversed the victim from the high left shoulder, along the chest wall to midline anterior chest.

After his recovery, the young man was convicted of resisting arrest and served a short sentence. Upon release he filed a complaint entered in district court for "unreasonable and excessive force and assault and battery under the Fourth, Fifth, and Fourteenth Amendments and Section 42 of the U.S. Code." The case was settled in his favor.

WORLDWIDE CIVIL/POLITICAL ABUSE

According to Amnesty International, statistics show that there are more than 100 countries where abuse of power against individual rights, up to and including torture, is either condoned or actual policy. Example of these excesses will be found in the following chapters.

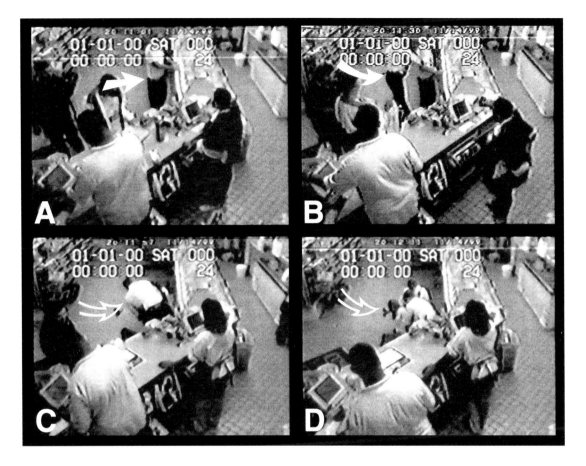

FIGURE 5.1 Sequence of frames from surveillance video camera. (**A**) Elderly man standing alone near convenience store counter (arrow). (**B**) Officer in light shirt (arrow) grabs man without warning from behind. (**C**) Officer throws him to the floor with classic takedown maneuver, officer in light shirt on top. (**D**) Cuffed man is lifted from floor by officer and his partner.

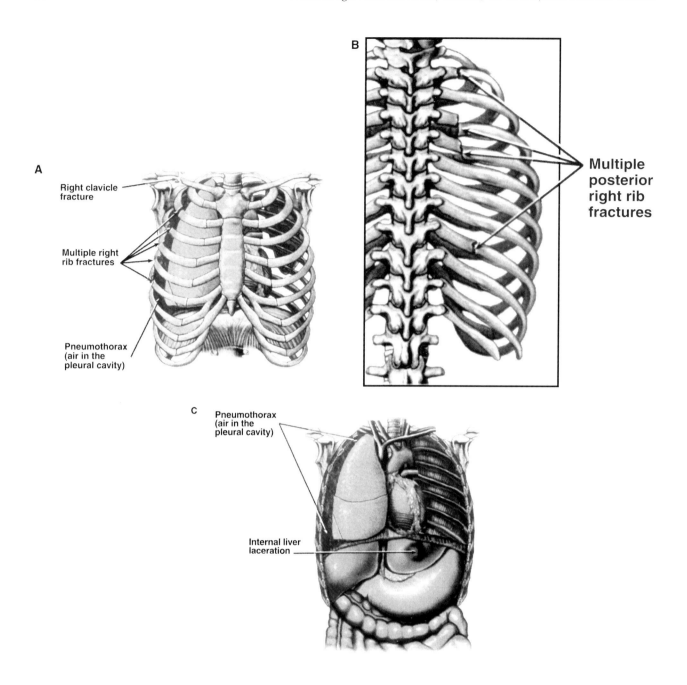

FIGURE 5.2 Artist's rendition of injuries disclosed by multiple x-ray and CT examinations. (**A**) Fractures of the right clavicle, right second through sixth ribs anterolaterally. (**B**) Fractures of the right second, fourth, fifth, and ninth ribs posteriorly. (**C**) Pneumothorax on the right. (The left lung had been removed previously for cancer.)

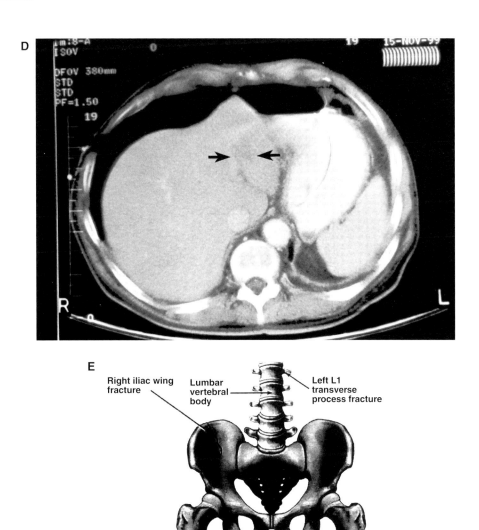

FIGURE 5.2 (Continued) Artist's rendition of injuries disclosed by multiple x-ray and CT examinations. (**D**) Liver laceration and contusion (arrow) shown by CT. (**E**) Fractures on the right iliac wing and left first lumbar transverse process.

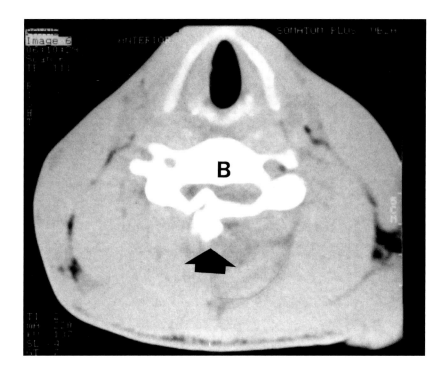

FIGURE 5.3 Axial CT view of C-5 vertebra. The spinous process and lamina (arrow) are driven into the neural canal, compressing the spinal cord against the posterior aspect of the vertebral body (B).

FIGURE 5.4 Officer's reenactment of his version of the shooting: on his back, feet up warding off his attacker, firing between his legs at the driver's chest.

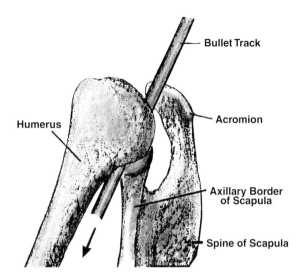

FIGURE 5.5 Course of the bullet entering high and posterior on the left shoulder and exiting the axilla. (Confirmed by entrance and exit wounds, x-rays, and CT.)

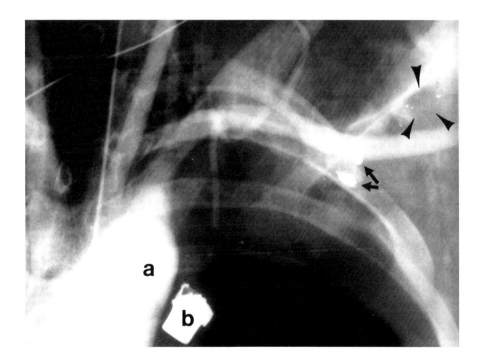

FIGURE 5.6 Aortagram shows the path of the bullet entering high on the left side of the back. An entrance hole in the scapula (arrowheads) is rimmed by tiny bullet fragments. Two bullet fragments were knocked off as the bullet passed over the left second rib posteriorly (arrows). The bullet (b) then passed downward and medially, coming to rest against the wall of the aorta (a).

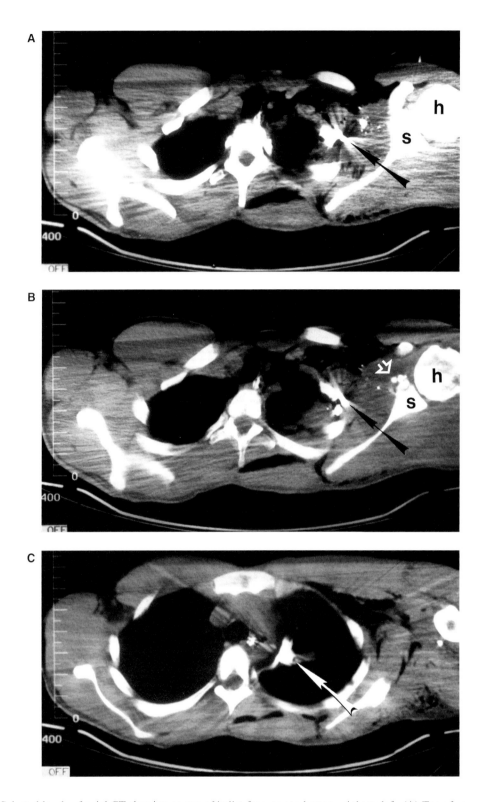

FIGURE 5.7 Selected levels of axial CT showing course of bullet from top to bottom, right to left. (**A**) Top of scapula (s) and head of humerus (h). The star pattern (arrow) marks the uppermost bullet fragment near the second rib posteriorly. (**B**) Slightly lower level, arrow points to lower bullet fragment near the second rib. Note the forward scatter of bone fragments from the inferior margin of the glenoid process of the scapula (open arrow), confirming that the high shoulder wound exiting the axilla came from the back. (**C**) Star pattern of the bullet (arrow) against the aorta.

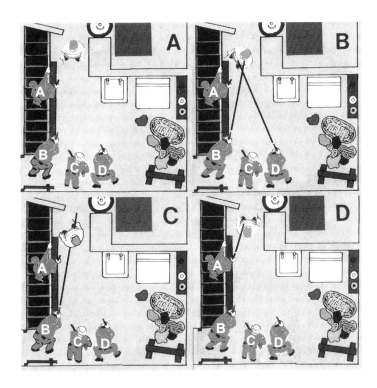

FIGURE 5.8 Sequential scenes of the action in the basement. A portion of the furnace room is at the top of each drawing. The officers are in the laundry room; the victim is in the doorway between. **(A)** Setting as the victim comes out of the furnace room. Patrolman Able is on the stairs. Sergeant Baker is at the front of the stairs. Patrolman Charlie is in the middle with the shotgun. Patrolman Delta is on the right.

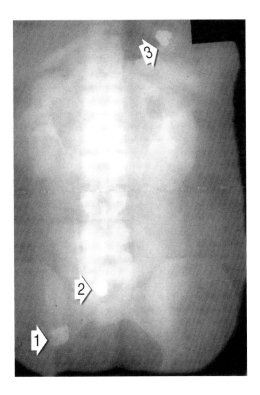

FIGURE 5.9 Abdominal radiograph showing three bullets within the body, numbered for descriptive purposes in text and captions.

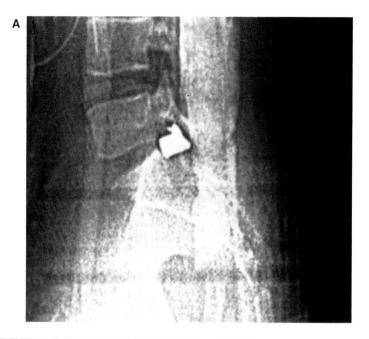

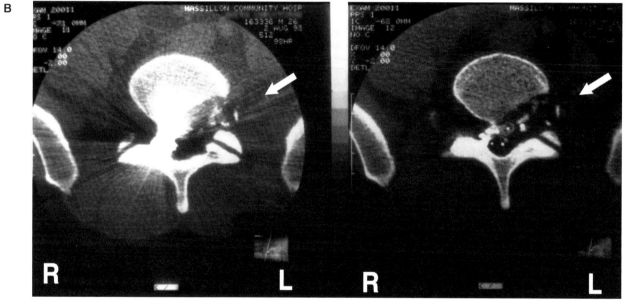

FIGURE 5.10 **(A)** Bullet #2 shown in the spine at the L-5, S-1 interspace on this lateral scout film prior to CT. **(B)** Sequential CT levels (the one on the right is uppermost) show that the bullet entered on the victim's left and was directed posteromedially and slightly downward (arrows).

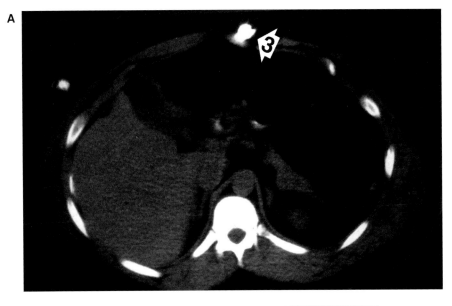
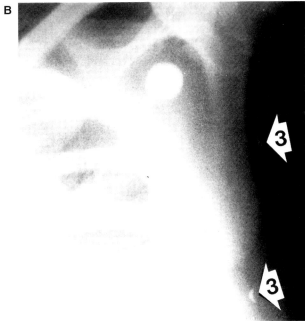

FIGURE 5.11 (**A**) Bullet #3 is very superficial in the lower anterior chest wall near the midline. (**B**) A chest film shows scattered fragments from bullet #3 along the chest wall, tracking from the high posterior shoulder wound toward its final position in the anterior chest wall.

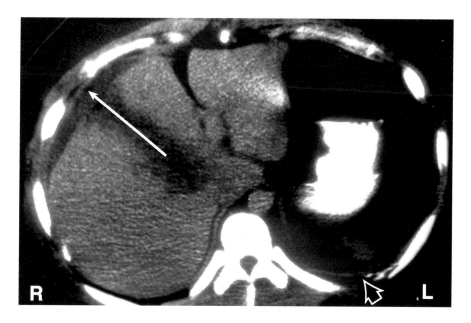

FIGURE 5.12 The bullet entered the left back and traversed the stomach and liver (arrow indicates the dark track through the liver), and exited low in the right chest. This was the bullet found on the floor from Sergeant Baker's weapon. Note the forward scatter of rib fragments (open arrow).

Section II

Torture

Those of us who grew up on a diet of American movies circa 1930–1960 are apt to think of torture as a means of forcible extraction of confessions from the bad guys or of information from the good guys – an inexcusable naiveté in today's world. Torture is a global reality employed as a political tool in more than 100 countries to systematically break the spirit and destroy the very identity and personality of its victims. It renders them docile and unable to resist or react to authoritarian or totalitarian desecration of human rights and human dignity.[1]

Encyclopedia Britannica[2] defines torture as:

> [T]he infliction of excruciating physical or physiological pain for such reasons as punishment, intimidation, coercion, the extraction of a confession, or the obtainment of information. Throughout history, governments have used torture against their enemies and as a part of the legal systems… Modes of inflictive pain range from physical devices to chemical injections to elaborate psychological techniques designed not only to break down resistance but to subvert personality… The modern techniques of torture include not only the traditional methods of physical pain but also the use of complex psychological and pharmacological methods that had been developed out of studies of medical research and the psychology of pain.

The World Medical Association Tokyo Declaration of 1975 defined torture as deliberate, systematic, or wanton infliction of physical or mental suffering by one or more persons acting alone or on the orders of any authority, to force another person to yield information, to make confession, or *for any other reason* [emphasis added].[3]

Torture has evolved throughout the ages to become more sophisticated. It usually is carried out in a clandestine fashion, often accomplished with a deliberate attempt to reduce any physical evidence of its practice. Therefore, documentation of abuse is difficult and often is based on historical accounts in the absence of physical findings at the time of examination. Ordinarily, most torture is carried out in the early stages of confinement and, if not initially fatal, the physical signs of torture are usually healed by the time the victim is released and can be examined.[4]

Torture that includes mutilation involves a high risk of the victim being killed. Victims who have torture applied to the trunk survive less often than those whose extremities have been tortured. Victims who escape their tormentors and come to the attention of rehabilitation centers in Europe, America, and elsewhere likely have been less severely tortured than those who are not permitted, or are unable, to leave.

Radiologic documentation of torture employs similar procedures, techniques, and modalities as are employed in the study of other forms of abuse. But imaging studies are usually scarce in countries where torture is common whether in times of peace or war. Therefore, imaging is an appropriate but exceptional method of record-keeping, or scientific analysis, of torture. Consequently, the literature on imaging and torture involves highly selective material. The reality is far more desperate than one can imagine.

Simplistically, torture can be classified as somatic, (bio) chemical (pharmacological), and psychological.[5] However, some forms of somatic torture are designed and applied in a manner to avoid telltale evidence by subsequent visual or radiologic inspection. Some somatic torture produces changes that can be demonstrated by imaging. In general, psychological and pharmacological torture does not lend itself to radiologic discovery. This section will be concerned with radiologically demonstrable somatic torture to include beating, electric torture, water torture, compression, stabbing and cutting, suspension, and other forms.

There are regional differences in the design and infliction of torture and mistreatment throughout the world and unfortunately, new forms of torture are constantly being invented. Consequently, this must be a general review.

Analysis of torture by imaging is rare in the acute phase. Often the victim is held in custody until the visible traces of torture have disappeared. Even after freedom is attained, the victim usually is frightened or shamed by the torture and is hesitant to seek diagnosis, treatment, or documentation of the trauma. This is especially true when torture is tolerated or performed by the state and when physicians and medical facilities are felt to be an active part of the system. Nevertheless, there have been isolated reports on the objective documentation of recent torture, for example, from Turkey.[6] In Syria, forensic physicians must examine a prisoner before he is brought before a judge for the first time and must differentiate between abuse and self-inflicted trauma, both in the acute stage.

While the majority of the physicians are devoted to preserving and defending human rights, unfortunately, and seemingly inevitably, some physicians become involved with abuse, torture, and other abridgements of human rights. In modern times this extends from Germany in the Third Reich, where 45% of German physicians (a higher percentage than for any other profession)[7] were members of the Nazi Party and a number of whom were convicted as war criminals at Nuremberg,[8,9] to present-day Turkey, where allegations of involvement in torture have been brought against 70 physicians and where 76% of physicians responding to a questionnaire did not consider beatings alone to constitute torture.[10]

Unquestionably, in regimes that countenance torture and other infringements of human rights, the medical community is under great pressures and coercion to look the other way, or to go along with the policy. In a retrospective case study of 200 alleged survivors of torture from 18 different countries, the Danish Medical Group of Amnesty International documented that 20% of those victims reported that medical personnel were involved in their torture.[11] Undoubtedly many of those were unwilling but silent accomplices. Physicians throughout the world have played an important role in opposition to torture and infringement of human rights, but this often has required great courage and the risk of professional and physical punishment. Physicians' groups and national medical societies must be constantly alert against any threat to human rights, particularly of a physical nature, and provide immediate and outspoken opposition before such practices and policies can take root.[4]

Radiologic studies can be particularly useful in evaluation of victims who have eventually come to rehabilitation centers where newer imaging modalities can be employed to access the late findings of torture. However, the cost of such procedures prevents wide-spread utilization.[4-7]

Computed tomography (CT) is used by centers for the rehabilitation of torture victims only in exceptional cases because of its cost and limited availability. Nevertheless, there are some strong indications for its use and, when employed, the findings can be quite impressive.

CT of the central nervous system is rarely employed early after torture has occurred. However, late studies can show sequelae such as subdural hematomas, hygromas, old intracerebral bleeding, and hydrocephalus.[12] Cerebral atrophy has been associated with previous beatings.[13]

Scintigraphy can verify that beating has indeed taken place, when clinical examinations and plain film diagnosis fail to document anything. In soft tissue, an increased activity can be demonstrated for days and even weeks; in bones it is demonstrated over months and even years, long after edema and hematoma have disappeared.[6,13,14]

The choice of examination depends on the form of torture, the region of the body affected, and the elapsed time. Various problems are faced when imaging suspected victims of torture. Some patients have claustrophobia and exhibit signs of aggression and fear (for example, general fear of people in uniforms). In addition, injuries such as scars due to cuts in African initiation rites have to be carefully distinguished.

Once obtained, diagnostic images must be carefully evaluated as to whether specific findings of forms of abuse or torture can be documented. Such evidence must be discussed and presented compellingly to physicians, lawyers, and officials usually not involved in the actual case.[4,15-18] While objectivity is required, one also must bear constantly in mind that the case is not theoretical, but actually represents a real human being.

Much of the evidence of torture comes from worldwide centers of rehabilitation for torture victims. Imaging sometimes demonstrates lesions so characteristic that they can be considered legal proof of previous torture and verify a presumed victim's claims.

Criteria that support claims of torture are:

1. Correlation between the type of torture and the findings derived from imaging procedures
2. Correlation between the date of torture and the imaging appearance of the lesion
3. Specific alterations, such as the periosteal reactions from palmatoria
4. Correlating findings in a particular situation, such as imprisonment and nutritional deficiencies or sequelae from denial of treatment or surgery
5. Patterns of beatings (proven by imaging) typical for a particular geographic location and corresponding with the victim's story

Unless otherwise indicated, illustrations in this section come from the private collection of one of the editors (H.V.) or, with permission, from his prior publication, *Gewalt in Röntgenbild.*

H.V.

B.G.B.

REFERENCES

1. Gaessner, S., Gurris, N., and Pross, C., Eds., *At the Side of Torture Survivors*, Johns Hopkins University Press, Baltimore, MD, 2001.
2. *Encyclopedia Britannica*, CD-ROM, 2001.
3. World Medical Association, The Declaration of Tokyo, 1975, in *Ethical Codes and Declarations Relevant to the Health Professions*, Amnesty International, New York, 1994, p. 9.
4. Brogdon, B.G., *Forensic Radiology*, CRC Press, Boca Raton, FL, 1998, chap. 17.
5. Genefke, I.K., *Torturen I verden: den angar os alle*, Hans Reizels forlag, Copenhagen, 1986, pp. 1–27.
6. Lök, V., Oral communication, International Torture Meeting, Istanbul, 1994.
7. Sidel, V.W., Commentary: the social responsibilities of health professionals: lessons from their role in Nazi Germany, *JAMA*, 276, 1679, 1996.
8. Grodin, M.A., Legacies of Nuremberg: medical ethics and human rights, *JAMA*, 276, 1682, 1996.
9. Lifton, R.J., *The Nazi Doctors: Medical Killing and the Psychology of Genocide*, Basic Books, New York, 1986.
10. Iacopino, V., Heiser, M., Pishever, S., and Kirschner, R.H., Physician complicity in misrepresentation and omission of evidence of torture in postdetention medical examinations in Turkey, *JAMA*, 276, 396, 1996.
11. Bro-Rasmussen, F., Henriksen, O.B., Rasmussen, O., et al., Aseptic necrosis of bone following falanga torture, *Ugeskr. Laeg.*, 144, 1165, 1982.
12. Hayes, E., MRI illustrates history of torture, *Diagn. Imaging Europe*, 13, 17, 1997.
13. Jensen, T.S., Genefke, I.K., Hyldebrandt, N., Pedersen, H., Petersen, H.D., Weile, B., Cerebral atrophy in young torture victims, *N. Engl. J. Med.*, 307, 1334, 1982.
14. Meier, J. and Andersen, J.G., Sclerosing of the calcaneus following phalanga torture, *Ugeskr. Laeger*, 147, 4206, 1985.
15. Kintzel, R., Röntgenbefunde von Folteropfern, dissertation, Hamburg, Germany, 1992.
16. Rassmussen, O.V., *Medical Aspects of Torture*, Laegeformenings forlag, Copenhagen, 1990.
17. Vogel, H., *Gewalt in Röntgenbildt*, ecomed verlagsgesellschaft mbH, Landsberg/Lech, 1997.
18. Vogel, H., Imaging helps unveil torture's dark secrets, *Diagn. Imaging Europe*, 37, 22, 1999.

6 Beating

Hermann Vogel, M.D. and B.G. Brogdon, M.D.

Physical beating is a widespread form of torture. The soft tissues bear the brunt of this form of torture and few, if any, radiological findings may be apparent upon delayed examination. In some countries, beating, caning, or lashing is used as an authorized form of punishment. Magnetic resonance imaging (MRI) studies shortly after such a legalized beating have shown massive edema and hemorrhage of soft tissue on the back over the thorax.[1]

Beatings may be generalized or localized.

GENERAL BEATINGS

Few specific findings will be detected radiologically from generalized beating since, as pointed out, soft tissue and bony injury usually has healed by the time the victim comes to sympathetic medical attention (Figure 6.1). Residual deformities of rib and spinal fractures may be present, as may be deformities due to ligamentous tears or ruptures. Defensive injuries sustained in the course of a generalized beating are common (Figure 6.2).

Fractures of the face and jaw are similar to those described in battering in Chapters 2 and 3.

Nondefensive injuries of the extremities may be inflicted in the course of a general beating (Figure 6.3).

LOCALIZED BEATING

Some types of localized beatings are widespread; however, beating often follows recognized patterns, some of which are typical for certain countries, regions, or even professions.

PALMATORIA

Palmatoria is an example of a method of localized torture that is virtually unique to a specific region—the small West African country Guinea-Bissau. Palmatoria involves repetitive blows to the shin where the tibia lies closest to the skin. Radiographic examination may show periosteal reaction from subperiosteal hemorrhage and hematoma. A laminar or onion skin periostitis can persist for weeks or even years (Figure 6.4). Somewhat peculiar endosteal and medullary changes may be seen as well.

Two recent case reports have shown that blows by a rod to this area of the tibia can produce a hidden endosteal fracture which is likely to be undetected on plain films

but obvious on computed tomography (CT) examination (Figures 6.5 and 6.6).[2,3] It is possible, perhaps likely, that some of the African cases would show similar findings with a more sophisticated imaging modality.

FALACA

Falaca, on the other hand, is a widespread form of torture, sometimes known as falanga and in Spanish-speaking areas as bastinado. Falaca means beating the foot, primarily (but not exclusively) on the sole of the foot. Falaca is perpetrated in the Near East, especially in Turkey and Iraq; in the Far East; and in some Spanish speaking areas. Falaca produces edema, hematoma, fractures and injuries to the ligaments, tendons, fascia, and aponeuroses of the feet and ankle (Figure 6.7). Shortly after torture, the clinical findings alone are usually diagnostic.

Radiography can confirm or exclude fractures and allows estimation of the time interval since torture was applied.[1,4–10] In my experience (H.V.), fracture can involve the toes, the metatarsals, the tarsals (especially the calcaneus), and occasionally the ankle. This pattern is found especially if the feet have been fixed during the beating. Fractures of the lateral malleolus seem to be an exception; nevertheless, the lower leg near the ankle may be involved. Scintigraphy initially shows increased soft tissue activity after the beating (Figures 6.8 to 6.12). Later, a generalized increased bony uptake with unusual degenerative changes may be found (Figure 6.13).

When available, MRI is better than CT in visualizing alterations of soft tissues including capsular thickening, atrophy, edema, and reparative changes. Delayed study may prove earlier torture by demonstrating thickened aponeurosis of the foot. MRI can also show bone bruises or edema (Figure 6.14).[11]

PRISONER'S SINUSITIS

In Chad, an uncommon form of torture involves a prisoner being beaten in the face producing fractures of the facial bones that can be demonstrated radiologically. Opacification of the maxillary sinuses is regularly seen due to bleeding, and subsequently sinusitis will develop. Somewhat similar injuries are seen in prostitutes in the Western world when pimps beat their women as a form of punishment, forcing them to continue to work despite hematomas and fractures.

HAND AND WRIST

In Zaire, fractures of the hands and wrists are particularly seen in journalists, writers, and artists. The aim is not only to hamper the victims' work, but also to cause physiological injury by mutilating the appendage that is their main instrument of livelihood and personality (Figure 6.15).

REFERENCES

1. Brogdon, B.G., *Forensic Radiology,* CRC Press, Boca Raton, FL, 1998, chap. 17.
2. Brogdon, B.G. and Crotty, J.M., The hidden divot: a new type of incomplete fracture? *Am. J. Roentgenol.,* 172, 789, 1999.
3. Petrow, P., Page, P., and Vanel, D., The hidden divot fracture: Brogdon's fracture, a new type of incomplete fracture, *Am. J. Roentgenol.,* 177, 946, 2001.
4. Genefke, I.K., *Torturen I verden: den angar os alle,* Hans Reizels forlag, Copenhagen, 1986, pp. 1–27.
5. Lök, V., Oral communication, International Torture Meeting, Istanbul, 1994.
6. Sidel, V.W., Commentary: the social responsibilities of health professionals: lessons from their role in Nazi Germany, *JAMA,* 276, 1679, 1996.
7. Bro-Rasmussen, F., Henriksen, O.B., Rasmussen, O., et al., Aseptic necrosis of bone following falanga torture, *Ugeskr. Laeg.,* 144, 1165, 1982.
8. Jensen, T.S., Genefke, I.K., Hyldebrandt, N., Pedersen, H., Petersen, H.D., Weile, B., Cerebral atrophy in young torture victims, *N. Engl. J. Med.,* 307, 1334, 1982.
9. Lök, V., Tunca, M., Kumanlioglu, K., Kapkin, E., and Dirik, G., Bone scintigraphy as clue to previous torture, *Lancet,* 337, 846, 1991.
10. Skylv, G., Falanga: diagnosis and treatment of late sequellae, *Torture Suppl.,* 1994.
11. Hayes, E., MRI illustrates history of torture, *Diagn. Imaging Europe,* 13, 17, 1997.

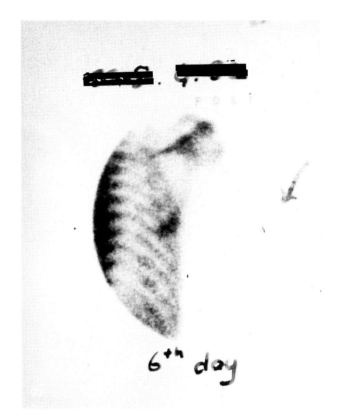

FIGURE 6.1 Rib contusion or fracture imaged by scintigraphy only 6 days after beating.

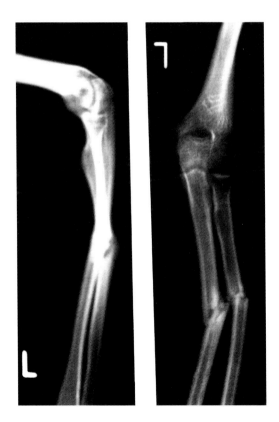

FIGURE 6.2 Angulated fractures of both bones of the forearm several weeks old. Defensive injury sustained during beating.

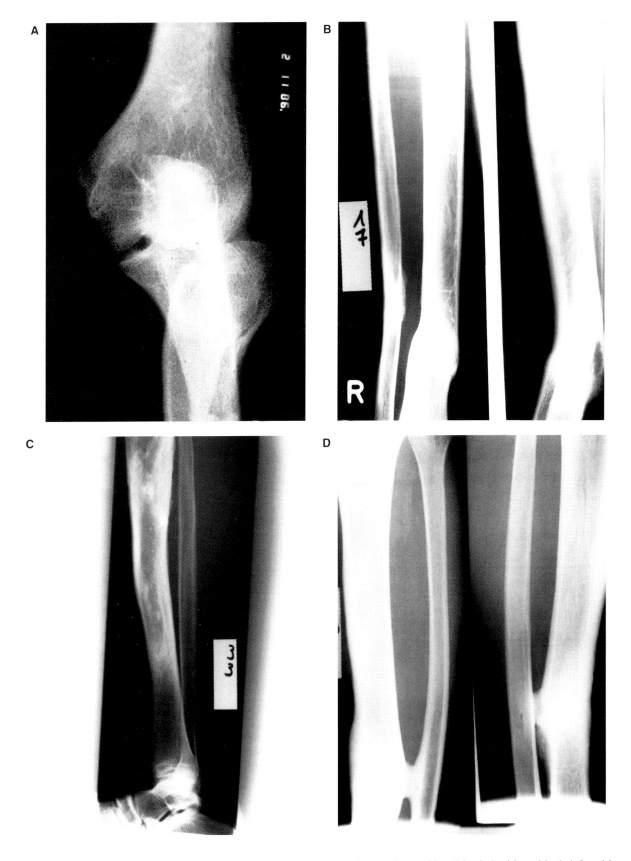

FIGURE 6.3 Fractures of extremities sustained during generalized beatings. All are old and healed with residual deformities. **(A)** Fracture dislocation of the proximal radius. **(B)** Both bone fractures of the lower leg. **(C)** Fracture of the tibia healed with residual angulation. **(D)** Fracture of the tibia healed with ankylosis to the fibula across the interosseous membrane.

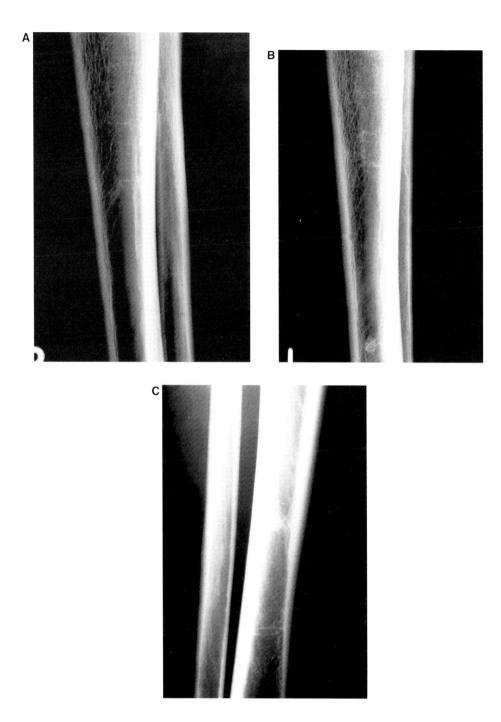

FIGURE 6.4 Close-up radiographs of the mid tibia and fibula of these victims of palmatoria. The anterior cortex of the tibia is thickened by periostitis, and there are peculiar endosteal and intramedullary changes.

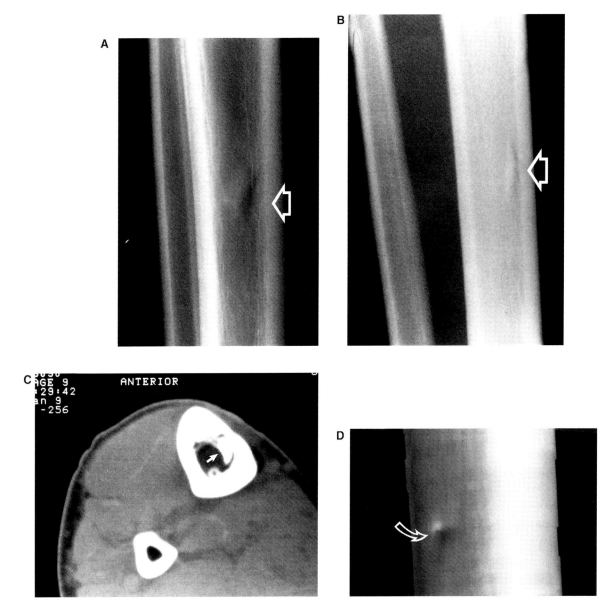

FIGURE 6.5 A young man was struck on the shin with a metal rod and sustained a laceration that was irrigated and sutured. (**A** and **B**) A worrisome finding on the radiographs prompted his recall. The wound was reopened and explored to reveal an intact periosteum. (**C**) A CT study showed an endosteal cone-shaped fracture fragment beneath an intact, slightly dimpled outer cortex. (**D**) 3-D reconstruction. (From Brogdon, B.G. and Crotty, J.M., *Am. J. Roentgenol.*, 172, 789, 1999. With permission.)

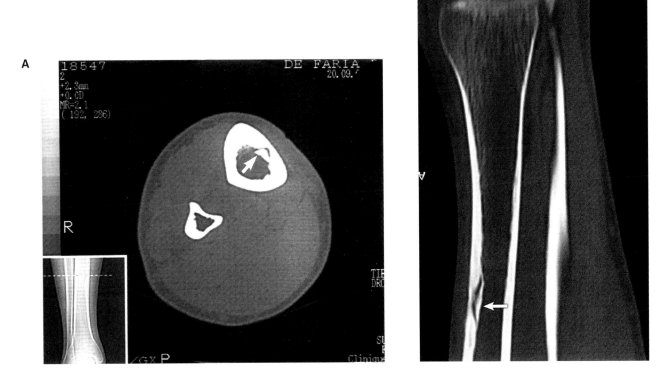

FIGURE 6.6 A young man was struck on the shin with a metal rod. This case, from France, presented identical findings as those of the preceeding figure. (A) Axial CT shows the internal fracture fragment. (B) Longitudinal demonstration of the endosteal fragment. (Courtesy of Dr. Daniel Vanel.) (From Petrow, P., Page, P., and Vanel, D., *Am. J. Roentgenol.*, 177, 946, 2001. With permission.)

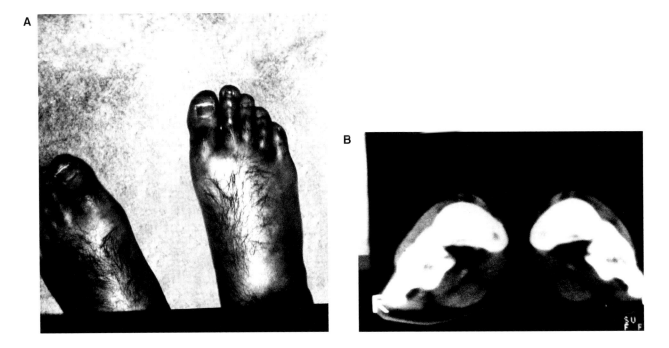

FIGURE 6.7 Falaca. (A) Photograph of feet after falaca. (B) Edema and hematoma, predominately plantar, after falaca (CT).

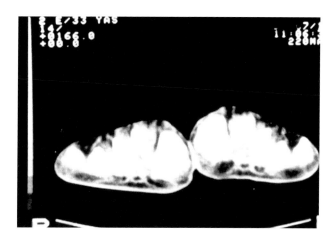

FIGURE 6.8 Chronic change after falaca, splay, and flat-foot deformities due to relaxed ligaments and aponeurosis (CT).

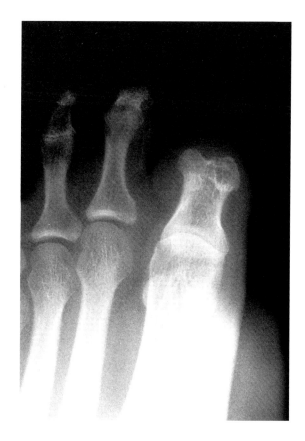

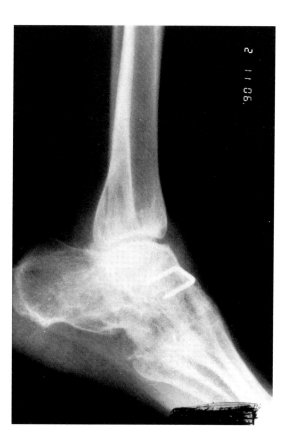

FIGURE 6.9 Amputation of the distal phalanx of the great toe required after its destruction by blows, falaca.

FIGURE 6.10 Intertarsal arthrodesis secondary to fractures during falaca.

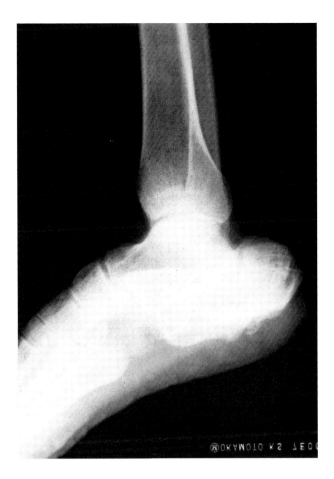

FIGURE 6.11 Multiple fractures of the calcaneus healed with residual deformity after falaca.

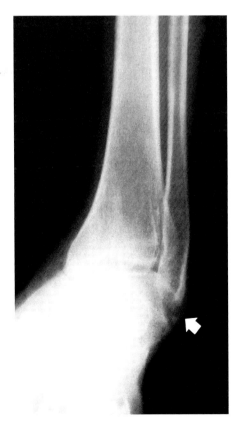

FIGURE 6.12 Fracture of the lateral malleolus healed with deformity, probably due to falaca.

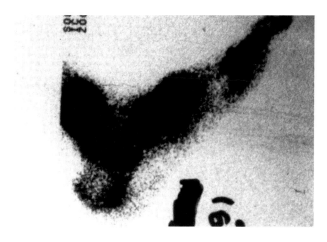

FIGURE 6.13 Very high uptake in foot on scintigraphy several weeks after falaca.

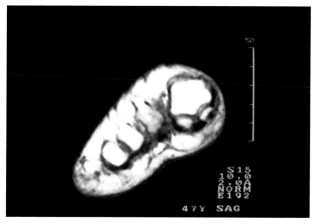

FIGURE 6.14 Thickening of the plantar aponeurosis, chronic changes after falaca.

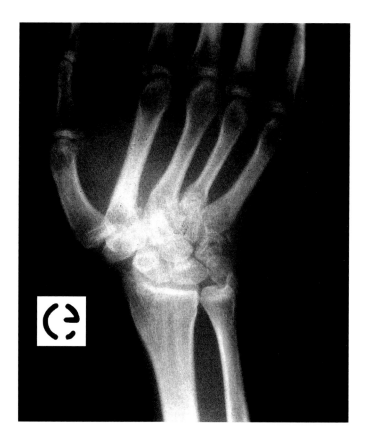

FIGURE 6.15 Crushed wrist of a journalist (Zaire).

7 Electric Torture

Hermann Vogel, M.D.

Electricity as an instrument of torture can be used in multiple ways. In the Near East, it is common to place the electrode between the toes (Figure 7.1), on the tongue, at the teeth, or on the penis. The location between the toes and on the tongue is chosen in order to hide the place of entrance of the electric current. The placement on the penis is selected not only to inflict pain but also humiliation. In Africa the electrodes are placed at the teeth. In the Near East large electrodes are used on wet skin and collar-like electrodes are placed on the neck.

Electric current induces muscle contractions. The consequences may be bone fractures (Figure 7.2) and soft tissue injuries, with secondary degenerative change in bony structures (Figures 7.3 and 7.4). Electroshock can produce compression fractures of the vertebrae (Figure 7.5) and along with grand mal seizures, is one of the few causes of high thoracic vertebral fractures.

For proving electric torture, local incision and microscopic evaluation can show characteristic necrosis that has been accepted as evidence by judges in Turkey (Figure 7.6).

If the victim were immediately available, it is likely that torture by electricity could be confirmed by magnetic resonance imaging (MRI). This inference can be drawn from the findings of high signal alterations on MRI examination of the chest in patients undergoing cardioversion (Figure 7.7).

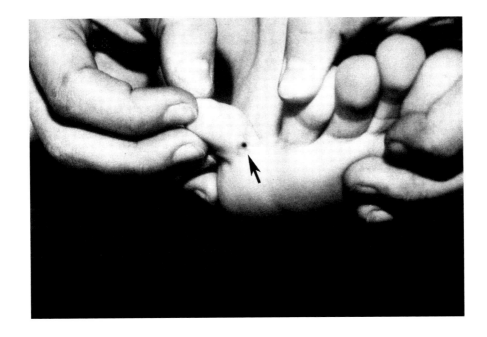

FIGURE 7.1 Interdigital point of entrance of electrode (Turkey).

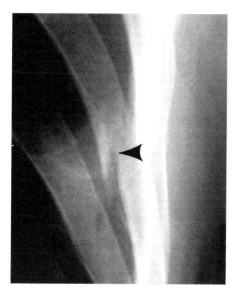

FIGURE 7.2 Fractured rib due to violent muscle contractions from electric torture.

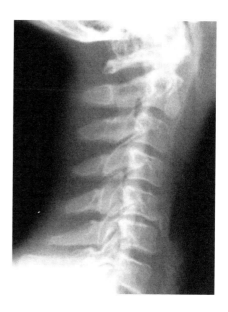

FIGURE 7.3 Straightened cervical spine (loss of cervical lordosis) due to muscular contractions during electric torture. An electrode in a broad metal band was placed around the neck of the victim (Cyprus). There also is disc compression at C-5, C-6 with secondary degenerative change.

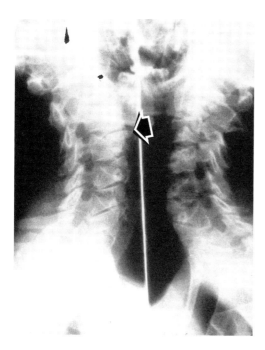

FIGURE 7.4 Degenerative arthrosis and osteophyte formation at C-3, C-4 on the right after compression fracture. This fracture is fairly common after blows to the side of the head or contractions from a collar-like electrode (Turkey).

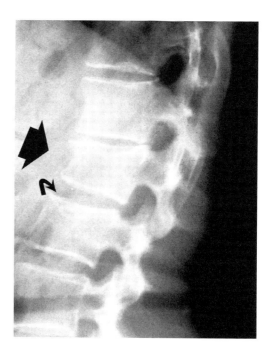

FIGURE 7.5 Compression fractures of L-1 and L-2 vertebral bodies.

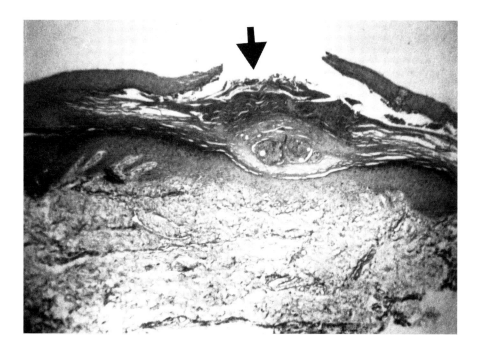

FIGURE 7.6 Interdigital skin necrosis at the site of entry of the electric current. Accepted as proof of torture by the court in Turkey.

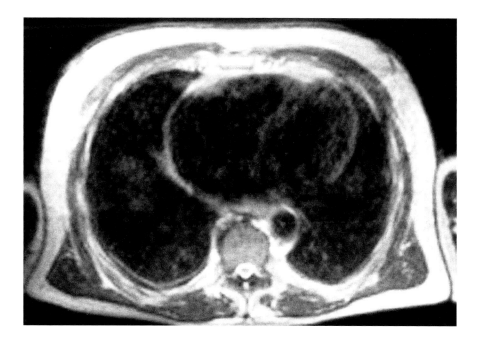

FIGURE 7.7 High signal on MRI at the region of the electrode paddle 5 days after cardioversion.

8 Water Torture

Hermann Vogel, M.D.

Water can be used as an instrument of torture in several ways.

SUBMERSION

In submersion, often called *submarino*, the victim's head is forced underwater until near-drowning. The water is often polluted with excrement. Aspiration is virtually inevitable and the subsequent radiography changes may vary from pulmonary edema to extensive pneumonia. The latter may eventuate in residual pulmonary scarring and adhesions. The findings are nonspecific.

DEPRIVATION

Deprivation of water can be an effective, even deadly, form of torture.

FORCED INGESTION

Victims from Chad, Africa have reported that they were bound with their arms behind them, then forced to ingest several liters of water in a very short time. Thereafter, they were thrown, or caused to fall, from a height of several meters to land on their anterior chest and abdomen, with the possibility of visceral rupture. One survivor was found to have a diaphragmatic hernia (Figure 8.1) that might have been induced by this forced trauma.

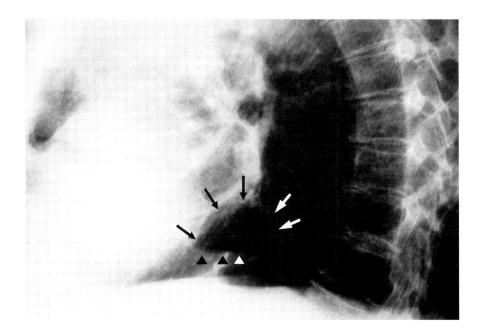

FIGURE 8.1 Diaphragmatic hernia perhaps due to a forced fall onto the belly after forced ingestion of a large quantity of water (Chad, Africa).

9 Finger and Toe Torture

Hermann Vogel, M.D.

Torture involving the fingers and toes is quite common and may produce both reversible and permanent anatomical alterations. In torture victims' rehabilitation centers one finds a variety of techniques.

FINGERNAIL TORTURE

The introduction of needles, wires, or wooden splinters beneath the fingernails is widespread. They are often directed to the distal interphalangeal joint or even farther. When retracted, splinters or fragments of the instrument may remain to be visualized on radiographic examination (Figure 9.1).

Extraction of fingernails has been practiced in South America and elsewhere.

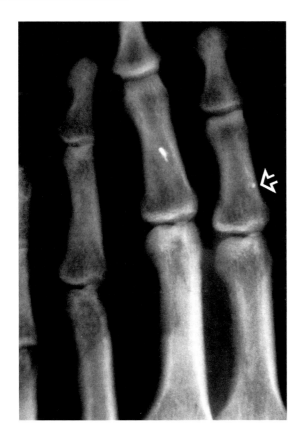

FIGURE 9.1 Metallic foreign body left in soft tissues of the middle phalanx of the second and third fingers. During torture, needles or wires were introduced underneath the fingernails. Splinters remained after they were withdrawn.

COMPRESSION INJURIES

Compression of digits by finger-, thumb-, and toe-screws has been applied since medieval times. Bony damage may be minor (Figure 9.2) or lead to complete loss of a phalanx or digit (Figure 9.3). Less mechanical compression injuries are accomplished by stomping or striking with rifle butts or other objects.[1]

PETITE GUILLOTINE

The *petite guillotine* was developed in Iran during the times of the Shah but persists to present times. The fingers, or parts of fingers, are cut off in succession (Figure 9.4). Fingers can also be lost or damaged by direct violence or by neurovascular loss as a result of suspension or squeezing. The latter is performed by putting a stick between the fingers and then compressing them against each other in order to damage nerves and vessels without leaving visible traces.

REFERENCE

1. Moreno, A. and Grodin, M.A., The not-so-silent marks of torture, *J. Am. Med. Assoc.*, 284, 538, 2000.

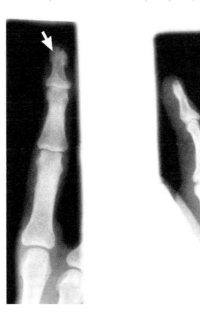

FIGURE 9.2 Ungual tuft fracture from screw device. (An almost identical radiograph has been published,[1] but the injury resulted from crushing with a rifle butt.)

A

B

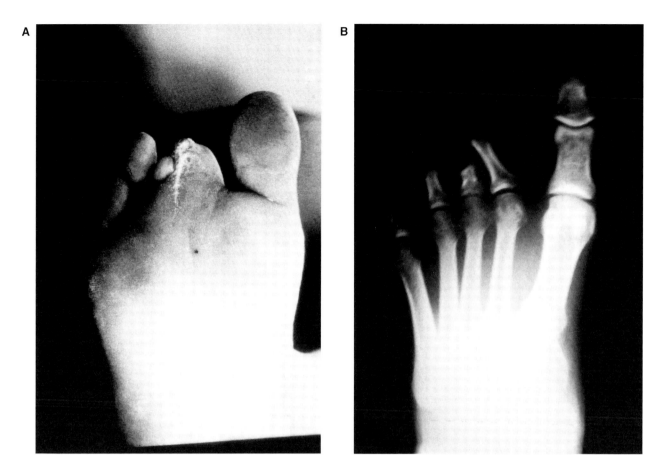

FIGURE 9.3 Destroyed toes after screw compression (Iran). **(A)** Photograph, **(B)** Radiograph.

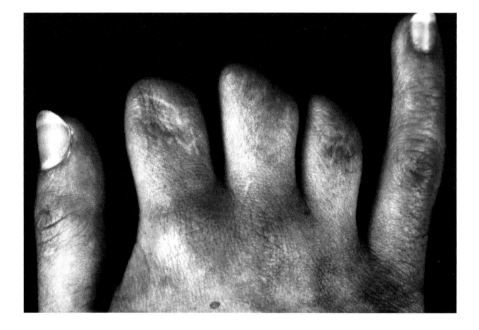

FIGURE 9.4 This 14-year-old girl was imprisoned by guards of the Islamic Revolution. Parts of her fingers were cut off in prison with the petite guillotine (Iran). (Courtesy of Professor Jacobsson, Stockholm.)

10 Stabbing, Cutting

Hermann Vogel, M.D.

Various forms and techniques of stabbing and cutting of victims is, and has been, performed all over the world throughout the ages. It can be used incrementally to demonstrate to the victim what is to be expected or it can be used with immediate intent to maim or kill.

STABBING IN THE TRUNK

Stabbing in the trunk incurs a high risk of injuring vital organs, with a consequent high probability of a lethal infection. Therefore, this method is less seen and reported. Sometimes fragments of the weapon or foreign bodies remain and can be documented by a radiologic method (Figure 10.1).

STABBING INTO THE HEAD

Since head wounds are often lethal they are rarely documented. A case in the Philippines involved torturers driving a long nail into the victim's head before killing him. This was to prevent the spirit of the victim from pursuing the murderers after death (Figure 10.2).

HIDDEN STAB WOUNDS

Stabbing into the anus is sometimes selected as a form of torture to make the victim suffer before his death. In the famous case of the murder of Edward II (1327), stabbing into the anus was selected in order to hide the wounds, and the murder, from the public who was entitled to view the corpse.

SELECTIVE STABBING

Certain forms of stabbing can be chosen to frighten or intimidate. In South Africa, I examined a young woman who was in shock for no apparent reason. An experienced surgeon suggested that I inspect the umbilicus which showed a tiny bit of blood. I learned this was typical for gangs hunting young women to torture them by introducing bicycle spokes into the umbilicus. A variant of this was stabbing into the spine with intent to produce paraplegia. In the former East Germany, a young man on his way to a disco was attacked by a gang and rendered unconscious. Upon being brought to the hospital it was discovered that mercury had been injected into his chest wall (Figure 10.3).

CUTTING

Cutting or slicing parts of the body can be used to intimidate or punish. In Sierra Leone, CNN reported that the hands of possible voters were cut off to prevent them from voting. This was a crude but effective method since the national vote was controlled by painting the fingers of individuals after they had voted.

Cutting off hands and feet of perpetrators of certain crimes is prescribed by Shari-ah, the law of the Koran. This punishment is applied in several Islamic countries where the Shari-ah is the official law of the land.

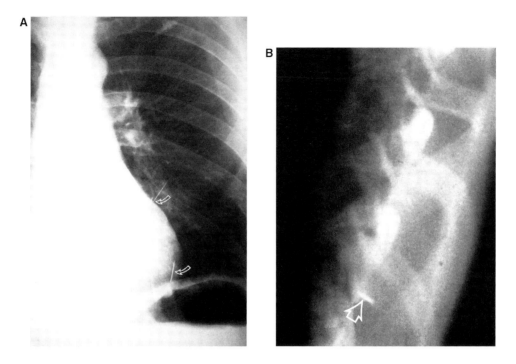

FIGURE 10.1 (**A** and **B**) Needle fragments remain in chest after stabbing with multiple needles.

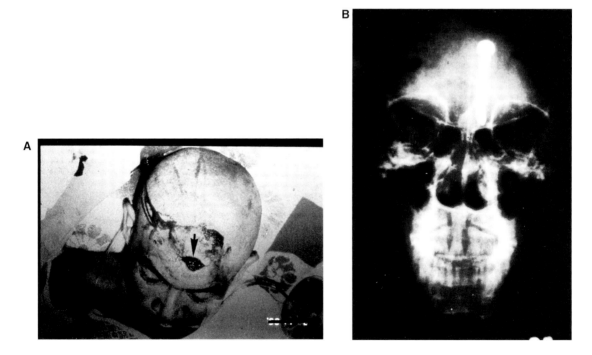

FIGURE 10.2 A large nail driven into the head was intended to prevent the victim's spirit from pursuing his torturers (Philippines). (**A**) Photograph shows nail in victim's head. (**B**) Radiograph.

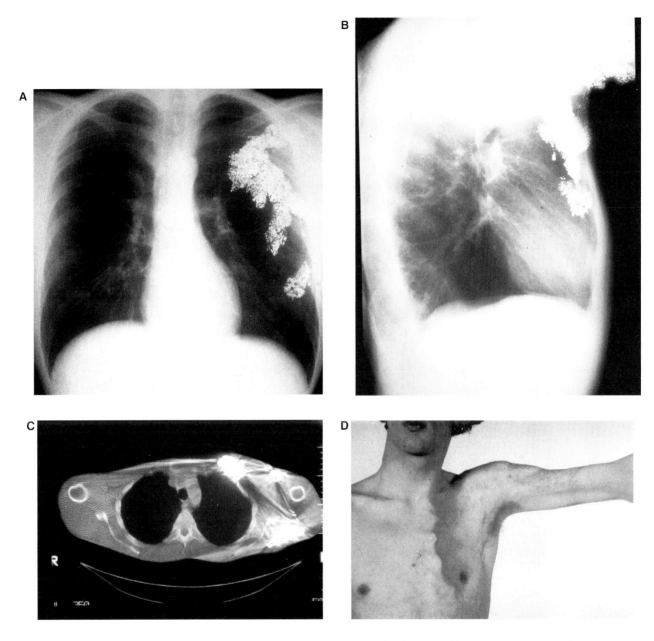

FIGURE 10.3 Young man rendered unconscious by gang attack was found to have opacifications in soft tissues due to mercury injections. (**A**) Frontal chest radiograph. (**B**) Lateral view. (**C**) Computed tomography. (**D**) Photograph shows darkened skin over injection sites.

11 Postural Torture

Hermann Vogel, M.D.

Requiring the victim to maintain a certain normal or awkward posture for long periods of time, binding the victim in various awkward and painful positions, or suspension of the victim are all widespread methods of torture that take many forms. Figure 11.1 demonstrates two common forms of postural torture and suspension from South America. Victims are sometimes suspended by the arms, which are bent backward and with sudden upward traction applied. Other forms use the hands and feet bound together at the back. Suspension is sometimes by one or a few fingers. In Syria, victims have been made to stand erect for long periods of time in a vertical cell that is sized and shaped somewhat like a coffin. A Kurdish refugee from Turkey claimed to have been made to walk across a floor strewn with shards of glass and then stand in salt. He also reported being forced to stand ankle deep in water after being beaten on the soles of his feet.[1]

Radiographic evidence of postural torture is sparse. Bone pathology is rare. Fractures and dislocations about the shoulder can sometimes be demonstrated (Figures 11.2 and 11.3). Magnetic resonance imaging and ultrasound may be able to demonstrate residual patterns of capsular injury and healing with scar formation from muscular contractions in the neck and shoulders of suspension victims. However, the results of these expensive examinations are probably no more contributory than a good examination by an experienced physiotherapist or physiatrist.

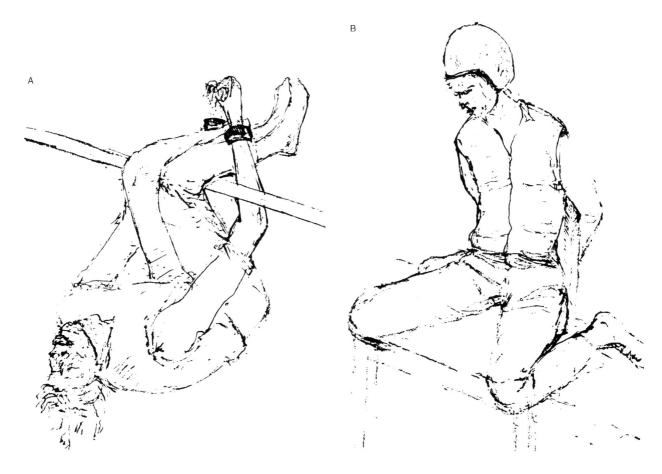

FIGURE 11.1 Examples of positional torture: **(A)** *"la barra,"* **(B)** *"la moto."* (From Rassmussen, O.V., *Medical Aspects of Torture*, Laegeformenings forlag, Copenhagen, 1990. With permission.)

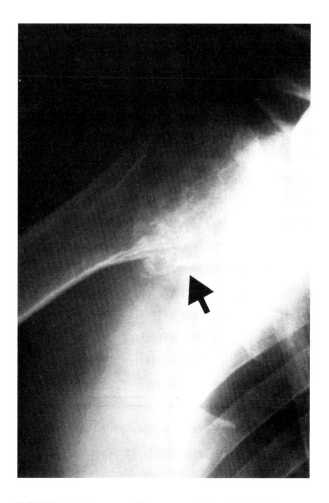

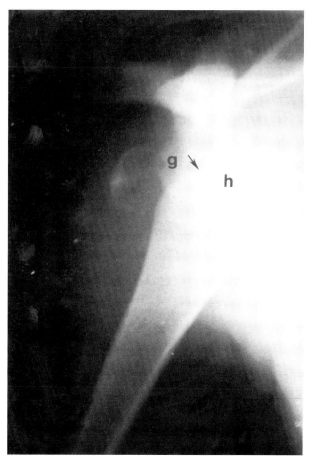

FIGURE 11.2 Fracture of the anatomical neck of the humerus with callus formation (arrow) due to sudden forceful upward traction on arms forced behind the back.

FIGURE 11.3 Dislocation of the glenohumeral joint: glenoid process of scapula (g), humeral head (h), Hill-Sacks lesion in proximal humerus (arrow).

REFERENCE

1. Gaessner, S., Gurris, N., and Pross, C., Eds., *At the Side of Torture Survivors*, Johns Hopkins University Press, Baltimore, MD, 2001.

12 Other Forms of Torture

Hermann Vogel, M.D.

Other forms of torture not lending themselves to broad categorization are included here.

KNEECAPPING

Kneecapping is a term originally applied to a gunshot wound in the knee, usually applied by a hand gun, in order to permanently maim or cripple the victim. In America, it has been attributed to mostly gang warfare. In recent years, it has been applied during the troubles in Northern Ireland. It is not certain which country is the importer and which the exporter. Kneecapping is no longer limited to the knee; other joints, particularly the ankle and elbow, are also targeted. In one known extreme case both knees, both ankles, and both elbows were shot. Occasionally, other parts of the leg are involved. Radiographs can easily document the extent of injury and frequently disclose the bullet path, trajectory of fire, and location of the bullet. Bullets are frequently found *in situ*, since low velocity weapons are ordinarily employed. Arterial damage is not uncommon, and angiography is frequently employed (Figures 12.1 to 12.5).

SQUEEZING

A former prisoner from Chad claimed his head had been squeezed in a screw clamp, but this could not be confirmed and his story was not entirely convincing. However, squeezing large joints is a torture method employed in Latin America. Sticks are placed at the elbow or knee, and the joint is forcibly bent and fixed in maximal flexion. This results in pressure lesions of the nerves and vessels with subsequent atrophy. The atrophy may be demonstrated, but the instruments of torture leave no visible trace.

Squeezing of the testes or other parts of the body can produce local damage demonstrable by scintigraphy days to weeks after the trauma (Figure 12.6).

TEETH

Teeth are often broken or dislocated during beating. They may be extracted or drilled as a form of pain induction.

These injuries, of course, can be demonstrated by direct inspection as well as radiography.

SURGICAL PROCEDURES

So-called research operations performed by Nazi physicians in the concentration camps sometimes left traces demonstrable by radiography.

OTHER COMMON FORMS OF TORTURE

Many common forms of torture leave no trace that can be demonstrated by imaging. These include:

1. Sexual abuse of both men and women
2. Sleep deprivation
3. Exposure to excess light or noise
4. Forced sitting on sharp edges for lengthy periods
5. La moto (Figure 11.1)
6. *Telefono* (blows to the ear to rupture the tympanic membrane)
7. Burns
8. Deprivation of food and water

Institutional alimentation can give rise to a variety of deficiency diseases, including Beri-Beri, scurvy, pellagra, and vitamin D deficiency with, at times, radiographically demonstrable lesions.

SHAKING

Reports in the popular press indicate that for some time the Israeli Security Service included the technique of violently shaking the suspect's upper torso. On occasion this produced intracranial lesions much like those found in the shaken baby syndrome. The practice has since been outlawed by the Israeli Supreme Court.[1]

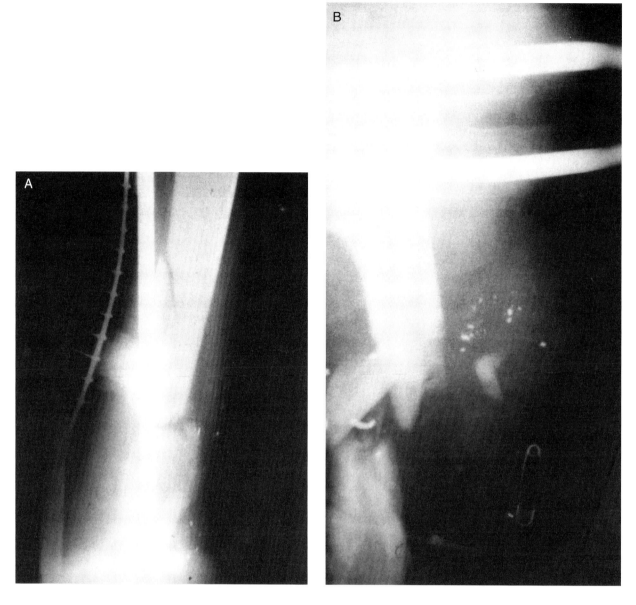

FIGURE 12.1 (**A** and **B**) Comminuted femoral fractures and marked soft tissue destruction from kneecapping (Northern Ireland).

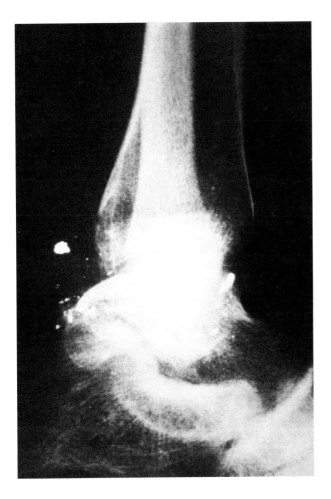

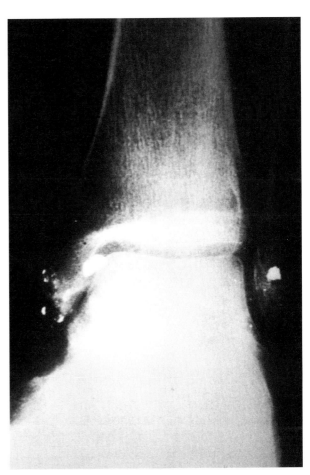

FIGURE 12.2 Total disruption of the knee joint and adjacent parts of the femur and tibia from kneecapping. Bullet fragments remain in the area (Northern Ireland).

FIGURE 12.3 Shot in the ankle joint with bullet fragments near the medial and lateral malleoli (Northern Ireland).

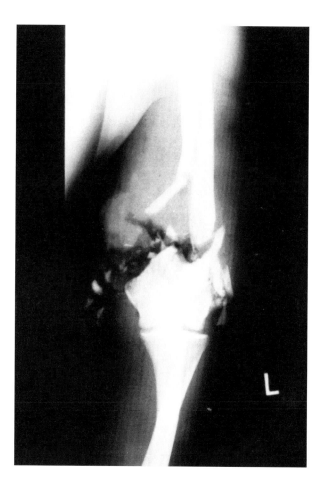

FIGURE 12.4 Punishment shot into the distal humerus with high velocity weapon. Almost total destruction of the distal humerus and adjacent soft tissues.

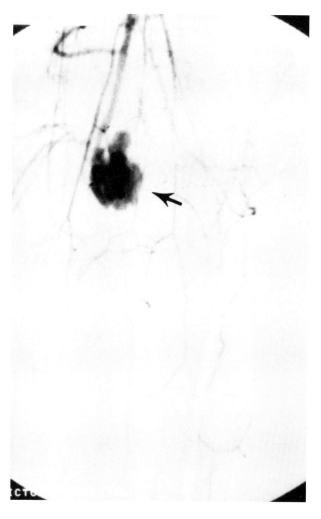

FIGURE 12.5 Kneecapping producing pseudoaneurysm of the popliteal artery (Northern Ireland).

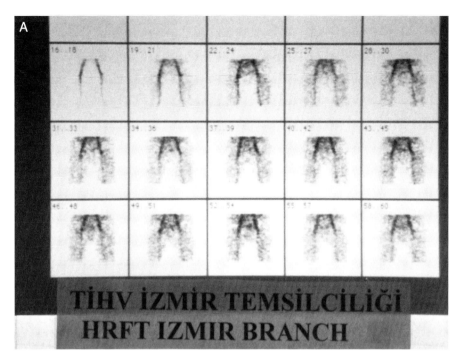

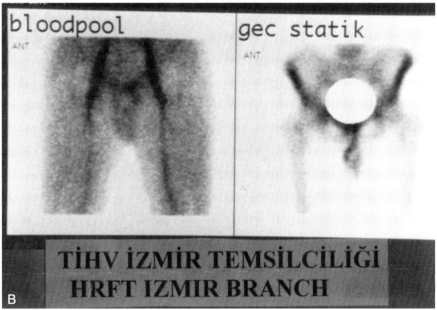

FIGURE 12.6 Scintigraphy to document squeezing injury to right testis. (**A**) Dynamic scan. (**B**) Blood-pool and static phases. Note increased uptake.

REFERENCE

1. Sonteg, D., A strike against brutality, *Mobile Register*, 9 Sept. 1991, 1.

Section III

Terrorism

The dictionaries of 30 years ago define terrorism as the systematic use of fear, threat, anxiety, or violence as a means of coercion, intimidation, submission, or dominance. How can one define, categorize, or generalize terrorism today? It is protean, ever changing, and ever present. It is random as well as systematized. It induces not only fear, but also hostility, panic, retribution, and resolution. The goals of terrorism have expanded to include revenge, protest, political advantage, and even paradise for true believers. Its perpetrators include misguided children, religious zealots, radical organizations, and organized governments. The tools and targets of terrorism are changing. The booby-trapped vehicle becomes the bomb itself at the Marines barracks in Kansas City and in the subterranean levels of the World Trade Center. The commercial airliner, long a target of terrorism, became the weapon of terrorism on September 11, 2001.

The terror may be directed at a single individual, a Lord Mountbatten, or at an entire religious or ethnic group (e.g., Kurds or Hindus). Consequently, the required response ranges from the treatment, identification, or disposition of a single body to the horrendous problems of a mass casualty situation.

The boundaries of terrorism are unfixed in any dimension, being determined only by the seemingly limitless imagination of the perverse minds of those who promote its practice.

This section deals mostly with some of the tools and methods employed in terrorism, with emphasis on the radiologic evaluation of its immediate effects on the human body. The radiologic evaluation for cause of death or injury and identification of victims is discussed and demonstrated in other sections of this Atlas.

Unless otherwise indicated, illustrations in this section come from the private collection of one of the editors (H.V.) or, with permission, from his prior publication, *Gewalt in Röntgenbild.*

B.G.B.

13 Explosives

Hermann Vogel, M.D.

INTRODUCTION

The explosives employed in terrorism are mostly home-made. However, when available, manufactured explosives produced for armed forces or industrial purposes are used. Terrorist organizations train their members in the construction of bombs. Instruction manuals can be purchased openly in many bookstores, and recipes are available on the Internet.

When military arms and military or industrial explosives are obtained, they will be used. Many explosives contain PETN (nitropenta, pentaerythrittetranitrat) which is also used in cardiology. PETN is the main component of the rapid detonative explosives (RDX) substance employed by the armed forces (Composition A; Composition B; Composition C, C3, and C4; HBX; H-6; Cyclotol and Semtex). Semtex (a combination of *Sem*tin—a town in former Czechoslovakia where it was produced—and *ex*plosive) is the most famous of the RDX. It is a plastic material, easily shaped and readily available on the international market.

The bombs obtained or produced by terrorists can be cataloged as:

1. Car bombs
2. Letter bombs
3. Parcel bombs
4. Nail bombs
5. Suicide bombs
6. Mortar bombs
7. Drop bombs
8. Buried bombs
9. Dirty bombs

LOCATION

Bombs can be exploded in a confined space or in the open, and the effect is usually influenced by the location. The power of the explosion, the heat or flame associated with the explosion, the distance from the explosion, and possible cover or protection available all modify the injury sustained. If the victims are very close to the bomb, either indoors or out, massive concussion injuries and even dismemberment are likely, and radiographs only have forensic purpose and value (Figures 13.1 to 13.5). Flash burns, smoke inhalation, and nonlethal concussion injuries are typical nonfatal effects of bombs exploded inside a room.

On the other hand, typical effects of terrorist bombs exploded outside on the streets or beneath a vehicle range from no physical injury but psychological trauma, to injuries from glass or metallic fragments, to serious or fatal somatic damage.

CAR BOMBS

Car bombs appear in two categories. In one, the car is the bomb. That is, the vehicle (not necessarily an automobile) is the carrier of the explosive. These can be made of fertilizers which are ignited by plastic explosives, often Semtex. The vehicle can carry several tons of explosives and the destruction can be gigantic. The explosion can be triggered by remote control or when the vehicle is opened. A car can also be booby-trapped. Typically, a lonely car, full of explosives, raises suspicion that is deadly to the unsuspecting investigator. Booby traps have important psychological as well as physical impact.

Secondly, the bomb can simply be attached to the car and set to explode when the engine is started, the door is opened, or remote control is activated. This bomb is usually small and the number of victims is limited to the driver and passengers and, perhaps, close bystanders (Figure 13.6).

LETTER BOMBS

Letter bombs, of necessity, are small. They usually contain a plastic explosive ignited by an electrical charge from small batteries when a circuit is closed by a simple switch activated upon opening the letter (Figure 13.7). Ordinarily, the worst damage is to the hands. The major damage is to the opening hand rather than the one holding the letter. Consequently, in the majority of people, it is the right hand that is most seriously injured.[1] Next to the hands, head injuries are the most serious and sometimes fatal (Figures 13.8 and 13.9).[2]

PARCEL BOMBS

These are on the same principle as letter bombs but can carry a larger charge. Figure 13.10 shows the virtually destroyed hand of a Peruvian police officer who tried to remove a parcel filled with dynamite. His armored vest saved his life, but he also lost an eye. Damage to the hands will ordinarily be worse than that from a letter bomb because of the size of the bomb and force of the explosion (Figure 13.11).

NAIL BOMBS

Nail bombs contain nails or other metallic objects that amplify the destruction. They may be placed in packages or can be constructed as small bombs to be thrown with an effect comparable to that of a hand grenade (Figure 13.12).

SUICIDE BOMBERS

Suicide bombers are much in the news from the Near East. Individuals turn themselves into bombs by carrying explosives. Since the explosives are carried and must be ignited, there are some opportunities for them to be apprehended, or to escape their intentions. For instance, on December 22, 2001, the British citizen Richard Reid, while trying to ignite 10 oz of Semtex hidden in his shoe, was thwarted by an attentive flight attendant and some passengers. Suicide bombers may also employ motor vehicles, boats, or airplanes filled with fuel or explosives against targets. Even when explosives are carried, the fuel on board has a significant additive effect. For instance, it is believed that the intense heat of the fuel-fed fire brought down the Twin Towers, not the impact or explosive force of the crashes.

MORTAR BOMBS

Mortar bombs are explosives that are thrown. In Northern Ireland, they have been used to attack police stations or military camps. They have a capable throwing distance of 20 to 30 m with a maximum height of trajectory of 8 to 10 m.

DROP BOMBS

Drop bombs are thrown from buildings or bridges onto armored vehicles because the roof is the most vulnerable point. They may also be hung from parachutes.

BURIED BOMBS

Buried bombs have an effect similar to the familiar land mine. Recently, in Palestine, an Israeli tank was destroyed by explosives hidden in the ground. The Israeli army thereafter changed its approach throughout neighborhoods, choosing access through buildings rather than along narrow streets and alleys.

DIRTY BOMBS

Dirty bombs have additives or contaminants which extend their effect over time. A case was reported from Israel where a bone fragment of a suicide bomber infected with AIDS was found in a victim. Radioactive isotopes of cesium, cobalt, radium, or plutonium are available from hospitals or reactors and can be added to an ordinary bomb. Even if the radiation risk is limited, the psychological impact can be disastrous.

RADIOLOGIC CAPABILITIES

In summary, in evaluating injuries due to explosives, radiologic investigation can show direct effects of the blast such as (Figures 13.13 to 13.15):

1. Contusion or laceration of the lung
2. Foreign bodies from the bomb
3. Foreign bodies from other sources (e.g., automobile fragments) transferred by the explosion
4. Fractures and dislocations of bones
5. Fractures and perforations of visceral organs
6. Arterial damage

REFERENCES

1. Missliwetz, J., Schneider, B., Oppenheim, H., and Weiser, I., Injuries due to letter bombs, *J. Forens. Sci.*, 42, 981, 1997.
2. Rothschild, M.S. and Maxeiner, H., Death caused by a letter bomb, *Int. J. Legal Med.*, 114, 103, 2000.

CREDIT

From Brogdon, B.G., *Forensic Radiology*, CRC Press, Boca Raton, FL, 1998. With permission. Figure 13.7

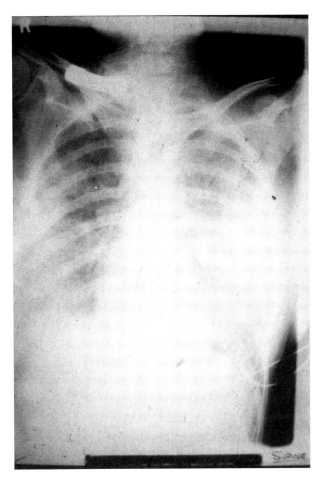

FIGURE 13.1 Bomb blast concussion produces extensive contusions in both lungs.

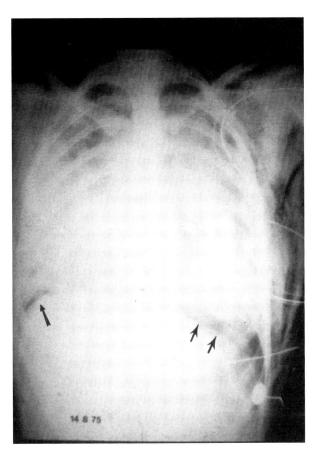

FIGURE 13.2 A more forceful bomb blast produces opacifications of both lungs from contusions and lacerations. Additionally, the air under the diaphragm (arrows) indicates perforation of abdominal viscera.

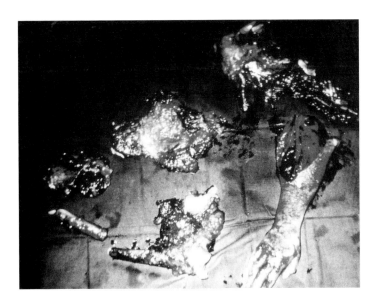

FIGURE 13.3 Photograph showing fragments of a totally dismembered body. A hand, wrist, and partial forearm can be identified at lower right.

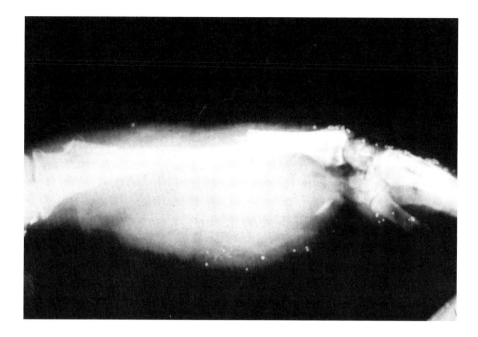

FIGURE 13.4 A portion of the upper extremity of a victim of a street bombing in Northern Ireland. The hand is on viewer right, the elbow on the left. Note the remarkable soft tissue swelling of the forearm, the fractures of both bones, and multiple small metallic fragments from the bomb.

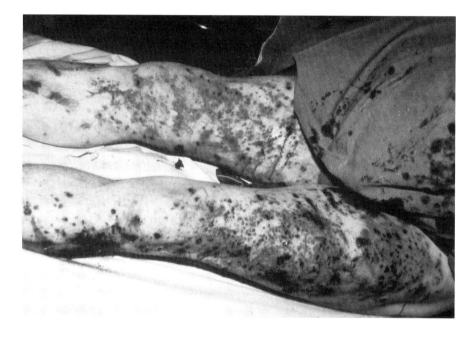

FIGURE 13.5 Photograph showing multiple injuries to the skin of the thighs and legs of a victim of the same explosion as Figure 13.4 (Northern Ireland).

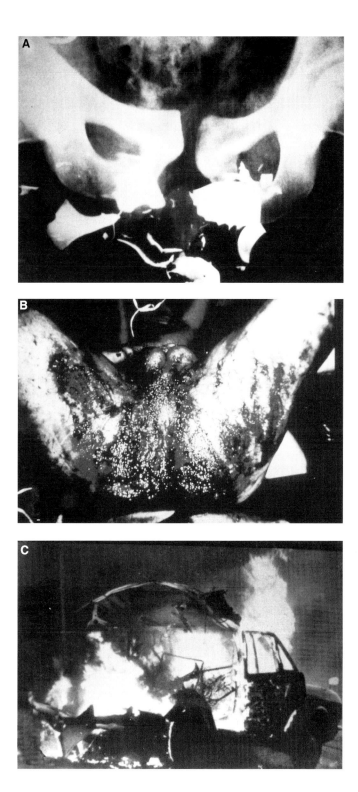

FIGURE 13.6 Effects of booby-trapped car bombs. **(A)** This is a radiograph of a portion of the pelvis of an arms dealer injured by a bomb placed underneath his car and exploded when he activated the ignition switch. Fragments from the floor of the car together with fragments of the bomb can be seen in pelvic and perineal soft tissues (Hamburg, Germany). **(B)** Photograph of the injuries to the buttocks and perineum of another victim of a bomb placed beneath his car (Northern Ireland). **(C)** Burning vehicle after a car bomb explosion.

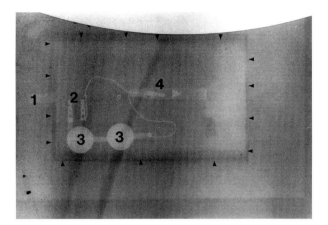

FIGURE 13.7 Radiograph of a letter bomb. Arrowheads indicate plastic explosive inside envelope. The triggering string (1) closes the contact (2) so that current from the batteries (3) energizes the detonator (4) (Lebanon). (Courtesy of Dr. Rafic Melhem.)

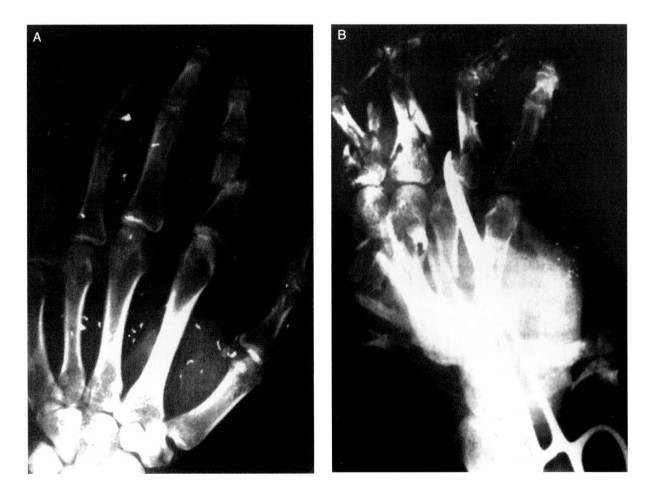

FIGURE 13.8 Radiographic effects of a letter bomb. **(A)** Left hand. **(B)** Right hand. (Copyright ASTM International. Reprinted with permission.)

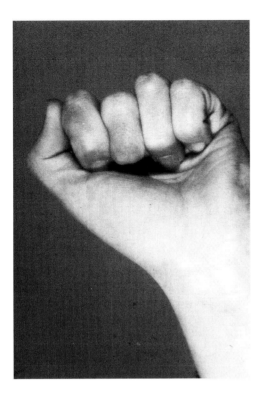

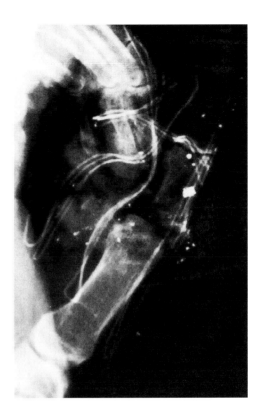

FIGURE 13.9 Disfigured, healed hand of a letter bomb victim (Northern Ireland).

FIGURE 13.10 Destroyed hand of a police officer who tried to remove a parcel bomb filled with dynamite (Peru).

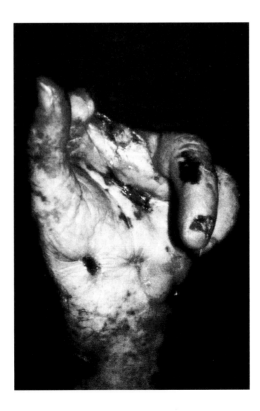

FIGURE 13.11 Photograph of injuries to the hand and wrist of a parcel bomb victim (Northern Ireland).

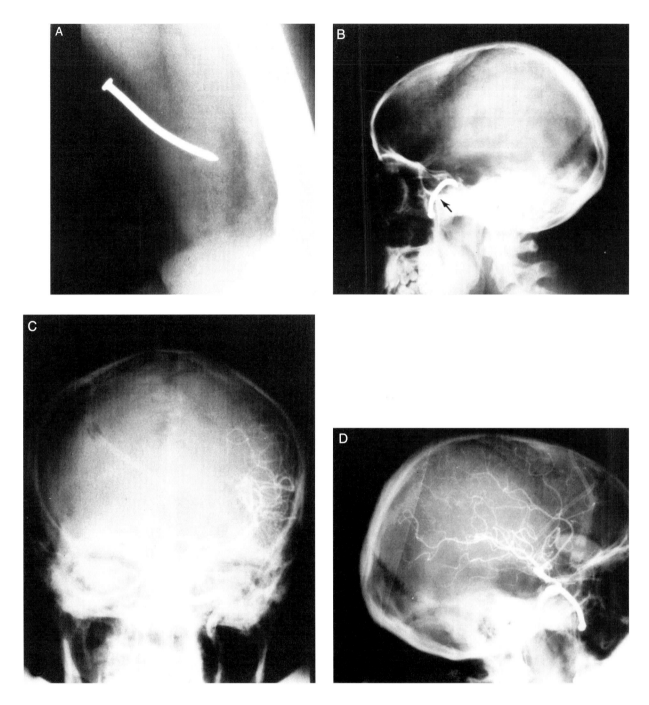

FIGURE 13.12 Nail bomb victim. (**A**) Large nail in the soft tissues of the thigh. (**B**) Lateral view of skull showing large nail overlying vital structures in this single view. (**C** and **D**) Carotid angiography in frontal and lateral planes shows the nail to have traversed the left maxillary sinus and penetrated the base of the skull to enter the left temporal fossa. Vital arterial structures are not damaged, but extensive damage to the temporal lobe can be anticipated (Northern Ireland).

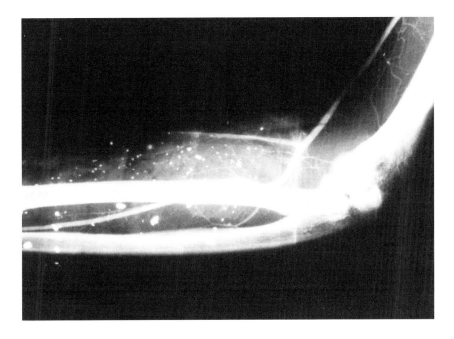

FIGURE 13.13 Soft tissue and arterial injury to the forearm with massive swelling and multiple bomb fragments of varying size (Northern Ireland).

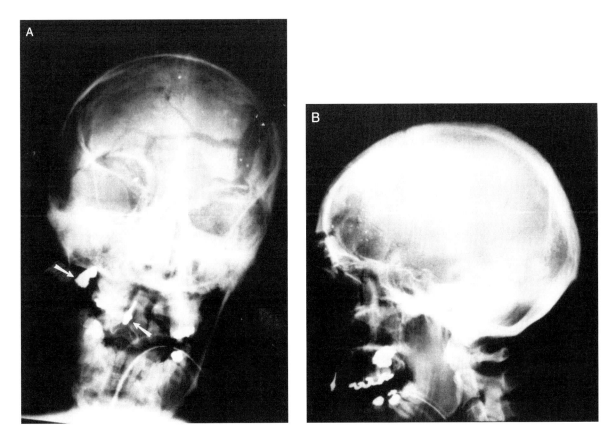

FIGURE 13.14 Massive blast injury to the head (Northern Ireland). **(A)** Frontal view and **(B)** Lateral view show multiple fractures in the frontal bone extending into both orbits. There are numerous metallic fragments that appear superficial to the calvaria. A displaced dental bridge is noted (arrows). The jaw is dislocated.

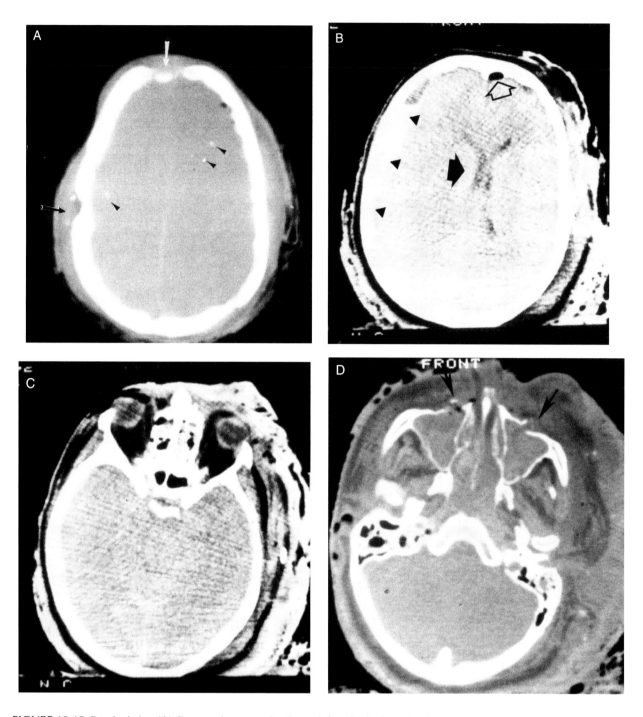

FIGURE 13.15 Bomb victim. **(A)** Computed tomography shows defects in the frontal and parietal bone (arrows) and bone fragments driven into the brain (arrowheads). **(B)** There is a large left subdural hematoma (arrowheads), acute cerebral edema, and a middle line shift to the left (broad arrow). There is air in the subdural space (open arrow). **(C** and **D)** Destruction of the orbits and facial bones (Northern Ireland).

14 Gas

Hermann Vogel, M.D.

Gases used in terrorist attacks are the same as those of chemical warfare. The term usually refers to the use of chemical agents, both lethal and nonlethal, that may attack one or more targets in the human body. These include nerve gases, which may induce temporary blindness, deafness, paralysis, nausea, or vomiting; caustic gases, which may cause severe burns to skin, eyes, or lungs; other types of gases, which may stifle respiration. Also included are chemical defoliants and herbicides for military purposes, such as those used in the Vietnam War.

Worldwide revulsion toward chemical weapons is embodied in the Geneva Protocol of 1925, prohibiting "the use in war of asphyxiating, poisonous or other gases, and of all analogous liquids, materials or devices." More than 140 states, including all major nations, are parties to the Protocol of 1925. Modern lethal chemical weapons employ the organophosphorus nerve agents first produced, but not used, by Germany during World War II. Related to certain insecticides, but much more toxic to man, they would cause intense sweating, filling of the bronchial passages with mucus, dimming of vision, uncontrollable vomiting and defecation, convulsions, and finally paralysis and respiratory failure. Death would result from asphyxia, generally within a few minutes after respiratory exposure or within hours if exposure was through a liquid nerve agent on the skin.

The U.S. stockpile of chemical warfare agents, loaded into munitions or stored in bulk, included the nerve agents sarin and VX, while the Soviet Union stocked the nerve agents sarin, VX, and soman. Of those three nerve agents (all liquids), sarin would evaporate the most rapidly and would pose mainly a respiratory hazard. VX, the least volatile, would act primarily as a contact poison. Soman, with volatility intermediate between that of sarin and VX, would pose both respiratory and contact hazards.

In addition to nerve agents, both nations stocked mustard gas and the irritant CS, which was also used by police. The Soviets also stocked lewisite, a blister agent developed but not used by the United States during World War I. Mustard gas and lewisite would not be nearly so lethal as the nerve agents, causing casualties principally from incapacitating blisters and temporary blindness. Their full effects would take several hours to develop, although lewisite, in contrast to mustard gas, would cause immediate pain to the skin and eyes. Liquid chemical warfare agents, such as mustard gas, lewisite, and the nerve agents, could be loaded into artillery projectiles, bombs, or missile warheads and be dispersed by an explosive charge as a vapor cloud or as a liquid spray. Liquid agents might also be carried in tanks and sprayed from aircraft at low altitude. Greater persistence and more controlled dispersion might be obtained by the addition of thickeners. Solid agents, such as CS, might be dispersed explosively or aerosolized from pyrotechnic mixtures in various munitions.

An innovation put into quantity production by the United States in 1987 was the binary sarin artillery projectile, in which two relatively nontoxic precursors of sarin were held in separate canisters. Upon firing, the two chemicals would mix and react to form sarin. One of the canisters might be stored and shipped separately, to be inserted into the projectile at the ammunition depot or the gun site. This built-in safety feature was intended to provide greater operational flexibility and safety in the storage and transport of the weapon. The binary principle could be applied to other types of chemical warfare agents. The amount of a chemical warfare agent required to create a hazardous cloud over a target area would be highly dependent on air movements. The weight of sarin, for example, required to produce a lethal respiratory hazard to unprotected persons over most of an open mile-square area could be between 0.3 and 10 t, depending on atmospheric conditions.[1–3]

Recently, the Japanese terrorist sect, AUN, used sarin in the Tokyo subway, killing several passengers. Iraq employed S-Lost in its war with Iran, killing and mutilating hundreds of thousands. By surface contact, S-Lost irritates the surfaces of the tracheobronchial tree, causing a hemorrhagic epithelitis as seen by bronchoscopy. The radiograph of the chest shows nothing until the appearance of infiltrates carries a serious prognosis. Emphysema develops rapidly in the early months after exposure.[4]

The defoliants used by the United States in Vietnam were known as agent orange, agent blue, and agent white, which referred to the color of their packing and not to their chemistry. One has to differentiate between the herbicides themselves and the accompanying substances like "dioxin", which is known to be carcinogenic and terratogenic.[5] During and after that war, the destroyed infrastructure and international isolation made it impossible, or at least difficult, to investigate the damages in Vietnam. Furthermore, the Vietnamese government had no means to decontaminate the country. Therefore, in Vietnam, the discussion of the problem and its effect on the population has been limited—a major consideration being not to cause public concern.

We have not had the opportunity or necessity to examine patients or victims exposed to these gases. We present one case of a young woman who worked on a plantation where an airplane sprayed parathion. She became ill and nearly died of asphyxia. Acutely, the radiograph showed an exudative reaction; after one year, the lungs were destroyed, with large bullae developing. She is permanently dyspneic. The clinical pictures probably are similar to exposure to phosgene, a toxic gas developed and used in World War I (Figure 14.1).

REFERENCES

1. Alibek, K. and Handelman, S., *Biohazard*, Econ, Munich, 2001.
2. *Encyclopedia Britannica*, CD-ROM, 2000.
3. Langenheim, K., Skalnik, C., and Smolek, I., *Bioterror*, DVA, Stuttgart/Munich, 2002.
4. Okhovat, C., Röntgenbefunde nach Lost-Exposition, Diss., Hamburg, 1992.
5. Vogel, H., *Gewalt in Röntgenbild*, ecomed verlagsgesellschaft mbH, Landsberg/Lech, 1997.

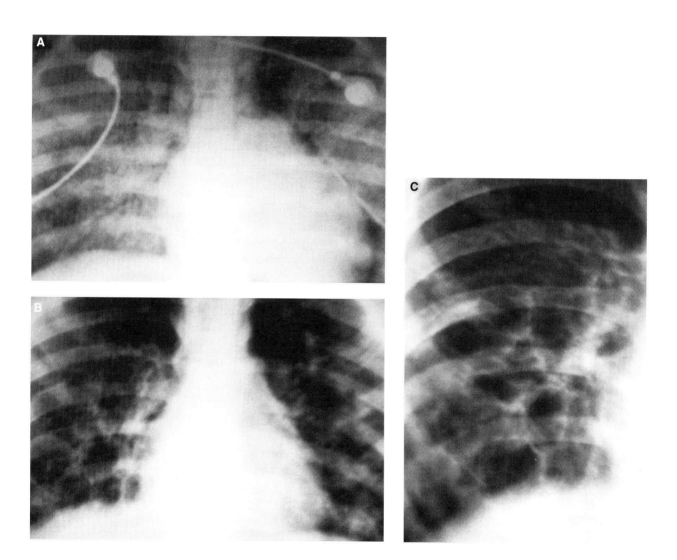

FIGURE 14.1 Parathion exposure. (**A**) Radiograph shortly after exposure shows an acute exudative pneumonitis bilaterally. (**B**) A year later she is dyspneic, with large bullae scattered throughout the lungs, effectively reducing her respiratory capacity. (**C**) Close-up view of the huge bullous changes in her lungs.

15 Biologic/Bacteriologic Terrorism

Hermann Vogel, M.D. and B.G. Brogdon, M.D.

The concept of terrorism using microorganisms exploded into public awareness in 2001 with the episode of the anthrax spore-bearing letters in the United States shortly after the destruction of the World Trade Center in New York City on September 11. However, the concept of biological warfare actually is very old. It has a long history in North America. After small pox-infected blankets had been distributed to one Indian tribe, it is said that in July 1763, Sir Jeffrey Amherst, the British commander in the American colonies, suggested in reference to an uprising among the Pontiac that, "could it not be contrived to send the small pox among those disaffected tribes of Indians." In 1781, the British general Alexander Leslie wrote up plans to use small pox against supporters of General Washington during the revolution by sending infected African Americans down the Potomac to infect the rebel plantations.

In 1933, the Japanese army developed a special bomb made of china (the "Uji") to transport plague-infected fleas—3,000 fleas to the gram! In the Gulf War, Iraq possessed tons of anthrax spores, but had no missile delivery system. Some biological agents can be cultivated easily, some can be stockpiled as dry powder or liquid slurry, and some of them can be put into missile delivery systems. Biological weapons designed to dispense airborne clouds of pathogenic microbes could kill or incapacitate unprotected civilian populations over very large areas. Their use could trigger a psychological impact even worse than the physical one. Fortunately, such weapons have never yet been used.[1–5]

Diseases classified as potentially dangerous and suitable for military use or terrorism have been classified as Category A: plague, anthrax, small pox, tularemia, and viral hemorrhagic fever; and Category B: Q-Fever, malleus, and brucellosis.

Recent clinical experience with anthrax and plague provides description of their radiologic findings (Figures 15.1 to 15.5).

Other possibilities for biological warfare include typhoid fever, Legionnaire's disease, and Clostridial infections.

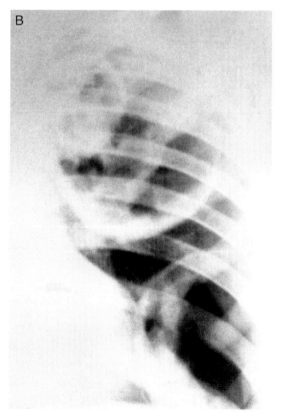

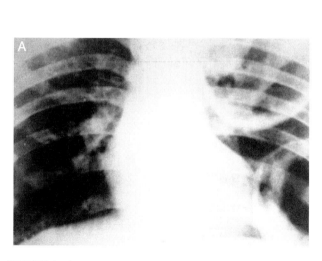

FIGURE 15.1 Pneumonic plague. **(A)** Large cavitary lesions are seen in the left lung without fluid levels. This is a rather unusual manifestation of pulmonary plague. **(B)** Close-up view of the left lung.

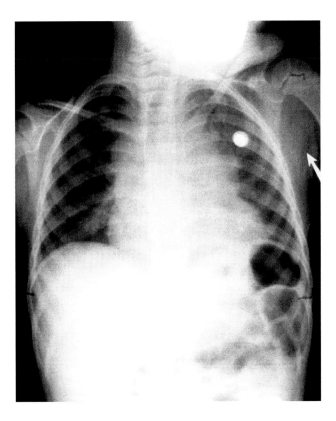

FIGURE 15.2 Three-year-old boy with bubonic plague. The chest radiograph demonstrates extensive mediastinal adenopathy. A buboe can be seen in the left axilla (arrow). (Courtesy of Dr. Loran Ketai, Albuquerque, NM.)

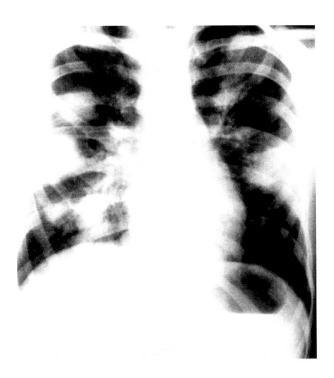

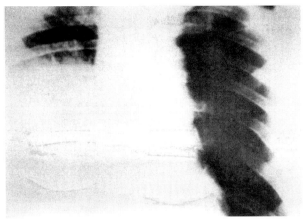

FIGURE 15.3 Thirty-year-old woman with secondary plague pneumonia. Chest radiograph shows left lower lobe airspace disease with formation of a large cavity occurring after 2 weeks of illness. (Courtesy of Dr. Loran Ketai, Albuquerque, NM.)

FIGURE 15.4 Pulmonary anthrax. There is consolidation of the right middle and lower lobes with a large pleural effusion on the right. There is mediastinal adenopathy bilaterally. (Courtesy of Dr. Severn, North Hampton, U.K.)

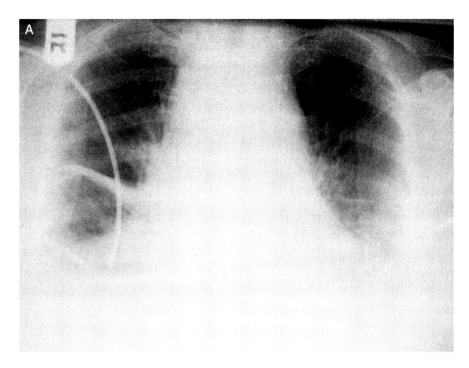

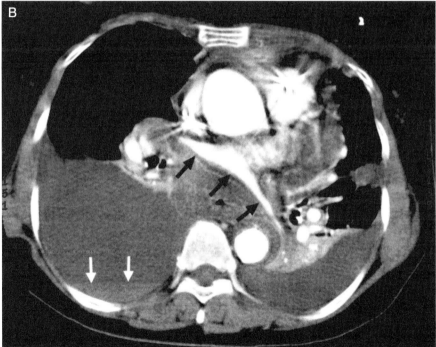

FIGURE 15.5 Pulmonary anthrax. A 61-year-old hypertensive female comes to the emergency room with increasing shortness of breath, resting dyspnea, and substernal pain for 3 days. **(A)** Bilateral mediastinal widening, bilateral perihilar infiltrate, and pleural effusions. **(B)** Dynamic CT scan 16 hours after **(A)** at the level of the left atrium shows bilateral pleural effusions, with high density material (white arrows) on dependent right pleural surface. Note heterogeneous material in mediastinum compressing the left atrium and hilar vessels (black arrows). (Courtesy of Dr. Christopher M. Krol.) (From Krol, C.M., Uszynski, M., Dillon, E.H., Farhad, M., Machnicki, S.C., Mina, B., Rothman, L.M., *Am. J. Roentgenol.*, 178, 1063, 2002. With permission.)

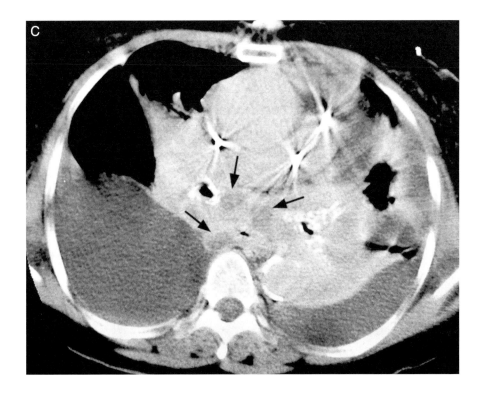

FIGURE 15.5 (Continued) (**C**) Computed tomography scan 20 minutes after contrast bolus at level of subcarinal region shows ill-defined, confluent ring-like areas of enhancement (arrows). Note central hypodensity associated with hemorrhagic lymphadenopathy. (Courtesy of Dr. Christopher M. Krol.) (From Krol, C.M., Uszynski, M., Dillon, E.H., Farhad, M., Machnicki, S.C., Mina, B., Rothman, L.M., *Am. J. Roentgenol.*, 178, 1063, 2002. With permission.)

REFERENCES

1. Alibek, E. and Handelman, S., *Biohazard*, Econ, Munich, 2001.
2. *Encyclopedia Britannica*, CD ROM, 2000.
3. Forquignon, F., *Radiology nach*, B-Waffen Einsatz, Diss., Hamburg, 1996.
4. Langenbein, K., Skalnik, C., and Smolek, I., *Bioterror*, DVA, Stahgart/Munich, 2002.
5. Vogel, H., *Gewalt in Röntgenbild*, ecomed verlagsge-sellschaft mbH, Landsberg/Lech, 1997.

CREDIT

From Vogel, H., *Gewalt in Röntgenbild*, ecomed verlagsgesellschaft mbH, Landsberg/Lech, 1997. With permission.

Figure 15.1.

16 Poisons

Hermann Vogel, M.D.

Different poisons can be used by terrorists, but there are few known cases. Potential biologic weapons include some toxins, noticeably those of botulism (Clostridium botulinum), staphylococcus enterotoxin B intoxication, and Rizin intoxication.

The Secret Service of Bulgaria is said to have used Rizin in 1978 in London to kill Oleg Markov, a writer living in exile. The toxin was injected into the leg of Mr. Markov via a needle hidden in an umbrella. The method was discovered by autopsy, when a small pearl of platinum-iridium containing the toxin was found. A similar attempt against Vladimir Kostov, an exiled politician, failed because the wax that closed the opening of the pearl did not dissolve. Such foreign bodies may be localized by ultrasound, less likely by plain film radiography.

The terrorist sect AUM sprayed botulism toxin from an automobile in Tokyo in 1993. The purpose was to create panic during the marriage of the Crown Prince. In March 1995, there was an attempt to liberate botulism toxin from three suitcases in the Tokyo subway system. The attempt failed because the release system was faulty.

It is said that Saddam Hussein had 12,000 l of botulism toxin and 8,500 l of Aflatoxin, a carcinogen, in Iraq at the end of the Gulf War. It is not known whether they were destroyed.

Radioactive substances can be considered as poisons. Radioactive isotopes of cesium 137, cobalt 60, radium, plutonium, and others are easy to obtain in highly industrialized countries because they are used in hospitals for treatment and in the manufacturing industry for nondestructive testing. Furthermore, radioactive decay products are stored all over the world and reports of thefts and smuggling of such substances are relatively common. An accident in Juarez, Mexico, gives an example of what can happen with decay products. A hospital with a radiation therapy unit was closed. The metal was bought by a scrap dealer who failed to remove the radioactive cobalt source from the therapy unit. The scrap was put into a furnace to produce new girders which were subsequently used in the construction of an office building where large numbers of employees became exposed to irradiation.

The distribution of radioactive material would be unlikely to produce many immediate deaths. However, there are long-term prospects of carcinogenesis and an immediate possibility or probability of panic in the population.

So far as is now known, diagnostic radiology has little to offer in the diagnosis of terrorist poisoning except in the long-term investigations of neoplasia potentially induced by the substances.

REFERENCE

1. Langbein, K. Skalnik, C., and Smolek, L., *Bioterror*, DVA, Stuhgart/Munich, 2002.

Section IV

Missile-Firing Personal Weapons

There is a broad range of weaponry, from fists to airplanes, applicable to the topics of this Atlas—abuse, torture, terrorism, and inflicted trauma. This section will deal almost exclusively with the gun, which also finds its place in all those categories. The United States has long been considered the example par excellence in personal use of the gun by its citizens. Indeed, the right to own and bear arms is guaranteed in our Constitution. It is a right that has been often abused, and our country has often been held up as a bad example in those countries where gun ownership is tightly controlled. The favorable results of such tight controls have been shown statistically. However, guns are ubiquitous throughout our world and are readily available to those who want them enough regardless of legal impediments. Guns are easy to transport and to use and can endow any user with deadly force or the threat thereof.

Evaluation of the gun and gunshot wounds by the radiologic method is essentially as old as radiology itself.[1] In one of his earlier experiments, Wilhelm Röntgen examined his favorite shotgun with the x-rays and found a few flaws, thus introducing the concept of nondestructive testing. Within 2 weeks of Röntgen's announcement of his discovery, x-rays were used in Canada to locate a bullet fired into the leg of Tolsen Cunning by George Holder, who subsequently was imprisoned for the assault. Within 3 months of Röntgen's announcement, x-rays were employed to locate the bullets fired into the head of Elizabeth Ann Hartley by her murderous husband, Hargreaves.

The oldest gunshot wound to be imaged by x-ray was sustained 117 years before Röntgen's discovery. On November 30, 1718, King Charles XII of Sweden died from a gunshot wound to the head while leading his troops in a siege of the Norwegian fortress, Frederiksen. It has since been questioned whether he was shot from the fortress or by one of his own. There were multiple motives for his murder. In 1917, on the fourth examination of his body, photographs and radiographs of the reconstructed skull were obtained. They show a left to right path of an 18 to 20 mm-jacketed projectile. Projectile size and distance from the fortress exonerates the Norwegians. It seems that the king was shot at close range by one of his own people with a specially made bullet   one fit for a king apparently (Figure IV.1)(courtesy of Dr. Hans P. Hougen).[2]

Today, applications of radiology in the investigation and interpretation of gunshot wounds are manifold and recognized to be of critical importance. This section will attempt to illustrate the scope of that process.

B.G.B.

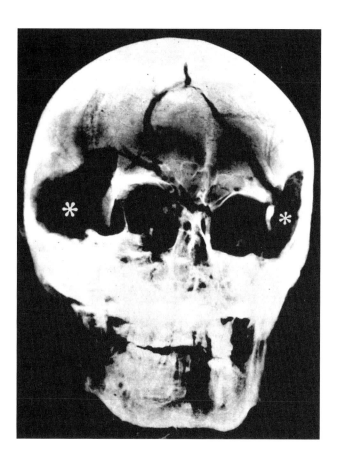

FIGURE IV.I Frontal view of the skull of King Charles XII of Sweden, died 1718, radiographed 1917. The smaller entrance wound is on the left (small asterisk) and the larger exit wound, with external beveling, is on the right (large asterisk).

REFERENCES

1. Brogdon, B.G., *Forensic Radiology*, CRC Press, Boca Raton, FL, 1998, chap. 10.
2. Hougen, H.P. and Munek, O., The death of King Charles XII: a forensic evaluation, Proc. Am. Acad. Forensic Sci., Colorado Springs, CO, 1999, p. 161.

17 Conventional Weapons, Including Shotguns

James M. Messmer, M.D., M.Ed., B.G. Brogdon, M.D., and Hermann Vogel, M.D.

BASIC RADIOLOGIC INFORMATION

X-rays can be used in evaluating gunshot wounds in several ways.[1,2]

LOCATION OF THE BULLET

Bullets frequently will end up at a site quite distant from their point of entry, particularly if they have struck bone. Radiologic examination will greatly expedite and simplify the search (Figures 17.1 and 17.2).

NUMBER OF BULLETS

The number of bullets is important and must be correlated with entrance and exit wounds (Figure 17.3). A discrepancy calls for a search for spent bullets at the scene or additional entrance wounds. More than one bullet can enter through a single entrance wound, particularly when automatic weapons are employed.

CALIBER OF BULLETS

Radiologic examination may reveal whether or not there are bullets of different caliber present, indicating more than one shooter. However, it should be noted that the precise identification of bullet caliber by radiography is fraught with difficulty and error (Figure 17.4).[3]

ANGLE AND DIRECTION OF FIRE

Small metallic fragments shed by the bullet may lead directly to the bullet and indicate its path (Figure 17.5). Forward scattered bony fragments provide similar information (Figure 17.6). Correlating this information with the scene can recreate the relative positions of the shooter and the victim (Figures 5.5 to 5.12 and 17.7).

The radiograph may reveal clues as to the type of weapon employed (Figure 17.8).

DISCOVERING A CONCEALED GUNSHOT WOUND

The fact that a gunshot wound exists may be entirely concealed when the body is decomposed, incinerated, immersed for long periods, or skeletonized (Figures 17.9 and 17.10). Normal creases may hide entry wounds. Retrieval of metallic fragments of whatever origin may help in identifying remains if there is an appropriate antemortem history.

WEAPON BALLISTICS

Radiologic interpretation of gunshot wounds is greatly aided by a general understanding of bullets, weapons, and the tissue damage bullets inflict. The three general types of guns are handguns, rifles, and shotguns. Rifles in general have the higher muzzle velocity. The bullets fired by rifles and handguns are similar and quite different from shotgun loads. Characteristic wounding patterns are found for each type of weapon. While high velocity bullets cause more damage than slow ones, speed is not the only factor in tissue destruction; the weight of the bullet, its construction, and its flight characteristics also play an important role in the amount of damage produced (Figure 17.11).

TYPES OF BULLETS

The ordinary load used for handguns and rifles is a cartridge consisting of a cartridge case (usually made of brass), a primer, a powder charge, and the bullet. The caliber of the bullet is expressed as a decimal corresponding to the diameter in inches or by the actual diameter in millimeters. Bullets of identical diameter may have different weights.

The common base metal for bullets is lead with antimony or tin added for hardness. (Bullets for military and other special uses may be made of other materials.) The lead bullet frequently is fully or partially covered by another metal, called a jacket, that hardens and lubricates the bullet and protects the weapon from leading.

The barrels of rifles and handguns have internal grooves which stabilize the flight of the projectile and helps insure its accuracy. These grooves are characteristic for each make and model of weapon, but each weapon also makes unique markings on the bullet or the jacket as it passes through the barrel. Therefore, for ballistic purposes, it is important to retrieve the jacket for testing for bullets that are fully or partially jacketed (Figures 17.12 and 17.13).

X-rays are quite helpful in this regard although the increasing use of aluminum jackets is a problem (Figure 17.14).

TYPE OF BULLET

The appearance of a bullet on a radiograph can give information about its type. For instance, "mushrooming" or flattening of the end of a bullet indicates a solid lead or partially metal-jacketed bullet (Figure 17.12). Several bullets have a uniquely identifying design (Figures 17.15 and 17.16).

TISSUE DAMAGE

The amount of damage done to the tissues of the victims is proportional to the amount of the bullet's kinetic energy that is expended in the tissue. Velocity, the weight of the bullet, internal composition and configuration, and yaw in the flight path are all contributing factors as well as yaw and rotation once inside the body.

Other factors that contribute to tissue damage are the elasticity of the tissue struck, bone fragmentation, and tissue cavitation (Figure 17.17). The brain, liver, or spleen, being less elastic, can incur more damage than muscle. Bone can deflect and fragment a bullet; then both bone and bullet fragments act as additional projectiles to cause more damage.

MILITARY GUNS AND LOADS

Military guns tend to be high velocity weapons. In general, they are of larger caliber than their civilian or sporting counterparts. Semiautomatic and automatic handheld weapons have the potential for more shots in the target and greater tissue damage.

The Hague Peace Conference in 1899 stipulated that bullets used in war be protected against deformation by a copper jacket, reducing tissue damage. As already shown, deformation is only one component of tissue damage. Other jacketing metals are used, but military rounds are still, for the most part, fully or partially jacketed. The tumbling action designed into some rounds, for instance, can produce ghastly damage to internal tissue. Armor piercing, even explosive shells, are available. One must assume that any handheld weapon and its projectile is available for nonmilitary or paramilitary or terrorist use. (Figures 17.18 to 17.22).

SHOTGUNS

The barrel of a shotgun is smooth inside and the load consists of a few to hundreds of metal spheres packed in a paper or plastic tube (Figures 17.23 and 17.24). The pellets, or shot, emerge from the barrel as a mass that disperses into a scattered pattern of shot determined by the range of fire, barrel length, and the degree of choke or constriction of the bore of the shotgun at its muzzle end. Instability of shot in flight is increased by its spherical shape.

Because of all these factors, the effective range of shotguns is measured in tens of meters as opposed to rifles, which have ranges of hundreds to thousands of meters. The caliber of shotguns is measured in gauges ranging from 8 to .410. The latter designation is actually the caliber of the barrel measured in thousandths of an inch; there is also a 9 mm shotgun named for its barrel diameter. For other gauges, the number represents the number of lead balls at a diameter equal to the diameter of the barrel that would weigh 1 lb. The lower the number of the gauge, the larger the bore. The size of the individual shot is expressed by a number ranging from 12 (smallest) to 000 (largest). The largest number of shot in any one shell depends on the size of the shot and the gauge of the shell.

Typically, shotgun wounds are among the worst in appearance of the wound (Figures 17.25 and 17.26) and can cause massive bone and soft tissue damage.

SUICIDE BY GUNSHOT

In the United States, the number of suicides exceeds the number of murders on an annual basis. As mentioned in Chapter 4, gunshot is the favored method, amounting to up to two-thirds of all suicides. Knowledge of the general characteristics of suicide gunshot wounds may help prevent unwarranted conclusions in some cases.

Gunshot wounds in suicide are usually contact wounds, and since most people are right-handed, enter on the right side of the head. Therefore, wounds to the right temple are most common. The bullet path usually has a posterosuperior trajectory (Figure 17.27). The nondominant hand is used often enough that it cannot be considered beyond the realm of possibility. Suicide wounds in the center of the forehead and to the top and even to the back of the head have been reported. Suicide wounds near the eye are uncommon, and suicide wounds in the mouth usually do not affect the tongue, which is placed out of the way of the barrel. If the tongue is involved, homicide is a possibility (Figure 2.17).

The head is the favorite target for suicide by gunshot, regardless of the type of weapon. In general, the larger the caliber of the bullet, the more damage done.[4] However, a fatal result does not necessarily correlate with caliber (Figures 17.27 to 17.30). The chest and abdomen follow in that order. The handedness of the suicidal person does not correlate in shotgun wounds to the head as with handguns. Shotgun wounds in the chest or abdomen are more apt to correlate with handedness with the shot path downward and to the left for a right-handed person and downward and to the right for a left-handed person. Multiple gunshot wounds, or the finding of more than one bullet, do not preclude suicide (Figure 4.23). There are reports of up to four suicidal gunshot wounds to the head and nine suicidal gunshot wounds to the chest.[5,6]

REFERENCES

1. Brogdon, B.G., *Forensic Radiology*, CRC Press, Boca Raton, FL, 1998, chap. 10.
2. Vogel, H., *Gewalt in Röntgenbild*, ecomed verlagsgesellschaft mbH, Landsberg/Lech, 1997, chap 2.
3. Messmer, J.M. and Fierro, M.F., Radiologic forensic investigation of fatal gunshot wounds, *RadioGraphics*, 6, 457, 1986.
4. Messmer, J.M., Massive head trauma as a cause of intravascular air, *J. Forensic Sci.*, 29, 418, 1984.
5. Jacob, B., Barg, J., Haarhof, K., Sprick, C., Wörz, D., and Bonte, W., Multiple suicidal gunshot wounds to the head, *Am. J. Forensic Med. Pathol.*, 10, 289, 1989.
6. Habbe, D., Thomas, G.E., and Gould, J., Nine-gunshot suicide, *Am. J. Forensic Med. Pathol.*, 10, 335, 1989.

CREDITS

From Brogdon, B.G., *Forensic Radiology*, CRC Press, Boca Raton, FL, 1998. With permission.
Figures 17.2, 17.5, 17.8, 17.9, 17.10, 17.15, 17.16, 17.27.
From Vogel, H., *Gewalt in Röntgenbild*, ecomed verlagsgesellschaft mbH, Landsberg/Lech, 1997. With permission.
Figures 17.4, 17.6, 17.17, 17.18, 17.20, 17.22, 17.23, 17.24.

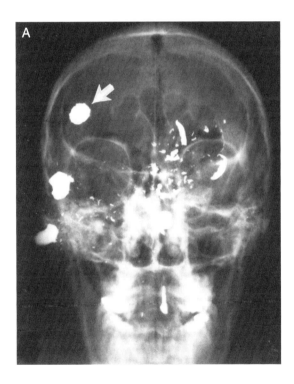
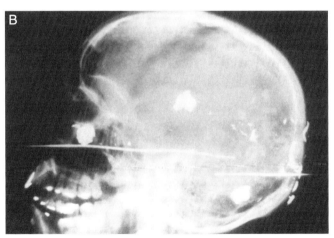

FIGURE 17.1 This is an execution-style murder in which five shots were fired into the back of the head. There is so much deformation and fragmentation of the bullets that it is hard to get an accurate count. **(A)** Frontal view shows a bullet overlying the right frontal sinus (arrow), which was the only bullet easily accessible. The remainder were lodged within the brain or the facial bones. **(B)** Lateral view shows the futility of probing for bullets. (From Messmer, J.M. and Fierro, M.F., *RadioGraphics*, 6, 457, 1986. With permission.)

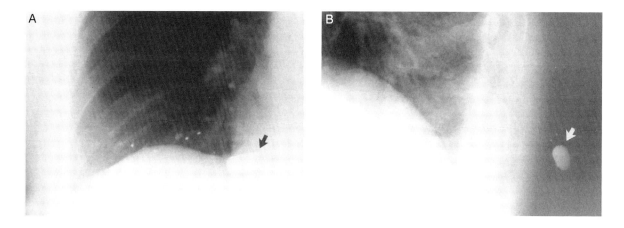

FIGURE 17.2 This felon, fleeing arrest, was shot in the back by a police officer. **(A)** Frontal view shows lead particles leading from the wound of entry, which is in the midportion of the right hemithorax just above the right hemidiaphragm, with small lead particles leading to the final resting place of the bullet behind the heart shadow (arrow). **(B)** The lateral view shows that the bullet is actually very superficial beneath the skin of the back. The bullet struck the rib, then followed its curvature to come to rest quite some distance from the wound of entry.

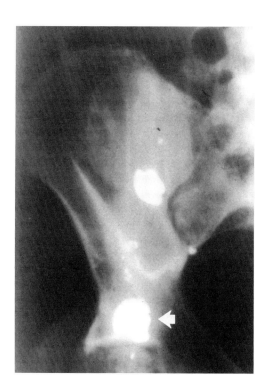

FIGURE 17.3 This man was shot only once. The radiograph appears to show two bullets. However, the lower density (arrow) is the separated jacket that was stripped from the mushroomed slug above. (From Messmer, J.M. and Fierro, M.F., *RadioGraphics*, 6, 457, 1986. With permission.)

FIGURE 17.4 Radiograph of a side view of several low velocity projectiles. On the left is a group of 9 mm bullets. The middle 2 are .45 caliber, and on the right are .38 caliber bullets. There is not much difference in their size and with variation in magnification, the difference would be very difficult to detect.

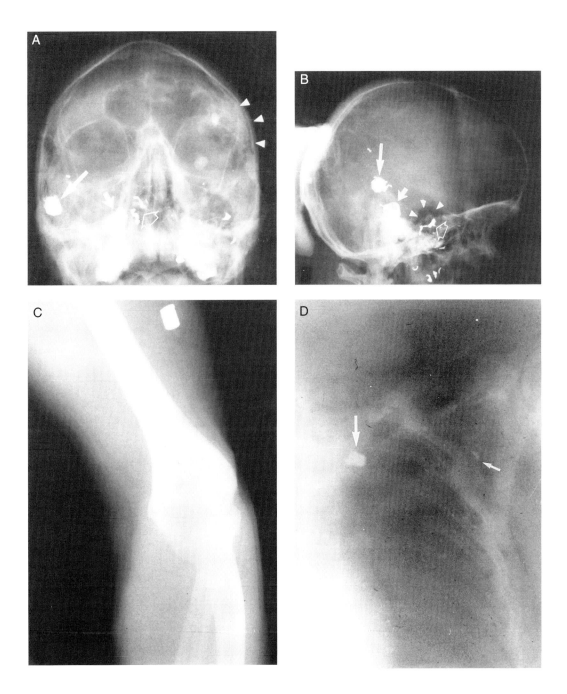

FIGURE 17.5 A body with multiple gunshot wounds was found on the side of the highway. All appeared to be at very short range, and all entered from the left side. This led to speculation that the victim might have been in the right-hand seat of an automobile, his assailant in the driver's seat. Later, the driver, stopped for speeding in a blood-stained car, confessed. **(A)** Frontal view and **(B)** lateral view of the skull shows a left temporal wound of entry (arrowheads). There are scattered bone and bullet fragments throughout. The bullet bounced off the sella (open arrows). The jacket (short arrow) separated and the bullet (long arrow) came to rest against the right parietal bone. **(C)** Nonfatal gunshot wound to the left upper arm. **(D)** Nonfatal bullet wound with trajectory from the left axilla (small arrow) to the left mediastinal border (large arrow).

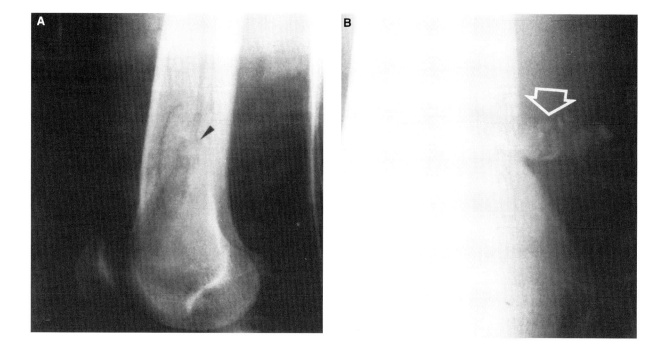

FIGURE 17.6 Low velocity gunshot through the femur. **(A)** Entry wound (arrowhead) is a circular bony defect with surrounding radial fractures. **(B)** A small cloud of bone splinters on the lateral view indicates the exit point of this fully jacketed bullet.

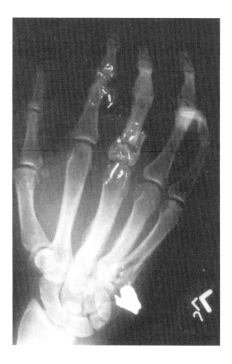

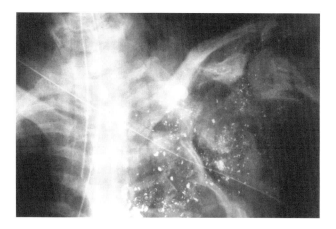

FIGURE 17.8 This is a typical lead snowstorm produced by an unjacketed bullet from a high velocity 30.06 hunting rifle.

IGURE 17.7 This bullet enters the tip of the index finger, passes through the base of the proximal phalanx of the third finger, and comes to rest at the dorsa of the hand over the base of the fifth metacarpal. This is a fending injury. The victim was obviously facing his assailant and futilely trying to fend off the bullet. (Courtesy of Dr. W.U. Spitz.)

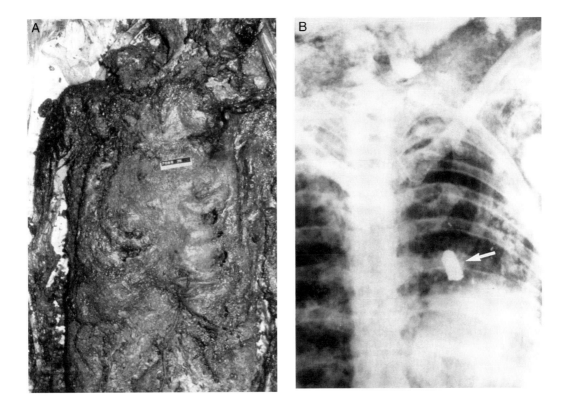

FIGURE 17.9 **(A)** A badly decomposed body gives no indication of cause of death by visual inspection. **(B)** Radiograph of the chest shows a large caliber bullet (arrow) in the left chest in the region of the former position of the heart.

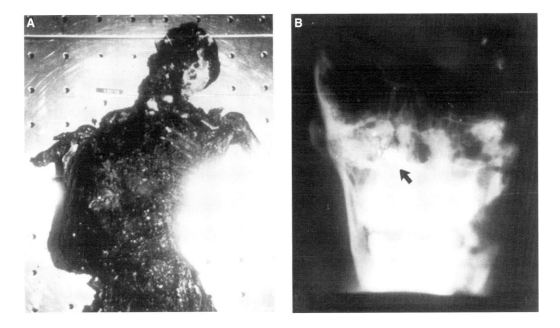

FIGURE 17.10 **(A)** An almost totally incinerated body with the extremities and half of the head missing. **(B)** A large caliber bullet (arrow) is found in the remaining portion of the skull by radiography.

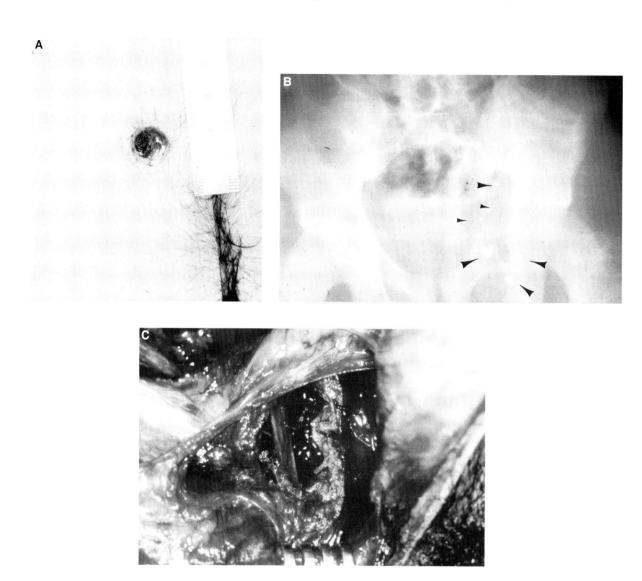

FIGURE 17.11 (**A**) Shows the small entrance wound in the lower abdomen caused by a high velocity M-16 round that (**B**) struck bone causing an extensive fragmentation seen on pelvic radiography and (**C**) massive soft destruction. (From Messmer, J.M. and Fierro, M.F., *RadioGraphics*, 6, 457, 1986. With permission.)

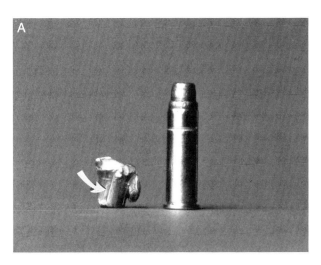

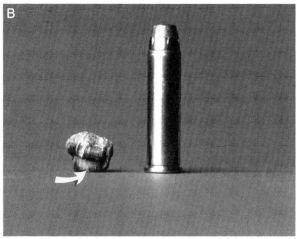

FIGURE 17.12 (A) A solid lead bullet shows the characteristic ballistic marking (arrow). **(B)** In the partially jacketed bullet, the crucial ballistic information is on the copper jacket (arrow) rather than on the lead component. (From Messmer, J.M. and Fierro, M.F., *RadioGraphics*, 6, 457, 1986. With permission.)

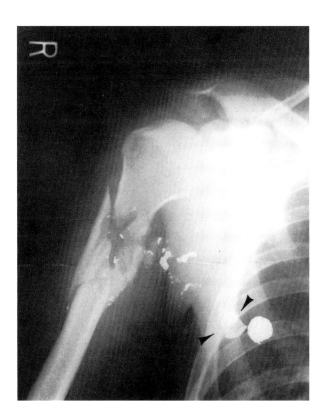

FIGURE 17.13 A partially jacketed bullet shatters the upper humerus and leaves scattered bone and lead fragments along its path before coming to rest in the chest. A large piece of the jacket is less dense (arrowheads) and lies next to the largest bullet fragment.

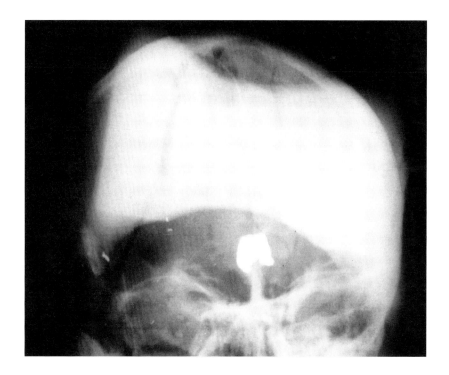

FIGURE 17.14 A frontal radiograph of the skull was taken with the victim on the autopsy table. The large white shadow is the head block used to maintain the position of the head. Large and small bullet fragments are seen as a result of the contact gunshot wound to the right temporal region. The aluminum jacket is not of sufficient density to be identified. (Courtesy of Dr. Kenneth S. Snell, Charlotte, NC.)

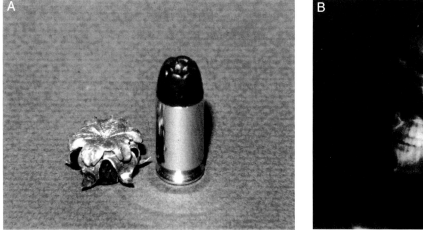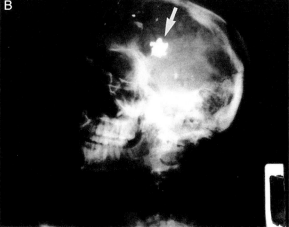

FIGURE 17.15 (A) Fired and unfired Black Talon rounds demonstrate the characteristic sharp projections that are exposed as the bullet mushrooms. **(B)** The radiograph of this homicide victim demonstrates the characteristic appearance of the Black Talon (arrow).

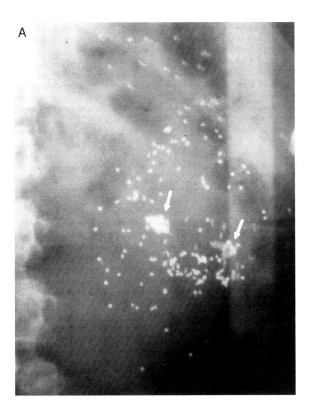

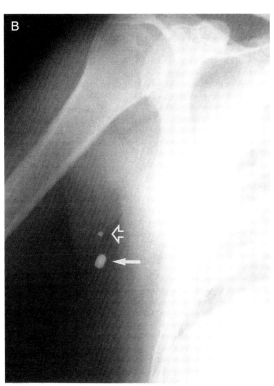

FIGURE 17.16 (**A**) A fatal wound to the flank from a Glaser safety slug, which mimics a shotgun wound to some extent. The shots are contained in a copper cup, fragments of which are shown with arrows. (**B**) Winchester-Western .25 caliber centerfire handgun load consisting of a copper-coated lead hollow-point bullet (arrow) containing a single No. IV steel birdshot pellet (open arrow). (Courtesy of Dr. J.C.U. Downs, Savannah, GA.)

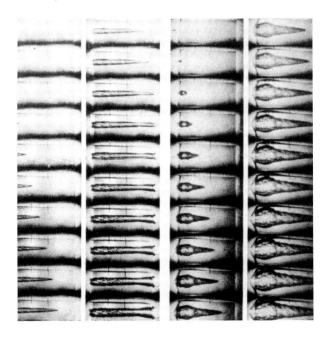

FIGURE 17.17 Examples of cavitation produced in a tissue-equivalent gelatin block. Those on the left are produced by a projectile with a complete steel jacket. Those on the right are produced by a projectile with a partial steel jacket which undergoes degeneration and produces a larger cavity.

FIGURE 17.18 Above is a cross section of a military hardcore projectile. Below is the cross section of an ordinary military projectile with a complete steel coat or jacket.

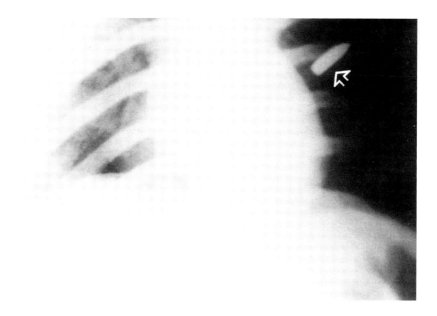

FIGURE 17.19 Fully jacketed .30 caliber projectile retained in the chest with no deformation or disintegration (Mexico).

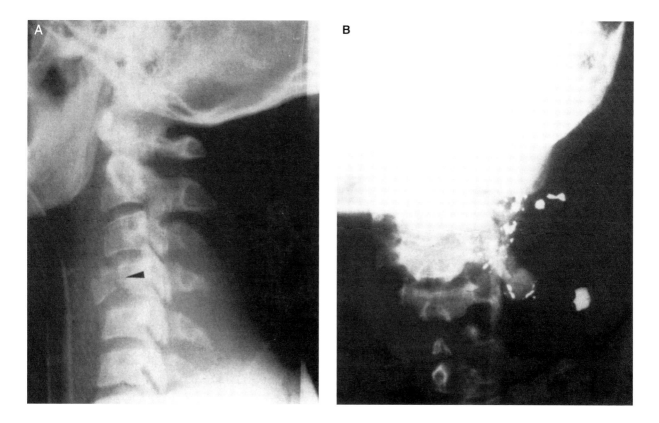

FIGURE 17.20 (A) Completely jacketed low velocity shot through the body of C-4 with no metal fragments and only moderate displacement of bony fragments. (B) Frontal view of a cervical spine hit with a partially jacketed low velocity bullet. Note the multiple bone and metallic fragments scattered in the exit path

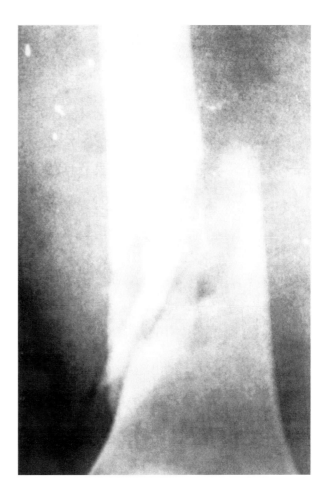

FIGURE 17.21 High velocity, jacketed projectile through the distal femur with limited destruction of bone and only a few shedded fragments (Peru).

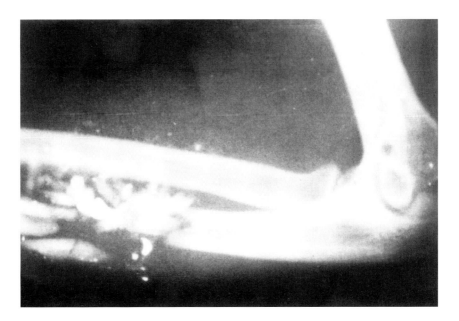

FIGURE 17.22 High velocity gunshot through the forearm. The exit cone is marked by multiple bone and metal fragments in a radiating pattern (Columbia).

FIGURE 17.23 Longitudinal section through several shotgun shells. The percussion cap is at the bottom. Above that is the powder chamber. Above that is the wadding and above that the shot chamber showing shots of varying size and the different shells. On the right is buckshot.

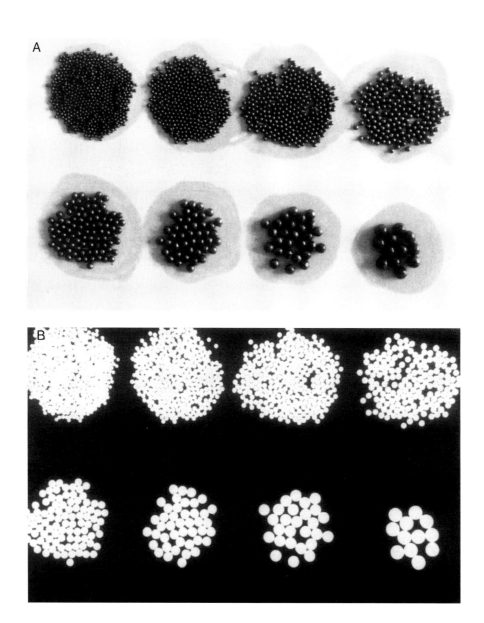

FIGURE 17.24 (**A**) Photograph and (**B**) radiograph showing shot content of shotgun shells of equal gauge. The range is from 2 to 7.5 mm. Note that as the size and weight of the pellet increases the number declines for shells of the same gauge.

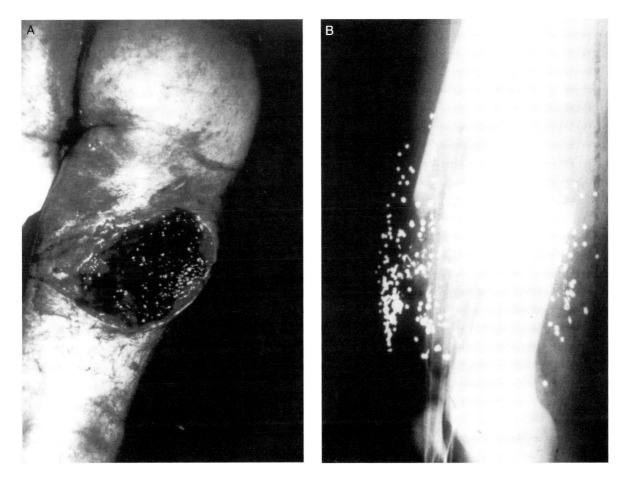

FIGURE 17.25 **(A)** Kneecapping shotgun wound exit (Northern Ireland). **(B)** Kneecapping radiograph. Notice how the elastic skin contains many of the small shot. Obviously, there is massive soft tissue and bony injury.

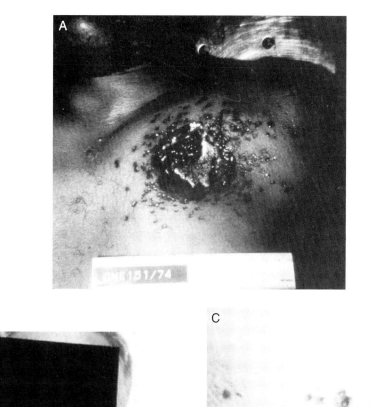

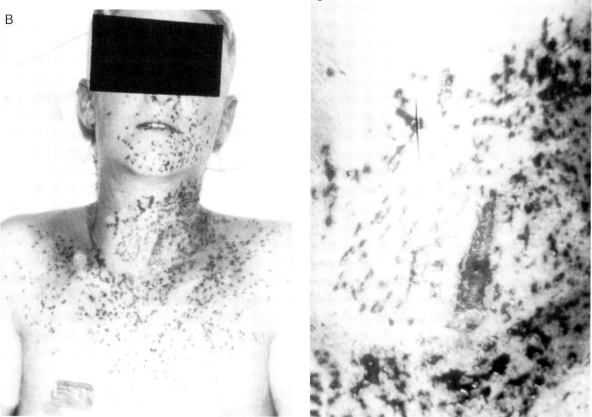

FIGURE 17.26 (A) Shotgun wound pattern at approximately 15 ft range of fire. The pellet pattern has just begun to disperse. (B) Shotgun blast at about 40 ft range of fire with a full dispersal pattern. (C) Close-up view of the multiple wounds. (From Messmer, J.M. and Fierro, M.F., *RadioGraphics*, 6, 457, 1986. With permission.)

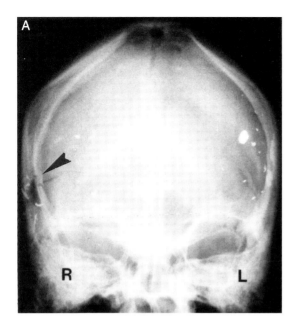

FIGURE 17.27 (A) Frontal radiograph of the skull demonstrates the entrance wound (arrowhead) in the right temporal region with metallic fragments scattered through the brain tissue. The main fragment comes to rest inside the skull at a higher level than the entrance wound. (B) The lateral radiograph shows the anterior to posterior distribution of the metallic fragments. A paper marks the entrance wound. Note the minimal calvarial fracturing related to the small caliber of the weapon.

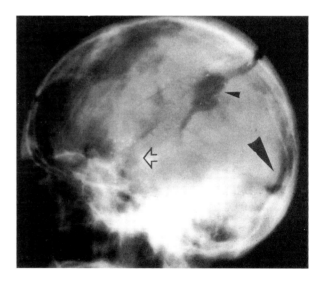

FIGURE 17.28 Lateral skull shot with a large caliber suicide gunshot wound demonstrates the entrance wound (arrow) and the larger exit wound (small arrowhead). Note the extensive fracturing. Also, air has been drawn into the sigmoid sinus (large arrowhead). (From Messmer, J.M. and Fierro, M.F., *Radio-Graphics*, 6, 457, 1986. With permission.)

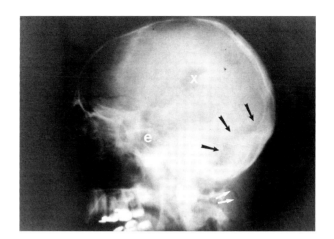

FIGURE 17.29 A self-inflicted .45 gunshot wound to the head shows a through and through injury (little e = entrance; little x = exit). There is air in the sigmoid sinus (arrows) and the occipital vein (white arrows). (From Messmer, J.M. and Fierro, M.F., *RadioGraphics*, 6, 457, 1986. With permission.)

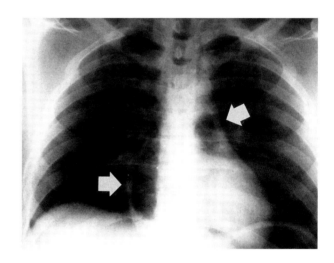

FIGURE 17.30 A postmortem view of the chest of a patient with a .38 caliber suicide gunshot wound to the head. Air entering the vascular system through the intracranial sinuses has been drawn into the right atrium and pulmonary outflow tract (arrows) during the agonal event. (From Messmer, J.M. and Fierro, M.F., *RadioGraphics*, 6, 457, 1986. With permission.)

18 Pitfalls in the Radiology of Gunshot Wounds

James M. Messmer, M.D., M.Ed. and B.G. Brogdon, M.D.

A number of pitfalls await the unwary, overenthusiastic or inexperienced interpreter of the radiologic examination of gunshot wounds.[1] The radiologist should give opinions only on what he is reasonably certain of, and should not exceed his level of competency or experience. Speculation and assumption can be the province of other members of the forensic team, but on the part of the radiologist represents a disservice to his colleagues.

SIZE OF THE MISSILE

There is a great temptation, always to be resisted, to estimate the caliber of a bullet or size of a shot by eyeballing the projectile on a radiograph. Any missile contained within the body will be magnified to some degree upon radiography, and only a small degree of magnification destroys any hope of accuracy (Figure 18.1). The actual difference in dimension between the caliber of weapons commonly used in both military and nonmilitary weapons is really quite close together in size. Moreover, the common designations of caliber are not really precisely accurate. Further, an entrance in the skin cannot be measured to accurately determine the caliber of the entering bullet. Even trauma specialists have difficulty in distinguishing entrance and exit wounds and the number of projectiles present.[2]

Determination of entrance and exit wounds in the skull is assisted by the rule of intersecting fractures,[3] which states that a linear fracture from an earlier blow will stop propagation of a fracture from a second blow.

NUMBER OF BULLETS

Surprisingly, the simple determination of the number of bullets expected or found within a body may be difficult (Figure 18.2). Entrance and exit wounds may be confused. It is possible that a bullet will enter the same wound made by a round fired earlier. Tandem bullets—when a bullet lodges in the barrel of a weapon and is propelled out by a second shot—is not an unknown phenomenon. Both bullets can enter the body through the same hole. Other metallic densities within the body or clothing can be confused with a bullet (Figures 18.3 and 18.4).[4]

MIGRATION OF MISSILES

Having once entered the body, bullets can travel for remarkable distances in tubular structures, such as the vascular system, the bronchial tree, the alimentary canal, the urinary tract, and the neural canal (Figures 18.5 to 18.14). They can also travel within less confined spaces, such as the pleural space (Figure 18.15) or the peritoneal cavity.[1,5] Being of metallic density, bullets and pellets are easily detected on radiographs. Thus, any missile not quickly located near its wound of entry or along an obvious track requires further investigation. In the dead, this can be time-saving for the medical examiner in recovering essential evidence and information. In the living, rapid location of migrating missiles can be life-saving as well as time-saving. In general, migrating missiles will follow the force and direction of blood flow, gravity, positional changes, and pressure changes (Figures 18.16 and 18.17). Sometimes the movement of missiles is not appreciated until serial radiographic studies are interpreted. Several examples are shown (Figures 18.5, 18.10, 18.15, 18.17).

PROBLEMS WITH SHOTGUN PELLETS

In the United States, shotgun pellets of all sizes are made of lead and subject to deformation (Figure 18.18). The exception is the steel load that is mandated for waterfowl hunting. Deformation of round pellets can lead to confusion. Large shot, particularly, upon flattening or fragmentation may suggest large-caliber bullets or jackets. Like large bullets, pellets can migrate to produce confusing clinical findings (Figure 18.10).

RANGE OF FIRE FROM PELLET PATTERN

Aerodynamically, the round or spherical pellet is unsound. It slows down rapidly, and groups of pellets exiting a shotgun muzzle spread out as they travel through distance. Most systems for determining the range of fire of shotguns (using information based on gauge, shot size, choke, and distance) are relatively inaccurate. Drawing general conclusions about range of fire from external inspection of wounds is reasonably accurate. There is a substantial pitfall in drawing those same conclusions from the pattern of shot on a radiograph. A dispersed pattern may suggest that the weapon was fired from a distance when it was actually fired from close range (Figure 18.19). This is the so-called billiard ball effect (Figure 18.20).

RANGE OF FIRE

Apart from spread patterns in shotgun wounds, range of fire assessment of bullet wounds may depend upon the composition and relative amounts of residue found on the skin. Residue deposits on excised skin have been examined with x-rays generated by the Faxitron® unit* or localization and further study by scanning electronmicroscopy or energy-dispersive x-ray analysis. Clothing may trap or redistribute gunshot residue and is also important for examination. Since blood, color, or patterns may render direct examination of cloth difficult, Faxitron examination can be extremely helpful in defining the presence, location, and distribution of gunshot residue, allowing further collection and analysis[1,6-8] (Figures 18.22 and 18.23).

DIFFERENT SIZE SHOT

With handgun and rifle shootings, the finding of bullets of different sizes suggests that there is more than one weapon or more than one shooter. This does not necessarily hold true for shotgun wounds since so many people reload their shells, sometimes mixing shot (Figure 19.24).

REFERENCES

1. Brogdon, B.G., *Forensic Radiology*, CRC Press, Boca Raton, FL, 1998, chap. 11.
2. Collins, K.A. and Lantz, P.E., Interpretation of fatal, multiple and existing gunshot wounds by trauma specialists, *J. Forensic Sci.*, 32, 1416, 1987.
3. Dixon, D.S., Pattern of intersecting fractures and direction of fire, *J. Forensic Sci.*, 29, 651, 1984.
4. Messmer, J.M. and Fierro, M.F., Radiologic forensic investigation of fatal gunshot wounds, *RadioGraphics*, 6, 457, 1986.

* Faxitron X-ray Corp., 1670 Barclay Blvd., Buffalo Grove, IL, 60089.

5. Hughes, J.J., Brogdon, B.G., and Eichelberger, R.F., Migrating Missiles, *Ala. J. Med. Sci.*, 21, 416, 1987.
6. Snell, K.S., Riddick, L., and Brogdon, B.G., Faxitron®: radiography in a forensic setting, *Proc. Am. Acad. Forensic Sci.*, Colorado Springs, CO, 1999.
7. Snell, K.S., Carter, R.D., Riddick, L., and Goodin, J., Identifying microscopic gunshot residue and evidence with the Faxitron®, *Proc. Am. Acad. Forensic Sci.*, Colorado Springs, CO, 2001.
8. Snell, K.S., Evaluation of gunshot residue with the Faxitron®, *Proc. Am. Acad. Forensic Sci.*, Colorado Springs, CO, 2001.

CREDIT

From Brogdon, B.G., *Forensic Radiology*, CRC Press, Boca Raton, FL, 1998. With permission. Figures 18.3, 18.5, 18.7, 18.10 (A and B), 18.12, 18.14, 18.15, 18.18.

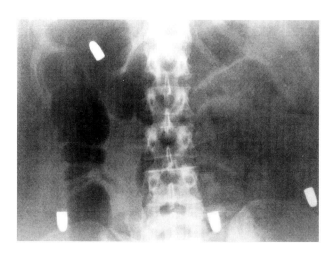

FIGURE 18.1 The effect of magnification on estimate of caliber. Bullets of .32 and .38 caliber were placed at different positions on a body and radiographed. All of the bullets appear to be about the same size because of the variation in magnification, which is related to the difference in object film distances for the different bullets. (From Messmer, J.M. and Fierro, M.F., *RadioGraphics*, 6, 457, 1986. With permission.)

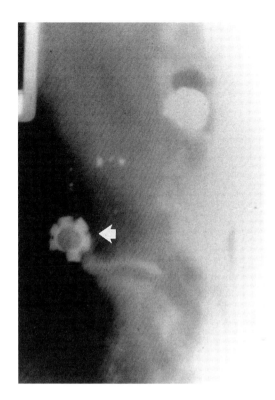

FIGURE 18.2 This is the same case as Figure 17.3, but the body has been turned slightly. It is now very clear that the lower density is not a second bullet, but the shed partial jacket (arrow) from the large bullet fragment above. (From Messmer, J.M. and Fierro, M.F., *RadioGraphics*, 6, 457, 1986. With permission.)

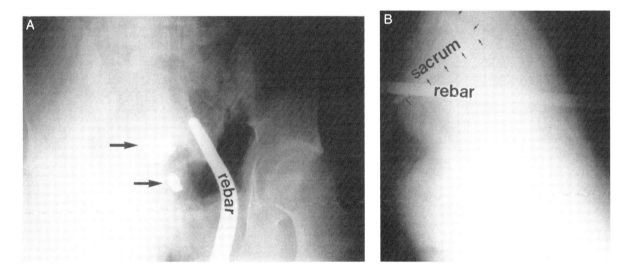

FIGURE 18.3 Articles of clothing can be confused with bullets. **(A** and **B)** This biker impaled himself on a length of rebar when he crashed into a bridge under construction. The initial frontal x-ray **(A)** showed two metallic densities that might be a bullet (arrows). Actually, the upper one is a waist fastener, and the lower one is a zipper pull.

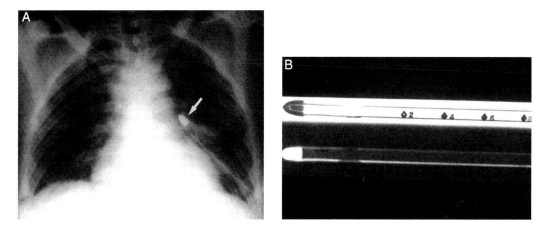

FIGURE 18.4 **(A)** A supine chest radiograph shows a bullet-shaped density at the tip of the chest tube. **(B)** Photograph (top) and radiograph (below) show that the bullet-shaped density is an integral part of the chest tube. (From Messmer, J.M. and Fierro, M.F., *RadioGraphics*, 6, 457, 1986. With permission.)

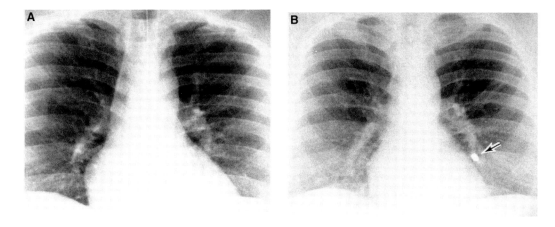

FIGURE 18.5 Intravascular, intracardiac migration. **(A)** Postoperative supine chest radiograph after surgery for a gunshot wound to the abdomen that disclosed a tear in the inferior vena cava. **(B)** Repeat study shows the bullet has traveled up the vena cava to the right heart and then out the left pulmonary artery to embolize a lower lobe branch (arrow).[5]

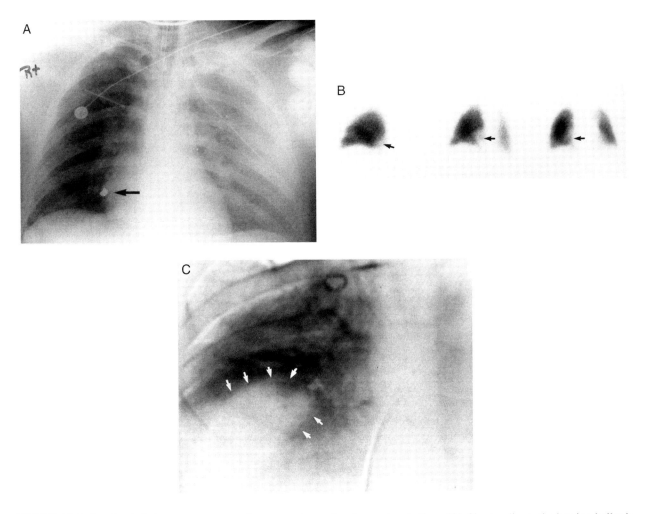

FIGURE 18.6 Another inferior vena cava to pulmonary artery migration and embolism. (**A**) Chest radiograph showing bullet in the right lower lobe (arrow). (**B**) Radioisotope lung scan showing perfusion defect of the right lower lobe posteriorly (arrows). (**C**) Pulmonary arteriogram subtraction image. The perfused lung is black; the nonperfused lung is clear (arrows).

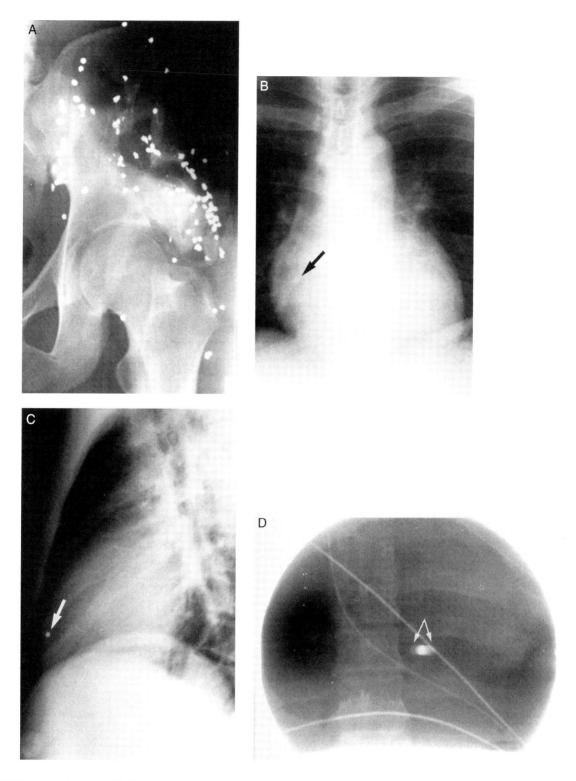

FIGURE 18.7 Venous migration. (**A**) Shotgun wound to the left hip. (**B** and **C**) Postero-anterior and lateral chest radiographs reveal a shot lying in the heart (arrow). (**D**) Spot film taken during fluoroscopy shows to and fro blurring of the shot as it moves with the heartbeat. This means it is either in the wall of the right ventricle or trapped in the chordae tendineae inside the right ventricle.

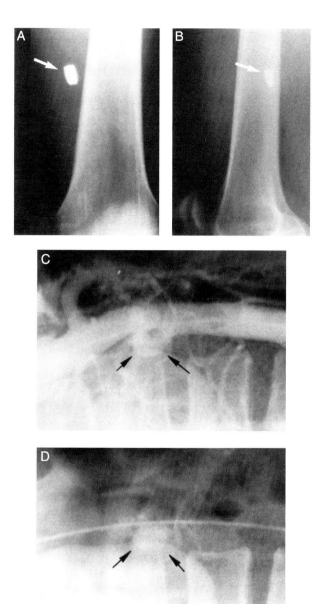

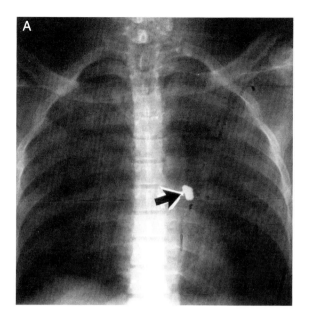

FIGURE 18.8 Aortic-arterial migration. (**A** and **B**) Bullet (arrow) from a left flank wound is found lodged in the superficial femoral artery in the thigh. (**C** and **D**) Early and late films from an aortogram (lateral view) show a pseudoaneurysm (arrows) arising from the posterior wall of the aorta.

FIGURE 18.9 Tracheobronchial migration. (**A**) This victim received two gunshot wounds to the face. A radiograph of the head (not shown) demonstrated only one bullet. Frontal chest radiograph shows a bullet (arrow) overlying the left hilum. (**B**) The autopsy shows the blackened bullet (arrows) had been aspirated and became lodged in the left mainstem bronchus. (From Messmer, J.M. and Fierro, M.F., *RadioGraphics*, 6, 457, 1986. With permission.)

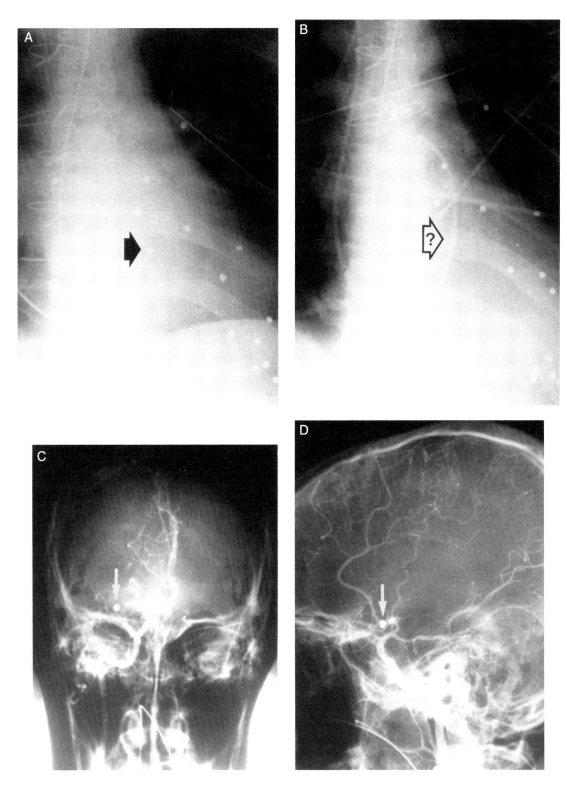

FIGURE 18.10 Cardiac to internal carotid artery migration. (**A**) A nonfatal shotgun wound to the chest is shown on an admission chest radiograph. Three days later, the patient had a sudden crisis in his hospital room and became paraplegic on one side. (**B**) Chest radiograph shows that one of the shotgun pellets on the initial study (black arrow) is no longer present on the follow-up study (open arrow). (**C** and **D**) Subsequent investigation shows that the pellet was lodged in the right middle cerebral artery which was occluded. (Figures 18.10 C and D from Kase, C.S., White, R.L., Vinson, T.L., and Eichelberger, R.P., *Neurology*, 31, 458, 1981. With permission.)

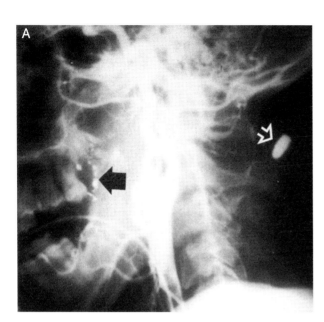

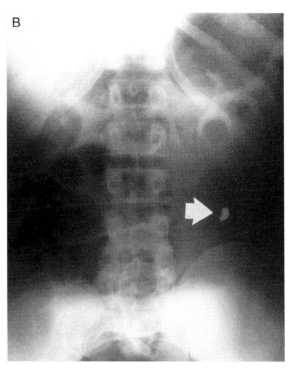

FIGURE 18.11 Migration in the gastrointestinal tract. **(A)** This man was shot twice in the face with a .25 caliber handgun. A lateral view during carotid arteriography shows a bullet in the soft tissues of the posterior neck (open arrow) and metallic fragments (arrow) around the coronoid process of the mandible. **(B)** Abdominal radiograph shows the second bullet, after having been stopped by the mandible, was swallowed and now lies in the left abdomen. It was eventually recovered in the stool. (From Messmer, J.M. and Fierro, M.F., *RadioGraphics*, 6, 457, 1986. With permission.)

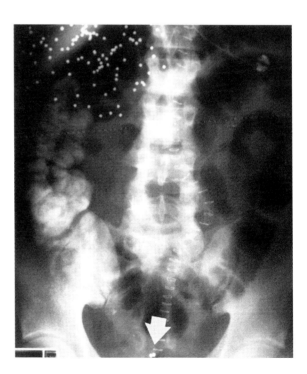

FIGURE 18.12 A shotgun wound to the right side of the back injured the right kidney. At the extreme inferior margin of the radiograph, there are two pellets in the bladder, after having entered the kidney and passed through the ureter.

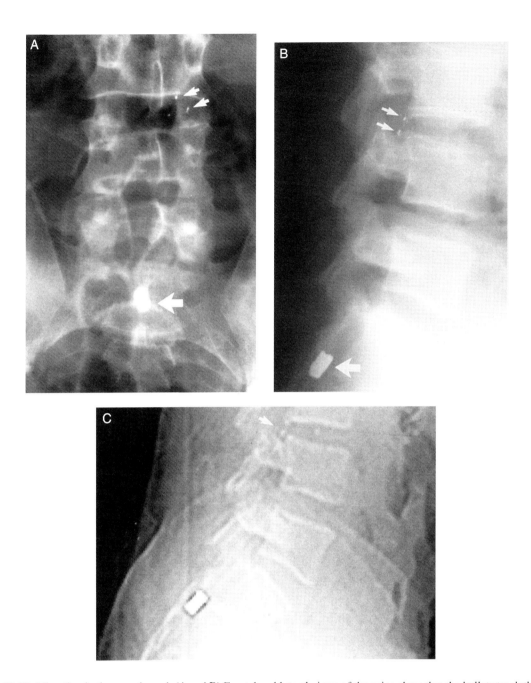

FIGURE 18.13 Migration in the neural canal. (**A** and **B**) Frontal and lateral views of the spine show that the bullet struck the inferior articular process of the L-3 vertebra, leaving two small fragments (arrows), then dropped through the subarachnoid space before coming to rest in the caudal sac (arrow). (**C**) A topogram, or digital scout film, for a computed tomography (CT) and is just as revealing as a standard lateral radiograph.

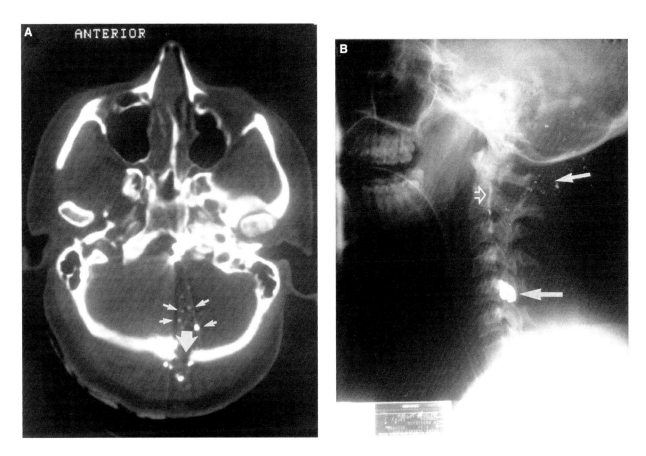

FIGURE 18.14 Migration from the skull into the neural canal. **(A)** A bullet was fired into the base of the skull, cutting a groove in the occipital bone (large arrow) and scattering fragments (small arrows) into the posterior fossa. CT examination. **(B)** A lateral view of the cervical spine shows that the bullet traversed the posterior elements of C-1 vertebra (small arrow), impacted on the posterior aspect of C-2 (open arrow), then dropped in the neurocanal before coming to rest at the C-5 level (large arrow).

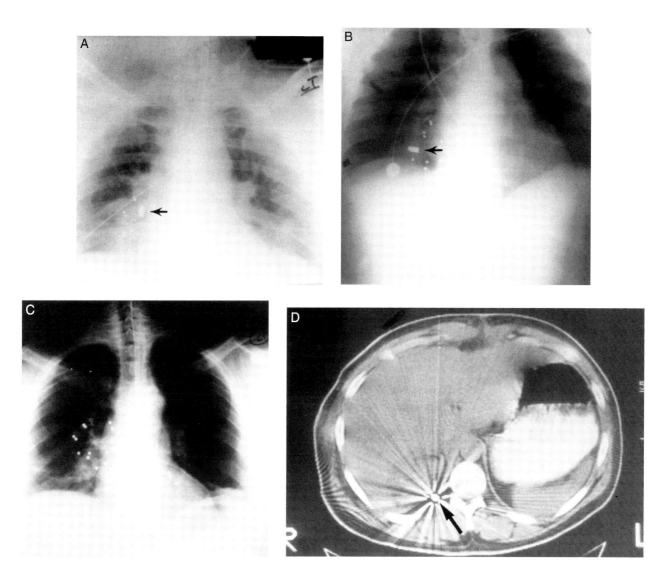

FIGURE 18.15 Migration in the pleural space. **(A)** Supine chest radiograph shows a bullet (arrow) from acute gunshot wound. The adjacent small shot is from an old shotgun injury. **(B)** Supine chest 2 days later shows that the bullet has moved and rotated. Therefore, it must be in the pleural space. **(C)** Two days later the bullet can no longer be seen on the chest radiograph. **(D)** CT reveals that the bullet is so deep in the posterior costophrenic sulcus (star pattern) that the bullet is obscured on routine chest radiography by the density of the full thickness of the liver.

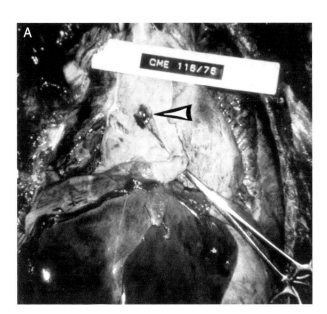
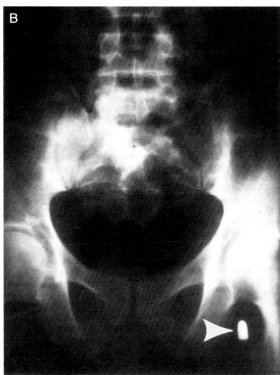

FIGURE 18.16 **(A)** The autopsy revealed a bullet wound to the anterior surface of the heart (arrowhead) although a chest radiograph had revealed no bullet. **(B)** Radiograph of the pelvis shows the bullet overlying the left groin in the left femoral artery. Forces of both gravity and flow probably affected this migration. (From Messmer, J.M. and Fierro, M.F., *RadioGraphics*, 6, 457, 1986. With permission.)

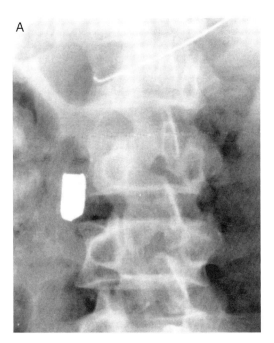
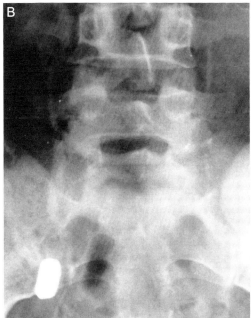

FIGURE 18.17 **(A)** Immediately after a gunshot wound to the midabdomen, a radiograph shows a bullet just to the right of L-3. **(B)** A subsequent study shows the bullet has migrated from its initial position consistent with the inferior vena cava *against* venous flow to a location consistent with the right iliac vein.

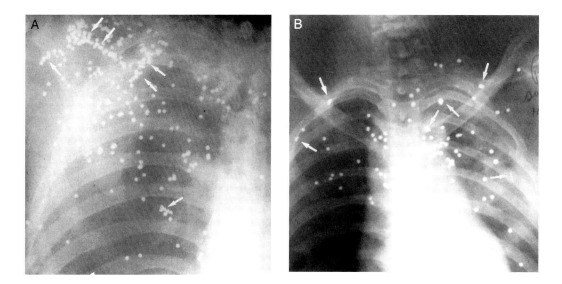

FIGURE 18.18 This young Native American died of exposure at the edge of the Sheriff's Trap and Skeet Range. His body was found decomposed in the spring. **(A)** Radiographs showed numerous pellets over the chest, but *none* are deformed and the clusters (arrows) are inconsistent with a shot pattern. These had merely drifted down over the body through the winter. **(B)** Typical relatively long-range shot pattern with many deformed pellets (arrows).

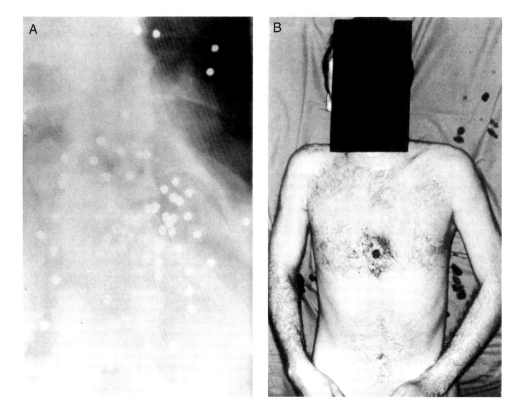

FIGURE 18.19 **(A)** Postmortem radiograph over the lower chest shows a spread pattern of shotgun pellets suggesting that the weapon had been fired from a distance. **(B)** The wound was, in fact, a contact suicide wound. (From Messmer, J.M. and Fierro, M.F., *RadioGraphics*, 6, 457, 1986. With permission.)

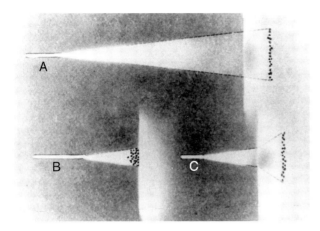

FIGURE 18.20 Schematic drawing of the billiard ball effect. (**A**) If the shotgun is fired at intermediate to long range, the pattern has a chance to form and the pellets enter the body through individual openings. A spread pattern will be seen on the radiograph. (**B**) If the shotgun is fired at close range, the leading pellets are slowed as they enter the body at the skin and are struck by the trailing pellets. (**C**) The colliding pellets ricochet to spread the shot pattern so that it can simulate the pattern of longer-range fire. (Redrawn from Messmer, J.M. and Fierro, M.F., *RadioGraphics*, 6, 457, 1986. With permission.)

FIGURE 18.21 Desktop model, Faxitron X-ray Unit. The controls are on top. The cabinet below contains the specimen and the film.

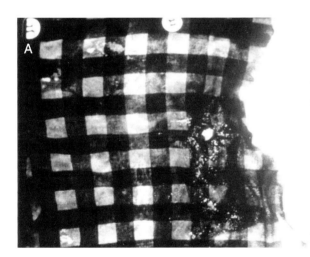

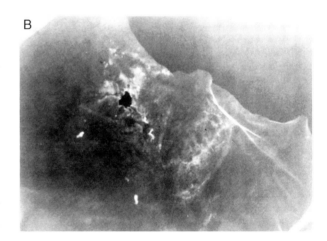

FIGURE 18.22 (**A**) This blood-soaked red and black plaid flannel shirt was almost impossible to examine for gunshot residue. (**B**) However, a low-energy radiograph with the Faxitron unit discloses the location and distribution of residue.

FIGURE 18.23 A young male was shot three times in the anterior chest, causing his death. He was wearing a T-shirt that became covered with abundant, thick blood. When submitted to the firearms examiner for evaluation, holes corresponding to the gunshots were identified. However, two additional large irregular holes in the middle of the back did not correspond to bullet holes in the body. Initial microscopic examination revealed no residue. Radiography with the Faxitron showed a wedge-shaped pattern of radiopaque particles extending from one of the holes (arrows). Reexamination with a microscope revealed numerous lead, bullet jacket, and bone fragments. This evidence established that a bullet had produced the two irregular holes. (Courtesy of Dr. K.S. Snell, Charlotte, NC.) (From Snell, K.S., Carter, R.D., Riddick, L., and Goodin, J., *Proc. Am. Acad. Forensic Sci.*, Colorado Springs, CO, 2001. With permission.)

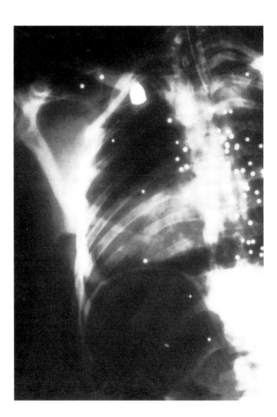

FIGURE 18.24 A radiograph of the chest of an individual with shotgun pellets of various sizes. In addition, a large caliber slug overlies the right upper chest.

19 Air Guns

Hermann Vogel, M.D. and B.G. Brogdon, M.D.

In the rural U.S. before and during World War II, almost every young boy acquired a BB gun. It was almost a rite of passage in an era, and an area, where almost every household contained one or more guns; hunting was not only a sport but a means of supplementing the family larder. The BB gun was named after the projectile (.177 caliber or 4.5 mm). It propelled a round sphere, originally made of lead and later copper coated. It was a low weight projectile and propelled with a low muzzle velocity (275 ft/sec) by compressed air. Most BB guns were Daisy Air Rifles manufactured by the Daisy Manufacturing Company in Rogers, AR. The weapon was charged and cocked by a lever that incorporated the trigger guard or, more rarely, by pump action or by breaking the barrel and stock as in a double-barrel shotgun. They were single-shot models. Some had a tubular magazine which would hold several BBs (current price: 350 BBs for 70 cents U.S.). The limited range and accuracy of the weapon made it relatively safe. The projectile would be stopped by most articles of clothing. Unprotected skin would be barely penetrated. The real hazard of the weapon was a wound in the eye (Figure 19.1).

The BB gun or air rifle seems to be disappearing from the American scene. This could be because of the fairly minimal hazard it represented or a general reluctance to accept the gun as a toy in our current society. The BB gun was a little of both. The sale of air guns is restricted in some U.S. jurisdictions. The Daisy Company will no longer ship a BB gun to anyone under 21 years of age, and the buyer must certify that it is a legal purchase where he lives.

There also is the pellet gun, frequently a handgun, and the projectile is shaped more like a sphere sitting on a truncated cone. Propulsion is provided by carbon dioxide cartridges. This truly is a weapon, with a reasonably high muzzle velocity (up to 650 ft/sec) that could injure. It was and is used primarily for target shooting and is definitely considered a weapon, not a toy. It can penetrate skin and even bone (Figure 19.2).

In Germany, air guns are a bit different. They are sold only to people older than 18 without restriction if they have energies of less than 7.5 J when leaving the muzzle. Their danger on short range is regularly underestimated, thus they are the weapon causing most of the accidents due to the use of arms in Germany. Ordinarily the calibers are 4.5 and 5.5 mm. There are several kinds of ammunition:

1. Round globes of a copper alloy, frequently found at fairs or similar events
2. *Diabolos* of a soft lead alloy, which have the form of an inverted egg cup
3. Pointed globes in the form of diabolos with an anterior tip of lead alloy
4. Pointed projectiles

The weight is normally 0.5 g for a caliber 4.5 mm. They are accelerated by gas in cartridges or by air compressed in a chamber. To stay below the limit of 7.5 J, the acceleration is not more than 175 m/sec. However, there are air guns for hunting with acceleration of 350 m/sec, corresponding to 30.5 J. In foreign countries, limits to acceleration and speed are the exception; powerful air guns are available. In recent years the acceleration, and thus the energy, has been increased with a result of more severe injuries.[1] These air guns are able to penetrate the calvaria and thus reach the brain and the ventricular system. Displaced bony fragments are removed as well as the projectile, if accessible. It is possible, however, that residual projectiles can cause additional damage from tissue reactions to lead. Pneumocephalus has been reported, requiring surgical treatment. Embolism of projectiles is also a possibility.

Radiographically, diabolos are easily recognized due to their typical configuration (Figures 19.3 to 19.6). Their point is nearly always deformed. When seen on end, they can resemble shotgun pellets. Penetration is usually superficial and bone lesions are the exception, except for the fingers. Eye lesions, of course, are severe. Radiography shows the projectile in relationship to neighboring and anatomic structures. The same can be accomplished with sonography or computed tomography. Magnetic resonance is not often employed because of the danger of dislodgement due to magnetic properties. Localization is most employed in the head and neck and in relation to superficial vessels. Intercostal penetration with pneumothorax has been reported.

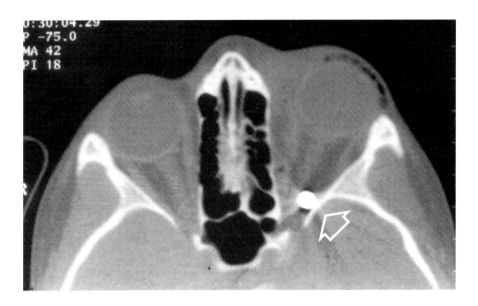

FIGURE 19.1 BB pellet in the apex of the left orbit. Remarkably, the optic nerve was not damaged.

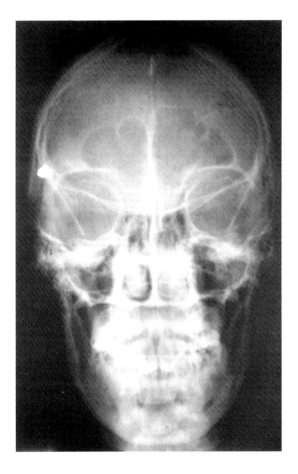

FIGURE 19.2 Pellet gun projectile stopped by the heavy bone at the upper outer margin of the orbit.

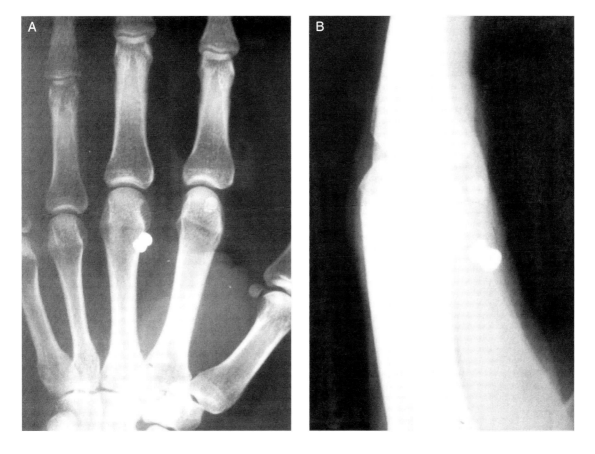

FIGURE 19.3 **(A)** "Diabolo" in the hand. There is no deformation of the projectile. The victim accidentally shot himself while handling the weapon prior to shooting for a prize at a fair. **(B)** Close-up view shows the characteristic configuration of the projectile.

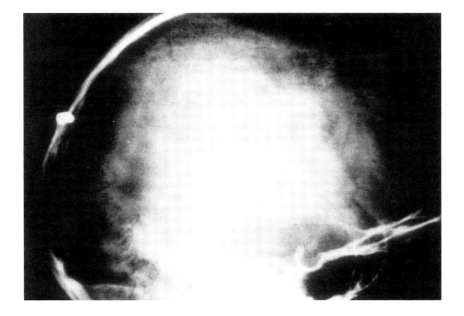

FIGURE 19.4 "Diabolo" with its typical narrow waist penetrating the calvaria near the lambda.

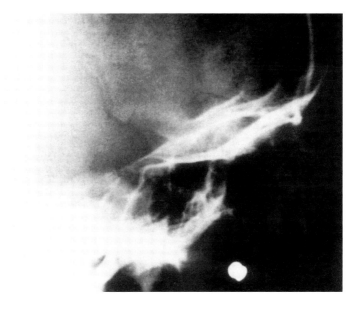

FIGURE 19.5 "Diabolo" in the face. Although there is no obvious bony lesion, there is some deformation and shortening of the projectile.

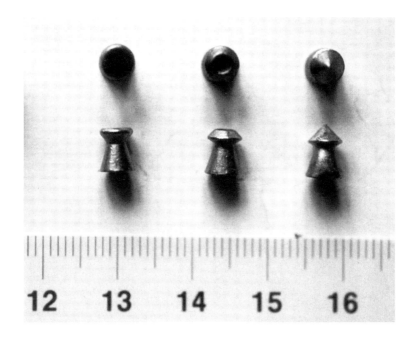

FIGURE 19.6 Different configurations of air gun projectiles.

REFERENCE

1. Jung, C., Röntgenbefunde bei Schussverletzungen, Diss., Hamburg, 1993.

20 Unconventional Loads and Weapons

Hermann Vogel, M.D. and B.G. Brogdon, M.D.

The transition between outright war and the limited enforcement of obedience of populations can be demonstrated by observing the utilization of rubber and plastic bullets.[1] Among others, they are used in Israel, Indonesia, and Northern Ireland. Rubber bullets contain a core of light metal and a coating of rubber. Thus, the term rubber bullet is misleading and can be regarded as a euphemism. The name implies harmless effects, at least not mutilation or death. The majority of reporting journalists know neither the makeup nor the real effects of these missiles. Not until the middle of 2001 did German TV start to refer to coated-bullets instead of rubber bullets, at least on occasion.

Plastic bullets are larger than rubber bullets. Originally, they were meant to stop or retard demonstrators in active protest or rioting. The idea was to aim at the ground about 30 m in front of the leading edge of the rioters, so that the leaders would be hit and immobilized by the ricochet. However, one has to keep in mind that it is possible to throw a Molotov cocktail more than thirty meters. Given that situation, a policeman or soldier will not aim at the ground in front of the mob, but will elevate his weapon and aim straight at the people. Direct hits are the consequence.

Special weapons were constructed. In Northern Ireland, projectiles of 10 to 15 cm in length and 3 to 4 cm in diameter were fired (Figures 20.1 and 20.2). Their trajectory is relatively unstable. Hitting the target directly transfers the total energy of the projectile to a small area of the body. The resultant lesions have a bull's-eye configuration (Figure 20.3). If the projectile hits parts of the body where there is superficial bone, the tissue cannot absorb and distribute the energy on impact, and open wounds result.

Ricochet bullets produce a long bruise with a blurred margin (Figure 20.4). They resemble the side view of the projectile. Hitting the chest, they may produce pulmonary contusions in varying sizes and configurations depending upon the impacted area (Figure 20.5). Of course, the eye and the face are the most vulnerable structures. Permanent damages can result from hits to the eyes. Hitting in the eye, the projectile can penetrate deeply through the orbit, destroying the eye and the orbital bony structure and entering the brain (Figure 20.6). Severe injuries to the calvaria are possible.

In Israel, the army and police forces employ different projectiles against Palestine insurgents. The generic term is either plastic bullet or rubber bullet. However, some of them have a rubber coat and a metal core, and they are fired either with a special arm or with a modified ordinary weapon. Multiple hits are possible. At 20 to 30 m these projectories can penetrate heavy musculature or penetrate bony structures to enter the abdomen, chest, or skull (Figures 20.7 to 20.9). Injuries to the jaw and teeth are not uncommon (Figure 20.10).

Some projectiles have a coat of light metal and are filled with glass and sand and are known as ceramic bullets. They are shot with a cartridge with ordinary high velocity capability, reaching a velocity of two to three times the speed of sound. At relatively short ranges, they burst or disintegrate, producing enormous amounts of tissue damage. At longer ranges, the ceramic bullets may not fragment (Figure 20.11).

In South America, the natives sometimes construct their own guns out of tubes which frequently explode with disastrous results to the face and hands (Figure 20.12).

In civil war or terrorist activities, any weapon that comes to hand is likely to be used. Figure 20.13 shows a tail fin rocket penetrating the pelvis.

Tasers are sort of an electric rifle. It is a firearm that uses gun powder to propel an electric probe or contactor. The Air Taser uses compressed nitrogen as a propellant. It is therefore classified as a nonfirearm and is legal for sale to the general public in some jurisdictions. They are restricted in some countries. The probes can carry some 50,000 v of electricity over a range of about 15 ft, and the victim will instantly lose his muscle control and become quite helpless (Figure 20.14).

Shah[2] reported a case where a pneumatic stud gun or nail gun (commonly used in construction work) was employed as a murder weapon. The victim was shot eight times through the left eye with 2 in. nails (Figure 20.15). We have seen one other, less extreme, shooting with a stud gun (Figure 20.16).[3] The use of a pneumatic hammer as a suicide weapon has already been described in Chapter 4.

Even crossbows or arbalests are sometimes used as weapons in modern Europe (Figure 20.17).

REFERENCES

1. Vogel, H., *Gewalt in Röntgenbild*, ecomed verlagsgesellschaft mbH, Landsberg/Lech, 1997, chap. 2.
2. Shah, M.B., Teed, H.G., and McDonough, M.D., Industrial homicide, *Proc. Am. Acad. Forensic Sci.*, Colorado Springs, CO, 2000, p. 182.
3. Brogdon, B.G., *Forensic Radiology*, CRC Press, Boca Raton, FL, 1998, chap. 11.

CREDITS

From Brogdon, B.G., *Forensic Radiology*, CRC Press, Boca Raton, FL, 1998. With permission.
   Figure 20.16
From Vogel, H., *Gewalt in Rontgenbild*, ecomed verlagsgesellschaft mbH, Landsberg/Lech, 1997. With permission.
   Figures 20.1–20.5, 20.8, 20.10–20.12.

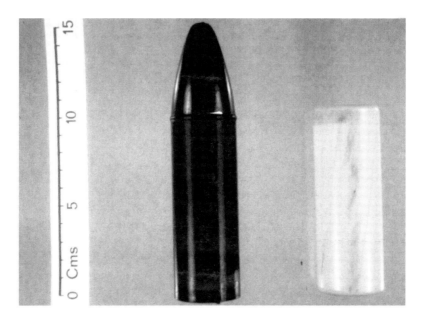

FIGURE 20.1 Plastic bullets (Northern Ireland).

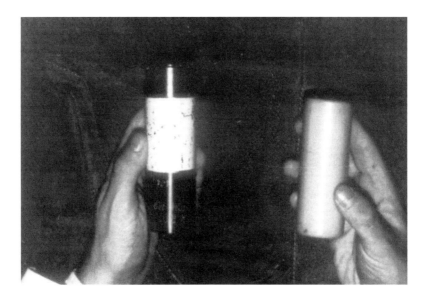

FIGURE 20.2 Plastic bullets (Northern Ireland).

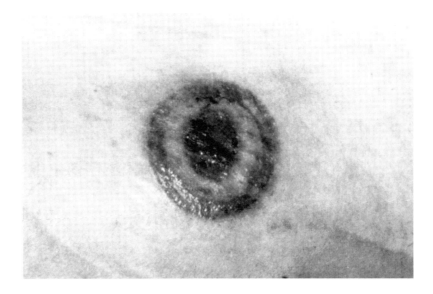

FIGURE 20.3 Bull's-eye or target lesion from plastic bullet hitting end-on.

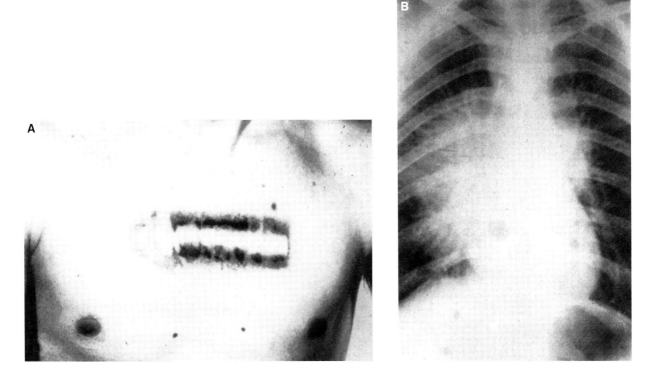

FIGURE 20.4 Typical bruise from lateral hit of a plastic bullet. **(A)** The bruise perfectly outlines the plastic missile. **(B)** Resulting pulmonary contusion.

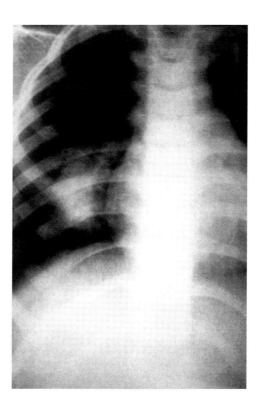

FIGURE 20.5 Focal pulmonary contusion from end-on hit from plastic bullet.

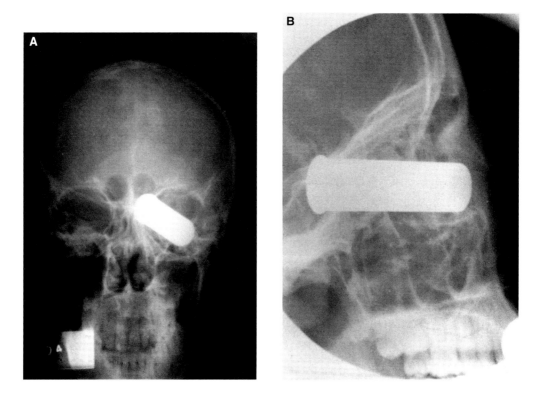

FIGURE 20.6 (**A**) Frontal and (**B**) lateral views of a plastic bullet penetrating the left orbit and entering the sphenoid bone.

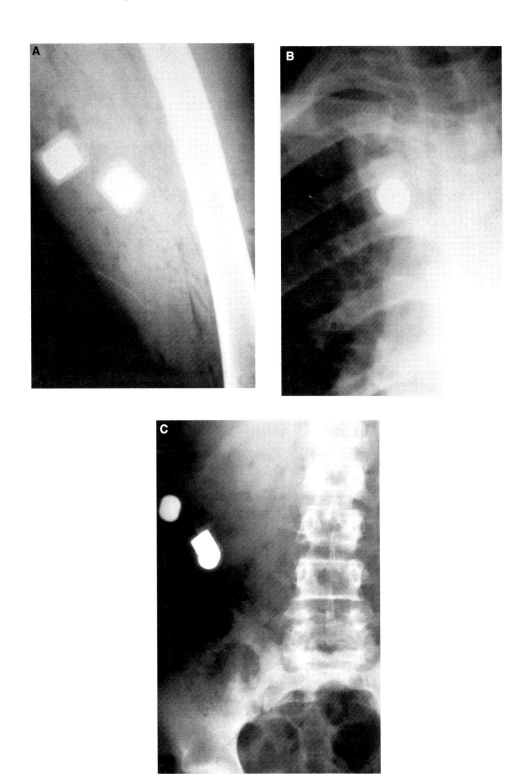

FIGURE 20.7 Rubber bullets. (**A**) Two rubber bullets in the thigh. One can see the halo of the rubber coating around the metallic core. (**B**) Rubber bullet that has penetrated the chest (Israel). (**C**) Three rubber bullets that have penetrated the right upper quadrant of the abdomen (Israel).

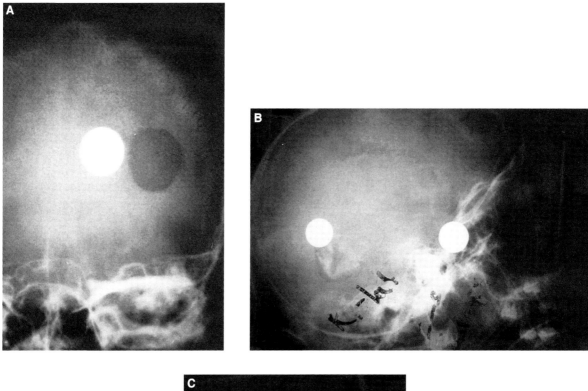

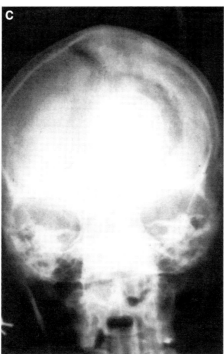

FIGURE 20.8 (**A**) Rubber bullet entering the frontal bone on the left and penetrating into the brain. (**B**) Two rubber bullets in the head. (**C**) Nonpenetrating rubber bullet producing massive fractures of the skull (Israel).

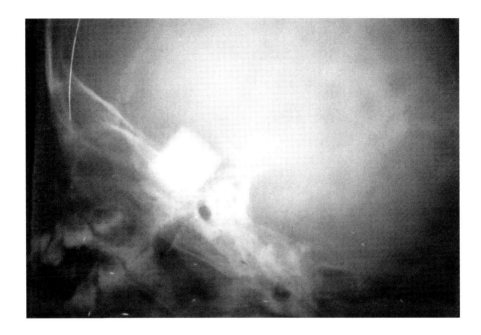

FIGURE 20.9 Toddler hit by a rubber bullet (Israel).

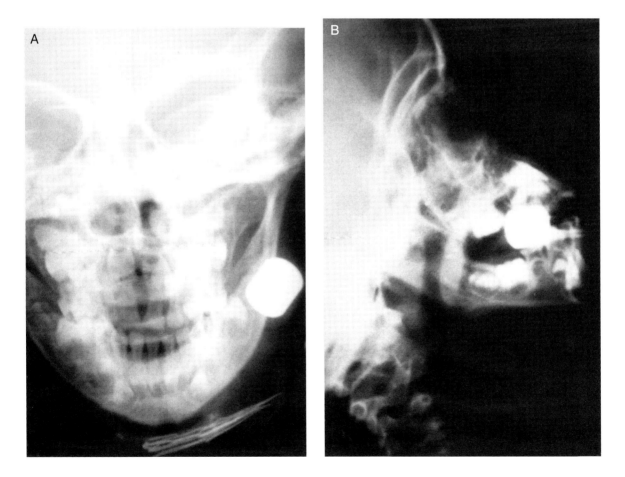

FIGURE 20.10 Rubber bullet penetrating the jaw of a child. **(A)** Frontal view. **(B)** Lateral view. Note the unerupted teeth (Israel).

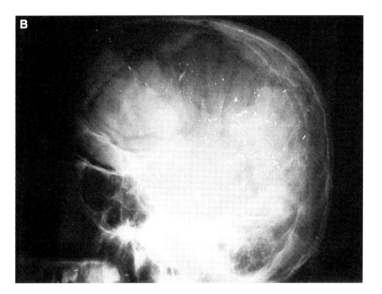

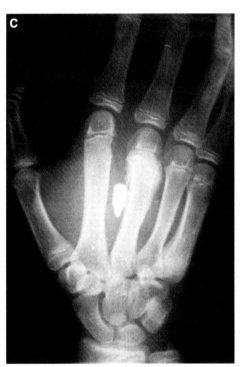

FIGURE 20.11 (**A**) Bullet in the thigh from a disintegrating ceramic bullet. (**B**) Tiny fragments of a ceramic bullet producing multiple radial fractures in the skull. (**C**) Intact ceramic bullet in the hand having traveled more than 100 m. The projectile had sufficient energy to injure the bone, but did not fragment.

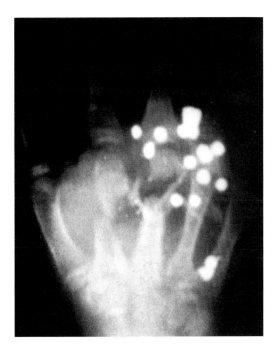

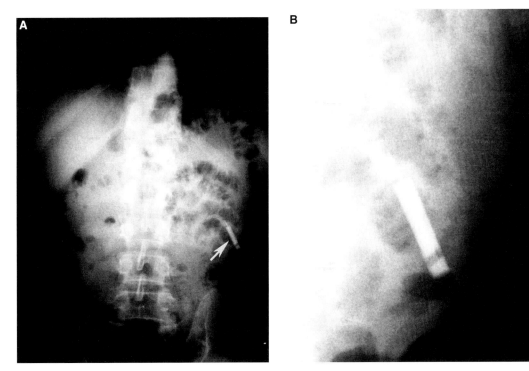

FIGURE 20.12 Extensive injury to the hand due to the failure and explosion of a homemade gun. The load was also homemade. Note the varying size and configuration of the metallic densities (Peru).

FIGURE 20.13 Tail fin rocket shattering the left pelvis and perforating abdominal viscera (Zimbabwe).

FIGURE 20.14 Air Taser. **(A)** The probe has snagged the abdominal wall and transmitted the electric current. **(B)** Close-up view. This device, ordinarily intended for police use, was used by a criminal gang during a robbery. The victim was totally incapacitated and had to be hospitalized (Hamburg, Germany).

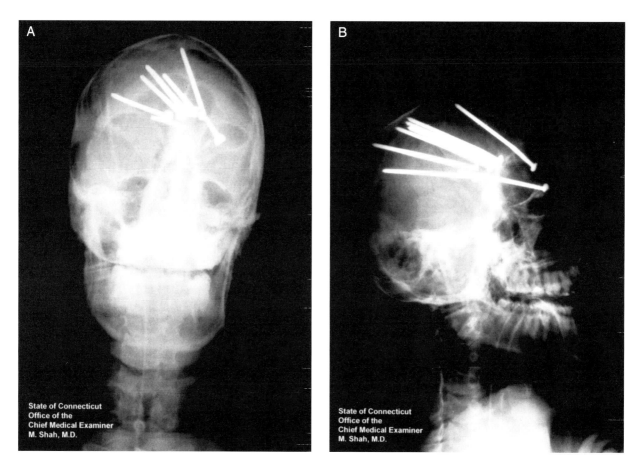

FIGURE 20.15 Murder with a nail gun. **(A)** Frontal view. **(B)** Lateral view. The victim was shot eight times through the left orbit with this tool ordinarily used in framing houses. (Courtesy of Dr. Malka B. Shah.) (From the office of the Chief Medical Examiner of the State of Connecticut. With permission. M.C. Sonntag, Forensic Photographer.)

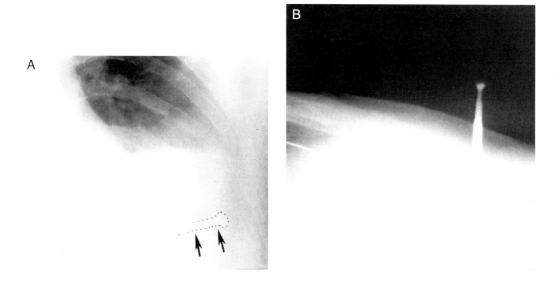

FIGURE 20.16 Wound from a stud gun. **(A)** The nail is barely seen within the density of the liver and blood or fluid in the left pleural space and is outlined for the reader's benefit. **(B)** Crosstable lateral view of the chest (head to viewer's left). The nail has entered at the level of the xiphisternum. The nail appears to enlarge, but actually does not, as it passes from being surrounded by air into surrounding soft tissue.

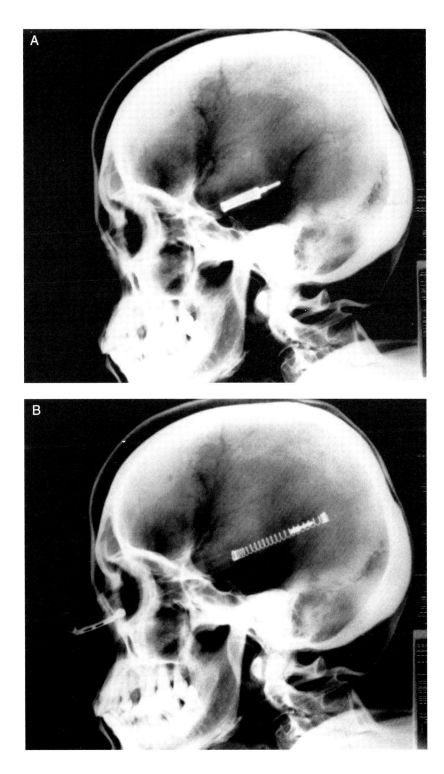

FIGURE 20.17 Death by ballpoint pen. A man was suspected of murder by shooting his mother through the eye with a mechanical writing pen that passed through the orbit into the brain stem. It was theorized that a mini crossbow or arbalest had been constructed to launch the missile. At the behest of the victim's father, the University Coroner of Groningen determined by experimentation that if the pen had been shot into the orbit, the spring and ink stem would have been propelled out of the holder as in (**B**). If the victim simply fell onto the pen, the holder and its contents would penetrate the orbit (**A**) as it has in this case. Verdict: not guilty. (Courtesy of Dr. Paul R. Algra, Alkmaar, The Netherlands.)

Section V

Inflicted Trauma

Inflicted trauma is defined here as action to cause damage or pain with intent and purpose. It may be caused by an individual or group against another individual or group. The distinction is made between inflicted trauma and accidental trauma. The latter may also cause damage or pain, but intent is missing.

The forensic pathologists like to categorize traumatic injuries as sharp or blunt, which really refers to the causative agent. Still, it is a useful classification and is adopted for the first two chapters of this section.

The final chapter in this section concerns war. It is perhaps the ultimate producer of damage and pain not only to contending armed forces personnel, but also to civilian bystanders. While the latter injuries are sometimes referred to as collateral damage, implying that it is accidental or unintended, it is difficult to argue lack of purpose. Unfortunately, war, in addition, all too often includes elements of abuse, torture, and terrorism. That, and the observation that certain types of warfare may produce typical or characteristic injuries demonstrable radiologically, prompts the inclusion of this chapter.

Unless otherwise indicated, illustrations in this section come from the private collection of one of the editors (H.V.) or, with permission, from his prior publication, *Gewalt in Röntgenbild*.

B.G.B.

21 Sharp Trauma

Hermann Vogel, M.D. and B.G. Brogdon, M.D.

SHARP TRAUMA, LOCATION

Radiologic examination of sharp trauma to the head is rather surprisingly fruitful. This is because the preponderant bony structure tends to entrap and retain the weapon, whereas sharp objects are more likely to cut or slice into and out of more fleshy parts. Blades are rarely found within the chest, abdomen, or extremities. However, they occasionally will be entangled in the ribs or vertebrae.

KNIFE WOUNDS

See Figures 21.1 through 21.14.

OTHER BLADES

See Figures 21.15 through 21.17.

OTHER SHARP OBJECTS

See Figures 21.18 through 21.23.

CREDIT

From Brogdon, B.G., *Forensic Radiology*, CRC Press, Boca Raton, FL, 1998. With permission. Figures 21.12, 21.21A, 21.22.

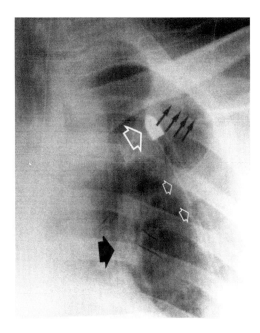

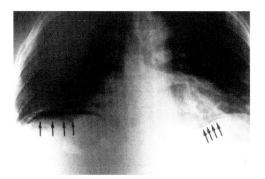

FIGURE 21.1 Chest after multiple stab wounds. There is pneumothorax (black arrows) and intrapulmonary hemorrhage (broad arrow). Note the bullet-tipped pleural drainage tube, a confusing medical device as described in Figure 18.4.

FIGURE 21.2 Stab wounds to the chest pierced the diaphragm causing a pneumoperitoneum. Free air under the diaphragm is indicated by arrows.

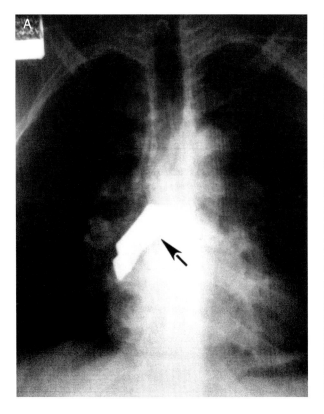

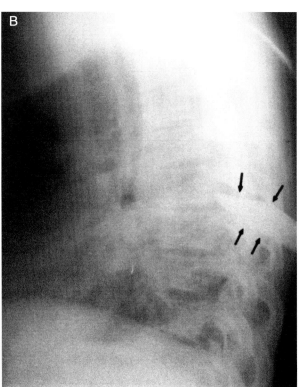

FIGURE 21.3 This knife was stabbed into the chest and stuck there between the ribs (arrows). **(A)** Frontal view. **(B)** Lateral view (Zimbabwe).

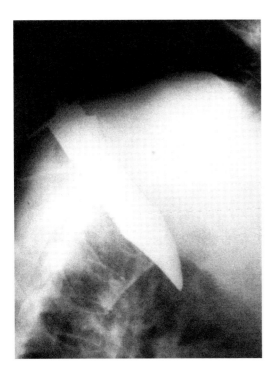

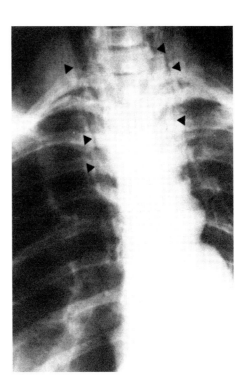

FIGURE 21.4 Stab wound in the back of the chest. The victim could not remove the knife (South Africa).

FIGURE 21.5 Stab wound perforating the trachea and producing pneumomediastinum. The streaky black shadows represent air escaping into the mediastinum and dissecting into the soft tissue structures of the neck (arrowheads).

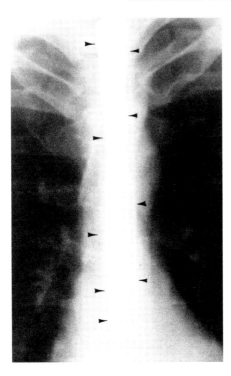

FIGURE 21.6 This prisoner partially succeeded in swallowing a knife (arrowheads) with the idea that it would get him transferred to the more desirable prison hospital.

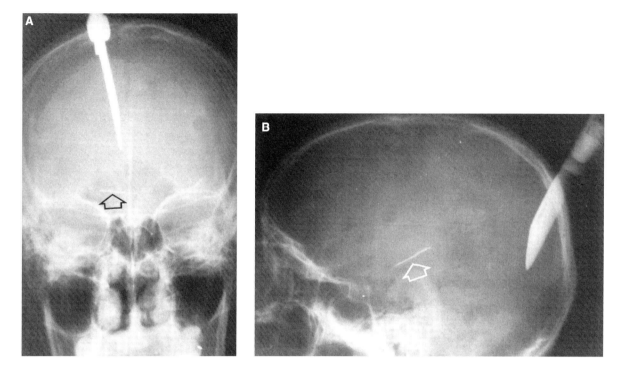

FIGURE 21.7 Stab into the head; the knife could not be removed. This is the second unsuccessful attempt to murder this victim. A preceding attempt has left a piece of wire (arrow) above (**A**) and posterior to the sella (**B**) (Mexico).

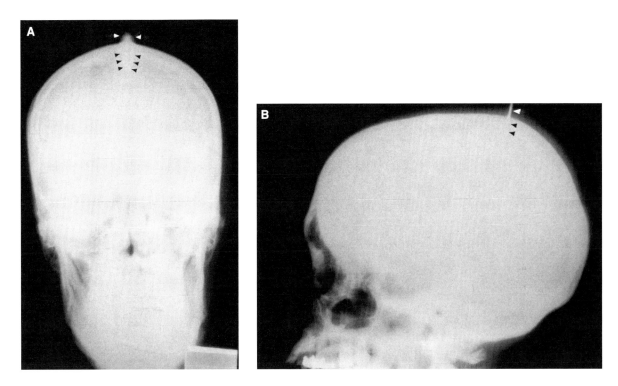

FIGURE 21.8 This convenience store cashier was stabbed in the head by a would-be robber. He drove him off, then walked into the emergency room for extraction of the knife (arrows). **(A)** Frontal view. The knife blade is optically widened by scatter in the adjacent soft tissues. **(B)** Lateral view (B.G.B., Mobile, AL).

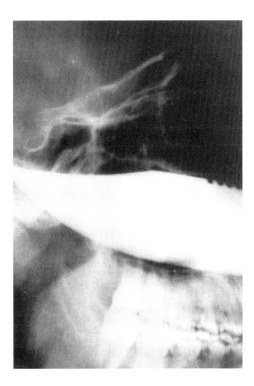

FIGURE 21.9 Knife piercing the maxillary antrum and orbital floor extends into the temporal lobe, the result of social fighting after payday or during a sporting event (South Africa).

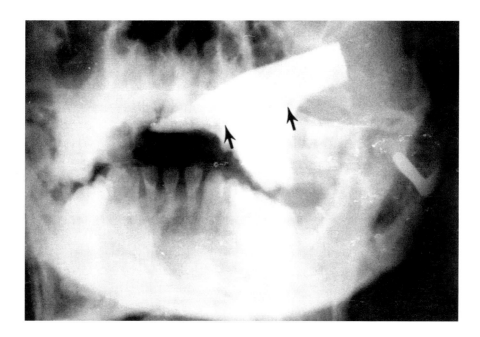

FIGURE 21.10 Broken knife in the face (arrows) (South Africa).

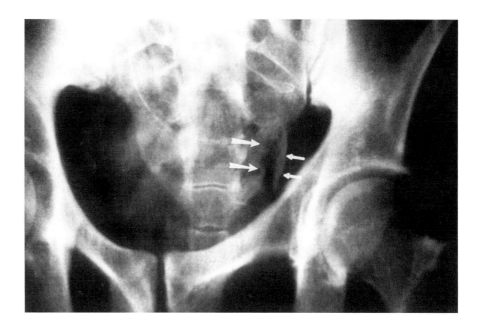

FIGURE 21.11 Knife fight in a bar between pimps. The sacrum is split on the left (arrows) after the knife first perforated the abdominal wall, bladder, rectum, and sigmoid colon. The victim died 3 weeks later.

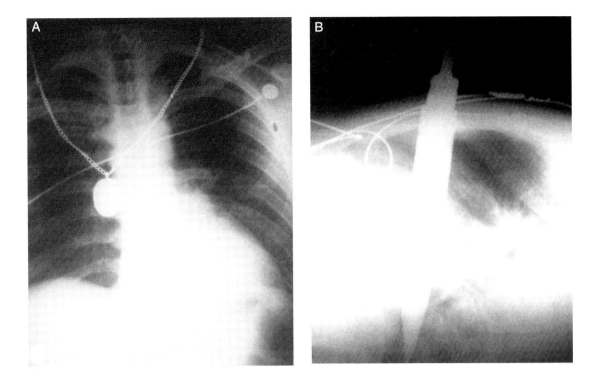

FIGURE 21.12 (**A**) Frontal radiograph of a corpse does not reveal a cause of death quite obvious to the autopsy surgeon. (**B**) The lateral view, while not required for the edification of the autopsy surgeon, makes a powerful display for the jury.

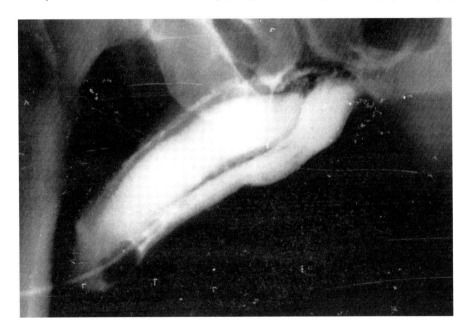

FIGURE 21.13 Stab wound to the penis. Retrograde urethrogram fills the corpora cavernosa, the corpus spongiosum, and the superficial veins. These injuries are common in South America and South Africa due to the use of knives in social fighting and the custom of stabbing upwards into the lower abdomen and genitalia.

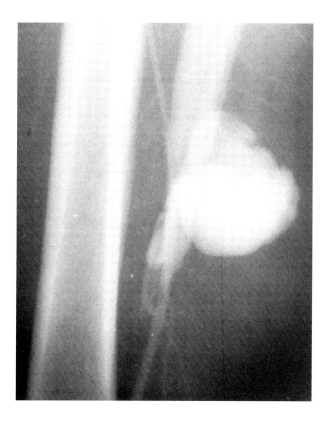

FIGURE 21.14 Stab wound to the thigh creating a pseudoaneurysm and arteriovenous fistula shown by angiography (South Africa).

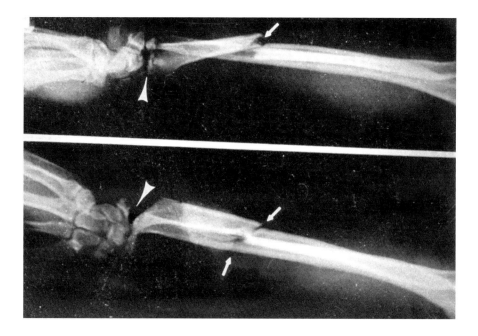

FIGURE 21.15 Two views of the forearm and wrist show results of a cane-worker's machete fight. There are fractures of both bones of the forearm (arrows) and through the wrist (arrowheads) (Columbia).

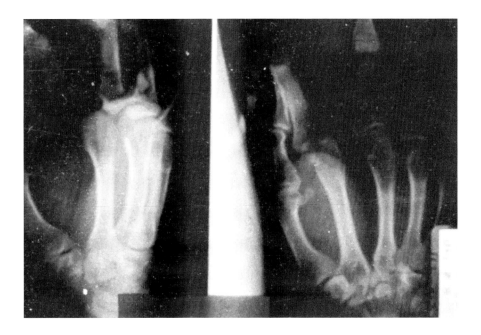

FIGURE 21.16 Machete wound of the hand, amputating the lateral three fingers, and destroying the second metacarpophalangeal joint (Columbia).

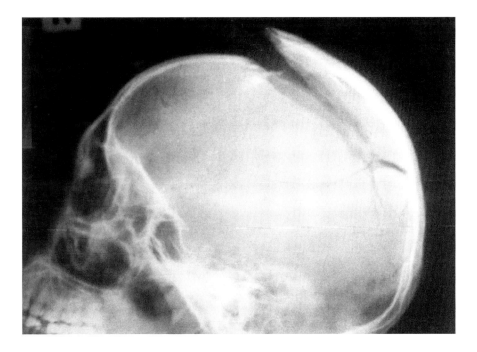

FIGURE 21.17 This man was struck on the head by a friend with an axe several weeks earlier. He complained of slight but persistent headaches. The fracture kept expanding and separating because of pulsation in the brain and collection of fluid. Such cases are remarkable, but not uncommon, in Africa, south of the Sahara.

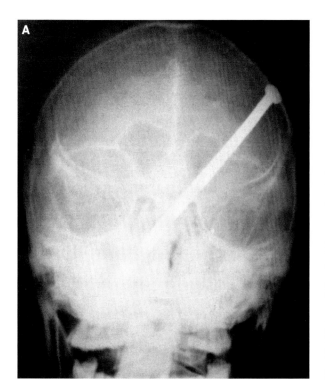

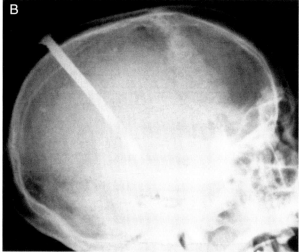

FIGURE 21.18 The victim was said to be possessed by an evil spirit. The healer chose to liberate his patient from this evil by putting a nail into his head. The victim died after some days in the hospital. **(A)** Frontal view. **(B)** Lateral view (Zimbabwe).

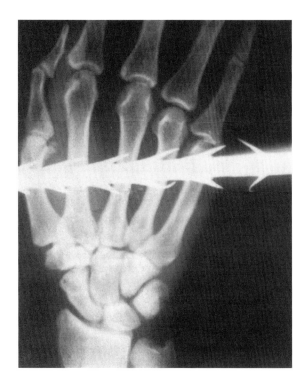

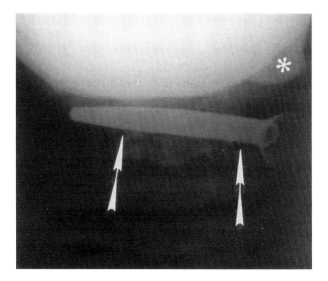

FIGURE 21.20 This victim was stabbed in the dorsal muscles of the neck with an umbrella. The ferrule (arrow) stayed behind. This is a frontal view. Large white shadow at the top of the image is the base of the skull. The small bulbous projection on the viewer's right is the left mastoid tip (asterisk). The cervical vertebrae beneath the ferrule are overexposed and do not show well.

FIGURE 21.19 Spear point in the hand. Note barbs pointed in both directions (South Africa).

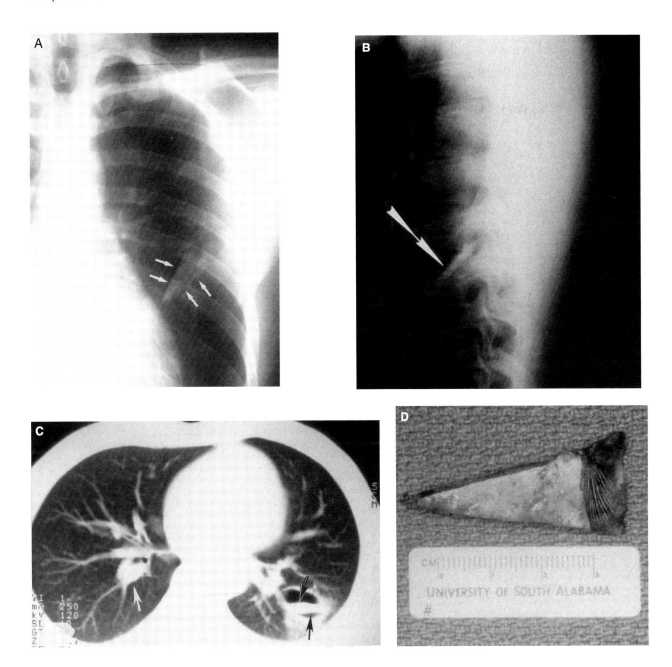

FIGURE 21.21 (**A**) Shard of glass (arrows) broken off in the left lung after the victim was repeatedly stabbed in the back with a broken beer bottle. (**B**) Lateral view of the chest shows the shard (arrow) lies in the lung after having slipped through between the ribs. (**C**) A computed tomography shows the shard of glass (black arrows) surrounded by a pneumatocele in the left lower lobe. On the right is another pneumatocele (arrow) from an earlier stab wound before the point of the broken beer bottle broke away. This pneumatocele is partially filled with fluid, probably blood. (**D**) Photograph of the shard of beer bottle glass removed from the left lung at surgery (B.G.B., Mobile, AL).

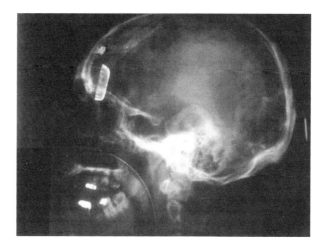

FIGURE 21.22 A full bottle of beer was driven into the victim's face. When withdrawn, the cap stayed behind (an unusual way to uncap a beer!).

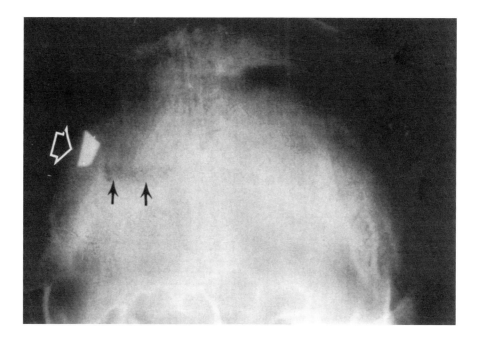

FIGURE 21.23 A beer bottle was smashed against the right frontal area of this victim, producing a fracture (arrows) and shattering the bottle as well. A piece of the bottle penetrated the scalp and stuck in the outer table of the skull (open arrow). (This is an example of both sharp and blunt trauma, which seems to be a good segue into Chapter 23.)

22 Blunt Trauma

Hermann Vogel, M.D. and B.G. Brogdon, M.D.

INTRODUCTION

Many examples of blunt trauma have been presented already in Section I, which addressed aggressive hurtful behavior targeted at specific population groups. This chapter is less discriminative, showing intentional injury to various anatomic areas with the assistance of a variety of implements ranging from fists to feet and from primitive clubs to manhole covers.

HEAD INJURIES

See Figures 22.1 through 22.8. For typical mandibular fractures, see Figure 2.2 through 2.9.

NECK INJURIES

Blows to the neck can cause vertebral fractures (Figures 1.23C and 5.3) and soft tissue injuries (Figure 2.16).

Included here are the blunt injuries of the throttling thumb and the more focused pressure of the ligature.

CHEST AND PECTORAL GIRDLE

See Figures 22.11 and 22.12.

ABDOMEN/RETROPERITONEUM

See Figure 22.13.

EXTREMITIES

See Figures 22.14 through 22.22.

CREDIT

From Brogdon, B.G., *Forensic Radiology*, CRC Press, Boca Raton, FL, 1998. With permission. Figures 22.6, 22.10A, 22.10B.

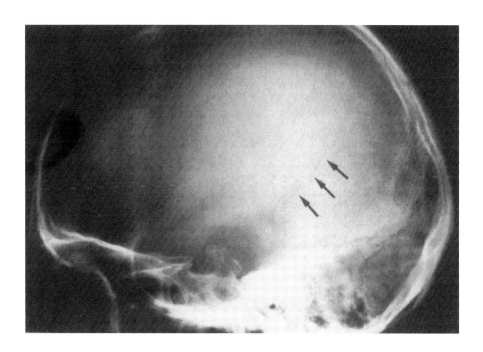

FIGURE 22.1 Simple fracture of the parietal bone from a blow. It is likely that there is no intracranial damage.

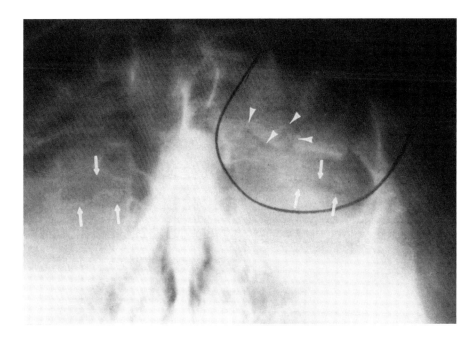

FIGURE 22.2 This is a somewhat unusual comminuted displaced fracture of the superior rim of the orbit (arrowheads) with extension into the left frontal sinus. Therefore, this fracture is susceptible to infection. The palpebral fissure on the left (arrows) is much more narrow than that on the right, indicating a great deal of soft tissue swelling. There may be intraorbital and ocular damage as well.

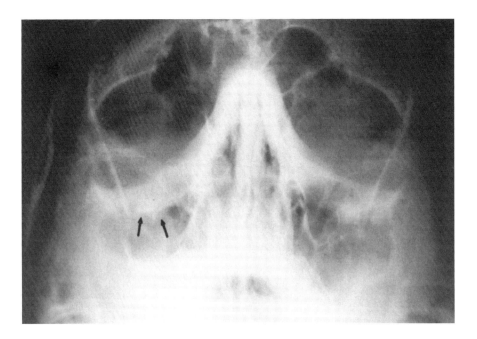

FIGURE 22.3 Blowout fracture of the right orbit. The orbital floor is depressed. There is herniation of orbital content (arrows) into the right maxillary sinus, which is partially filled with blood. Compare to the opposite side. See also Figure 2.11.

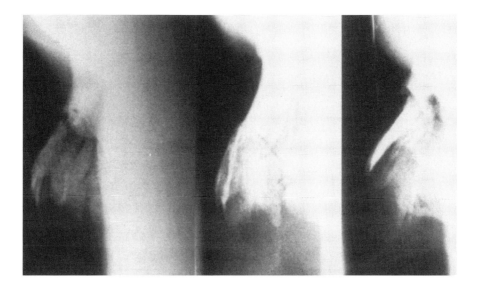

FIGURE 22.4 Three different victims with nasal bone fractures. In Germany, these fractures are most often seen after sports events with ritualized fighting between fans of competing teams.

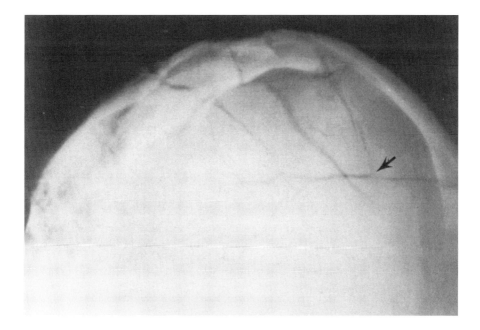

FIGURE 22.5 Multifragmented fissural fractures through the top of the skull (lateral view) with a hammer club. The patient was conscious. We are seeing both sides of the skull, so the law of intersecting fractures is not abrogated. An arrow points to an example of where one fracture did not propagate across a preexisting fracture.

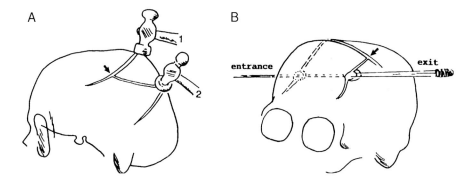

FIGURE 22.6 Schematic drawings indicate that: **(A)** a linear fracture from an earlier blow stopped propagation of a fracture from a second blow; **(B)** a linear fracture from an entrance wound travels faster than the bullet causing it—a fracture from the exit wound will terminate on meeting the preexisting fracture. (This rule can help in deciding the sequence of blows in cases of blunt trauma and between entrance and exit wounds in gunshot wounds where beveling is inconclusive. (See Dixon, D.S., *J. Forensic Sci.*, 29, 651, 1985.)

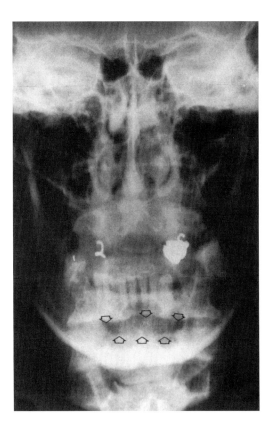

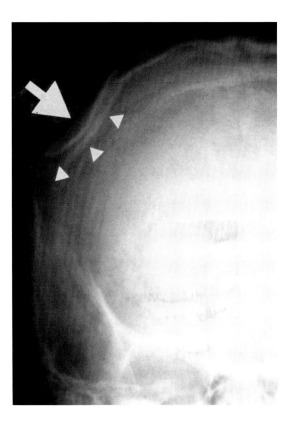

FIGURE 22.7 A most unusual fracture of the mandible separating the mandibular alveolar ridge and central teeth from the body of the mandible (open arrows).

FIGURE 22.8 Massive impression fracture of the parietal bone conforming to the size and shape of the weapon. This type of fracture is typical for Africa south of the Sahara. In some areas, it could be due to a coconut. In this case, it exactly corresponds to the wooden club used in the assault (South Africa).

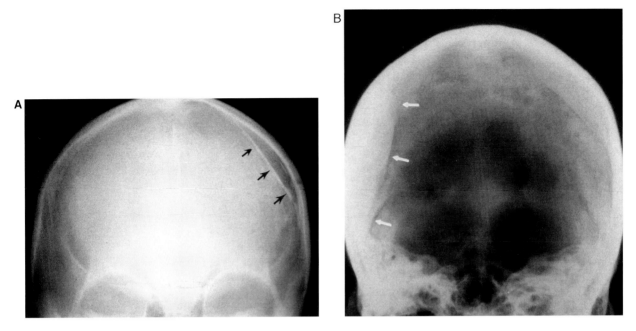

FIGURE 22.9 Calcified subdural hematomas from previous blows to the head in two different victims. **(A)** Marginal calcification. **(B)** Solid calcification.

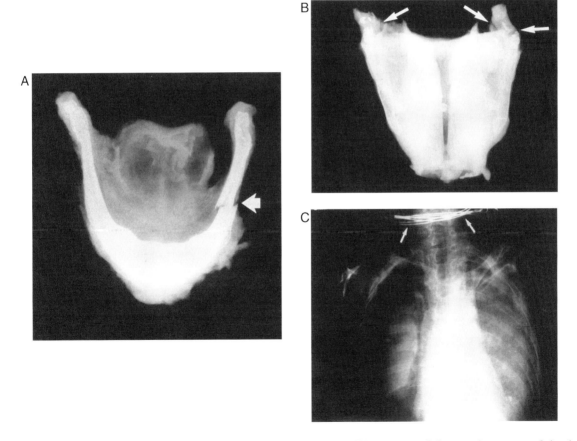

FIGURE 22.10 (A) Fracture of the hyoid bone (arrow) from strangulation. **(B)** Fractures of the superior cornua of the thyroid cartilage from strangulation. (Both (A) and (B) courtesy of Dr. J.C.U. Downs, Savannah, GA.) **(C)** This woman was found burned beyond recognition in a house fire. It was assumed she had died in the blaze. A chest x-ray was obtained to try for a match with the presumed decedent's antemortem chest radiograph. The postmortem film disclosed several coils of wire as a ligature around the neck (arrows). The fire was set in an attempt to obscure the real cause of death.

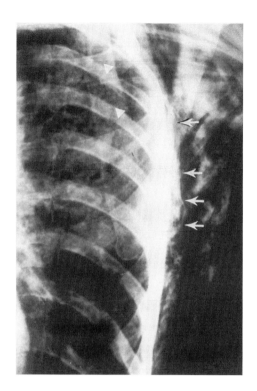

FIGURE 22.11 This woman was badly beaten and suffered multiple rib fractures (white arrows). She has a pneumothorax (white triangle) and extensive subcutaneous air in the chest wall and the axilla.

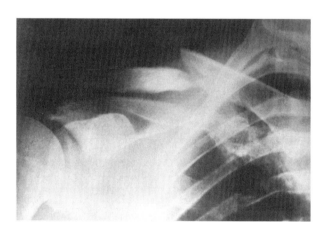

FIGURE 22.12 Fracture of the clavicle by a directed downward blow. The medial fragment is elevated because of the pull of the sternocleidomastoideus muscle.

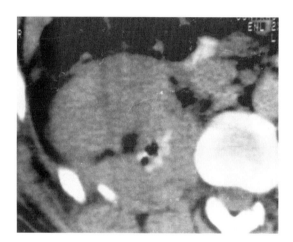

FIGURE 22.13 Fracture of the left kidney with hemorrhage from a kick to the right flank shown on computed tomography examination.

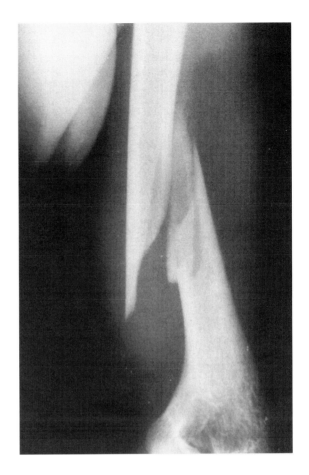

FIGURE 22.14 Fracture of the humerus from a direct blow. A similar spiral fracture, without comminution, has been seen as the result of the sport of arm wrestling.

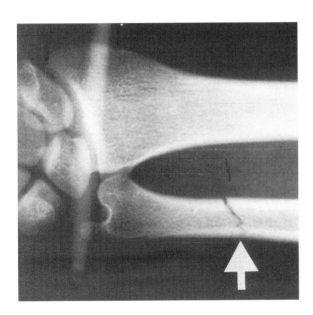

FIGURE 22.15 A fracture of the ulna by an iron bar, a typical defensive injury or fending fracture.

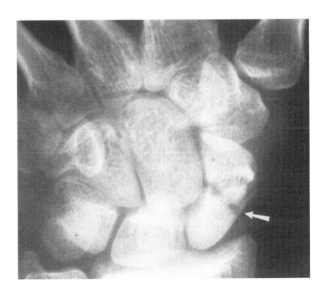

FIGURE 22.16 Fracture of the scaphoid sustained during a fight.

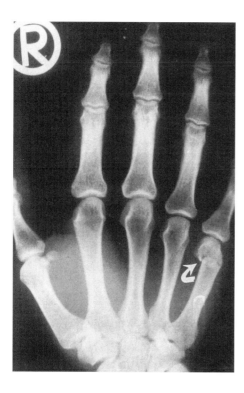

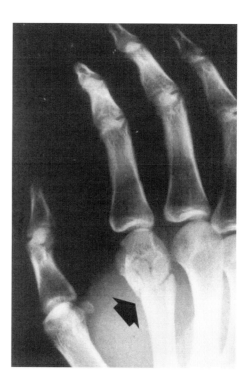

FIGURE 22.17 Angulated fracture of the distal metaphysis of the fifth metacarpal, a typical "boxer's fracture".

FIGURE 22.18 Communited fracture of the distal end of the second metacarpal during a fight. This is a somewhat unusual bone to be broken during fisticuffs. However, it appears that the second metacarpal is longer than the third, which is unusual, and may explain why this bone was broken.

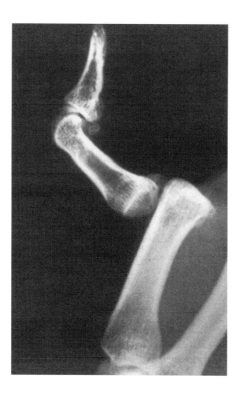

FIGURE 22.19 Total dislocation of the metacarpo-phalangeal joint of the thumb during a fight.

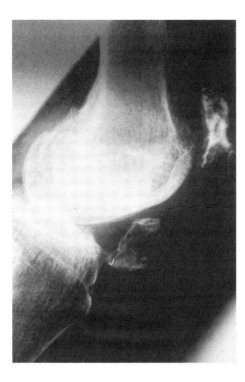

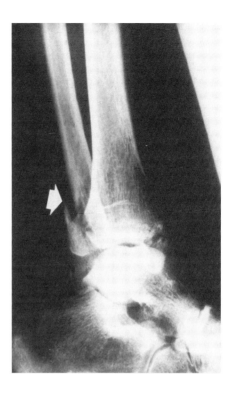

FIGURE 22.20 Old fracture of the patella with rupture of the patellar capsule allowing wide separation of fracture fragments. This was never repaired and now shows changes of degeneration and aseptic necrosis.

FIGURE 22.21 Fracture of the distal fibula sustained during a fight.

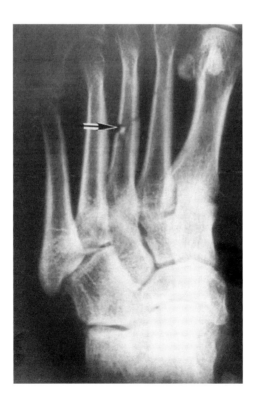

FIGURE 22.22 Transverse, slightly comminuted fracture of the third metatarsal due to having a manhole cover thrown on the foot.

23 War

Hermann Vogel, M.D.

INTRODUCTION

It is possible to differentiate between several forms of warfare to some extent by the radiologic findings of the casualties produced. *Typical* findings are encountered also, but less often, in other forms of warfare. *Characteristic* findings are those lesions that are exceptional in other forms of warfare. The forms of warfare to be dealt with in this chapter are:

1. Air warfare
2. Guerrilla warfare
3. Desert war
4. Gas war
5. Conventional warfare
6. Annihilation warfare
7. Terrorist and city guerrilla warfare
8. Occupation and population control

Contemporary examples of these forms of warfare can be found today or in the recent past.

In the same war there may be differences between the opponents. The soldiers and civilians of the side that has air superiority will have injuries other than those of the opposite side that does not have air superiority. The weapons, their use, and the medical equipment (including radiological facilities) will differ. This can be seen radiologically. A typical example is the Vietnam War or the wars of France, Great Britain, the former Soviet Union, and Israel during the last decades. Even if both sides have a similar military starting point, there may be differences. For instance, in the last war between Serbia and Croatia, Serbia had air superiority; thus, its injured soldiers were transported with helicopters very quickly to specialized hospitals. On the contrary, due to transportation difficulties, Croatia had important losses during the first battles. The losses decreased when emergency treatment units were established near the front. The radiographs of both sides show the difference.

AIR WARFARE

The air warfare in North Vietnam was among other things characterized by large bombs. The explosions produced shockwaves that led to pulmonary lacerations with hemoptysis. In Hanoi, pulmonary surgery was impossible under war conditions. Consequently, Vietnamese radiologists treated pulmonary bleeding by transcatheteral occlusion of bronchial arteries (Figure 23.1).

GUERRILLA WAR

In Zimbabwe, the war was characterized by blocking traffic routes and territories by mines—mostly antipersonnel mines. The typical findings documented on radiographs is the destroyed foot (Figure 23.2) or dislocation of the sternum by jumping mines, which will explode after jumping to a height of 1 to 1.5 m (Figure 23.3).

DESERT WAR

In Chad, desert war is characterized by transporting troops over large distances on small vehicles such as jeeps. Typical are extremity lesions documented by radiography (Figure 23.4). Victims with wounds of the trunk and head usually do not survive the long transport and do not get radiologic examination; consequently, there are essentially no radiographs.

GAS WAR

In its war against Iran, Iraq used S-lost, which by contact and inhalation produces corrosive lesions of the skin and the respiratory tract. Radiographs may show pulmonary infiltrates (Figure 23.5A), which at first may not appear too threatening but have a bad prognosis (Figure 23.5B). If the patient survives, emphysema appears in a matter of weeks or months (Figure 23.5C) and pulmonary hypertension and myocardial insufficiency may occur (Figure 23.5D).

The effects of other toxic gases are more speculative (see Chapter 14).

CONVENTIONAL WARFARE

In the recent Balkan wars, arms and tactics similar to those of World Wars I and II were used. Radiographs showed lesions due to conventional arms like hand grenades (Figure 23.6), fired projectiles, and bombs.

ANNIHILATION WARFARE

Annihilation war was and still is being carried out in Africa, for example, in the Sudan and Rwanda. This involves systematic killing of large groups of population either by direct force or indirectly by starvation—a characteristic of this type of warfare. There are signs of starvation with protein and vitamin deficiencies (Figure 23.7).

CITY AND GUERRILLA WARFARE

There are many radiographic findings from the types of weapons used in city and guerrilla warfare. Examples are shown in Chapter 13.

OCCUPATION AND POPULATION CONTROL

Characteristic injuries are seen from humane rubber and plastic bullets (see Chapter 20). One may also see injuries due to caning or beating (see Chapter 6).

SPECIAL FORMS OF WARFARE

Chemical warfare and biological warfare are special forms for which the radiology is not yet entirely described or understood. Both have been mentioned in earlier chapters. Some of the diseases proposed in bacteriological warfare have recognizable, although nonspecific, radiological findings. Others, such as small pox, have practically disappeared from the collective memory and collective medical literature in most parts of the world. New hybrid or genetically engineered bacteria and viruses are not beyond the realm of future possibility (Figures 23.8 to 23.12). Note: For examples of radiographic examination in plague and anthrax, see Chapter 15.

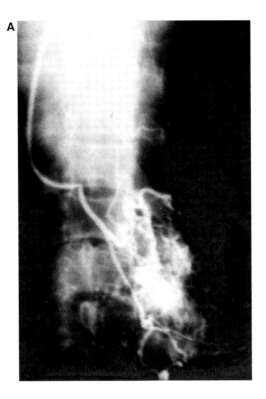

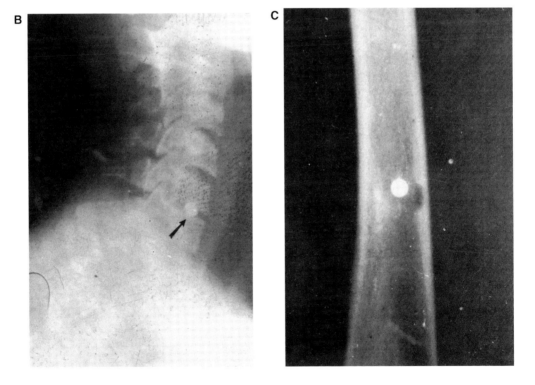

FIGURE 23.1 (**A**) Pressure waves from a large bomb caused pulmonary lacerations. This is an attempt at transcatheteral vascular occlusion. More than 300 patients were treated in that way in Hanoi during the Vietnam War. (**B** and **C**) Cluster bombs also were used extensively. These are small antipersonnel bombs casting out many small, nonexplosive metal balls with a characteristic appearance on radiographs.

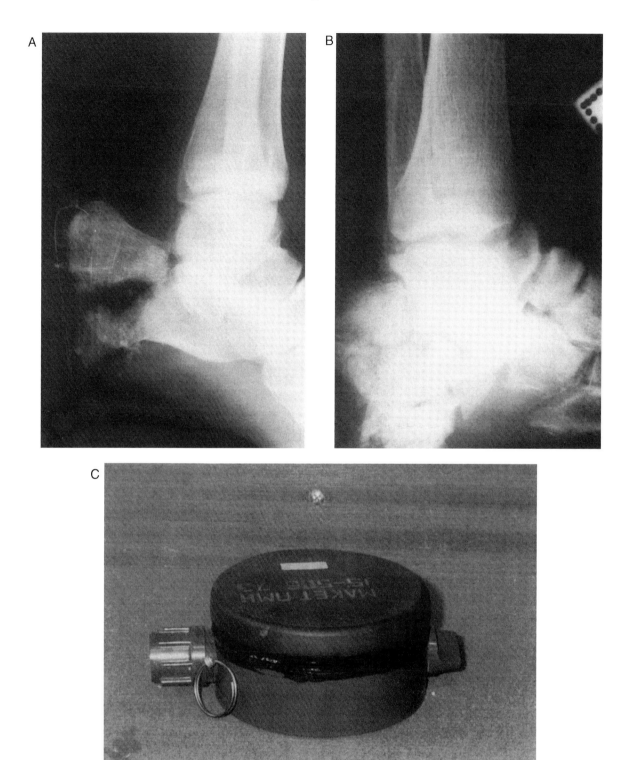

FIGURE 23.2 (**A**) Destroyed os calcis by a land mine (Zimbabwe). (**B**) Massive fractures and dislocations of the hind foot by a land mine (Zimbabwe). (**C**) Example of a land mine. This antipersonnel mine was deployed on the inner borders between East and West Germany.

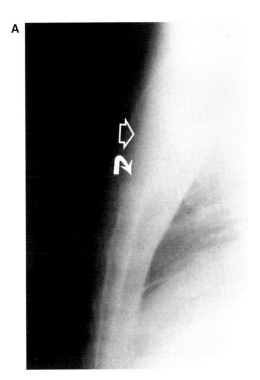

FIGURE 23.3 **(A)** Dislocations of the sternum at the sternal angle. The upper border of the gladiolus or body of the sternum stands clear (arrow) of the manubrium which is displaced posteriorly (open arrow). The injury was caused by a jumping land mine. **(B)** Jumping mines. The mine can be triggered by contact or a wire. The mine is propelled 1 to 1.5 m into the air, where it explodes.

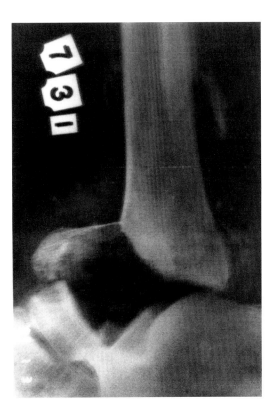

FIGURE 23.4 This is a high velocity bullet wound of the foot with a large defect in the talus and articular surface of the tibia, both dislocated. This distal portion of the fibula has been carried away. This victim survived transport through the desert back to the capital of Chad.

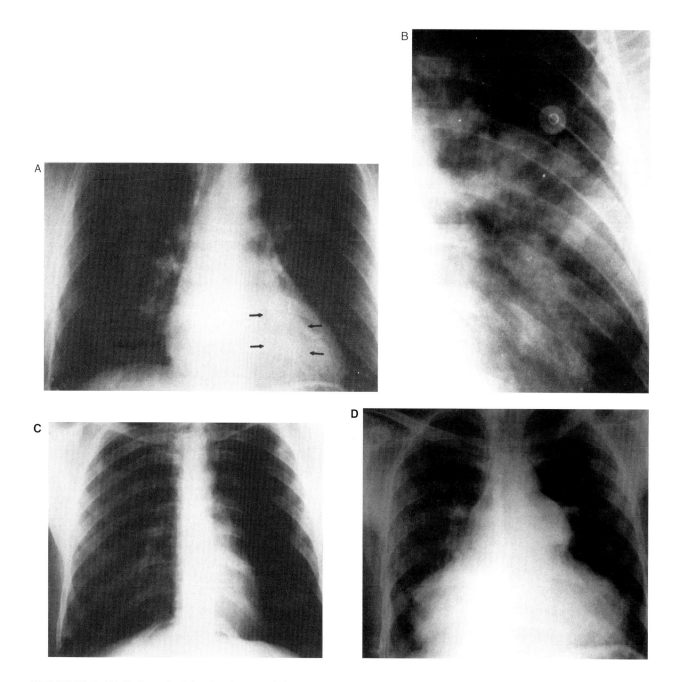

FIGURE 23.5 (**A**) Early and minimal pulmonary infiltrate behind the left side of the heart (arrows) after S-Lost exposure. (**B**) Progression of the extent and severity of infiltrates in the left lung. (**C**) Late emphysematous change with marked hyperexpansion of the lungs. (**D**) A different patient progressed to the more uncommon sequelae of pulmonary hypertension. (Note the enormous pulmonary artery outflow tract and the enlarged heart with myocardial failure, particularly on the right.)

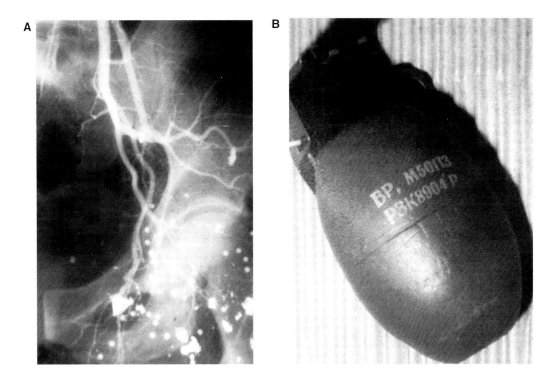

FIGURE 23.6 (**A**) Multiple irregular hand-grenade fragments. The findings of round metal balls in combination with irregular metal fragments from the grenade coating is typical (Croatia). (**B**) Example of a hand grenade from the Serbia/Croatia War.

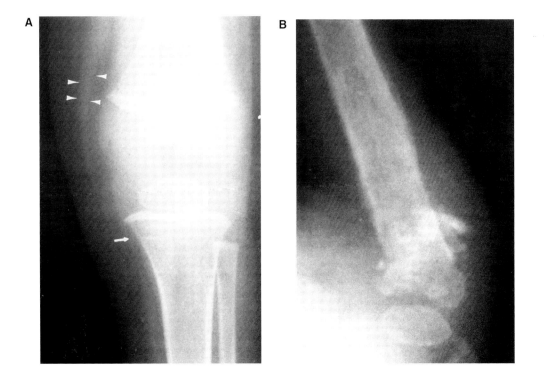

FIGURE 23.7 (**A**) Kwashiorkor (severe protein deficiency) and scurvy (vitamin C deficiency) with marked osteoporosis of bone, growth arrest lines (small arrow), soft tissue swelling, and muscle wasting (arrowheads). (**B**) Vitamin D deficiency (rickets) with marked osteomalacia, widening and fragmentation of the metaphysis, and absent zone of provisional calcification.

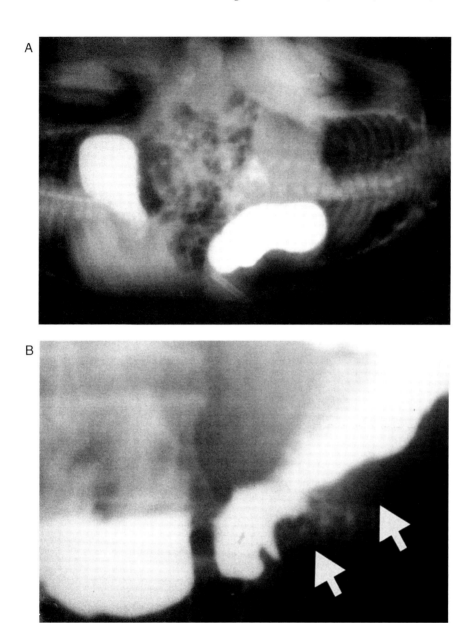

FIGURE 23.8 (A) This is a Siamese twin with an individual thorax on either side of the picture, separate stomachs filled with contrast, but some shared organs and only three legs. This baby comes from an area where herbicides were disbursed in large quantities during the Vietnam War. Dioxin was discussed as a possible etiologic factor in this massive malformation. It is purely speculative, of course. The twins were successfully separated in the Viet-Due Hospital in Hanoi. **(B)** A case of carcinoma of the gastric anthrum (arrows) in another person exposed to herbicides and their associated dioxin. The carcinogenic qualities of dioxin are recognized, but cannot be specifically applied to an individual case such as this. However, a number of gastric carcinoma cases were noted in Hanoi since the war.

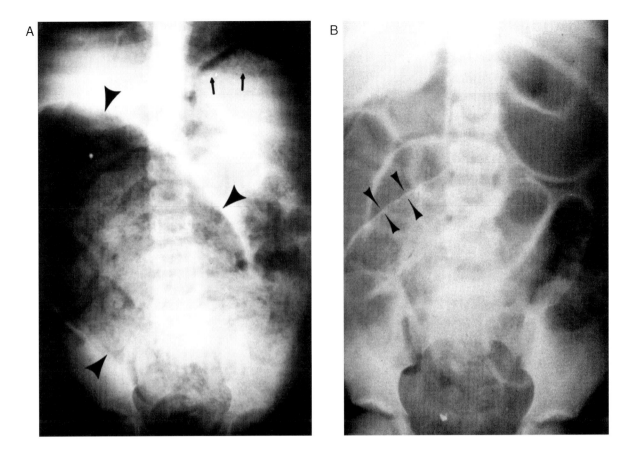

FIGURE 23.9 **(A)** Typhoid fever (salmonellosis) with perforation of the bowel and consequent free air underneath the diaphragm (arrows). There is massive dilation of the colon (arrowheads), perhaps a toxic megacolon. **(B)** Another case of typhoid fever with perforation of the bowel. Note the clarity with which both the intraluminal and extraluminal surfaces of the bowel wall are seen (arrowheads). This is the so-called double-wall sign, an indicator of free intraabdominal air.

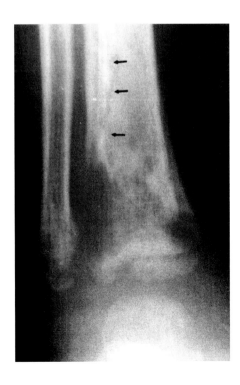

FIGURE 23.10 Salmonella osteomyelitis with massive destruction of the metaphysis and epiphysis in both the fibula and the tibia. There is little bone response to this rapid destructive process. The white densities in the medullary portion of the tibia (arrows) are pieces of dead bone or sequestra.

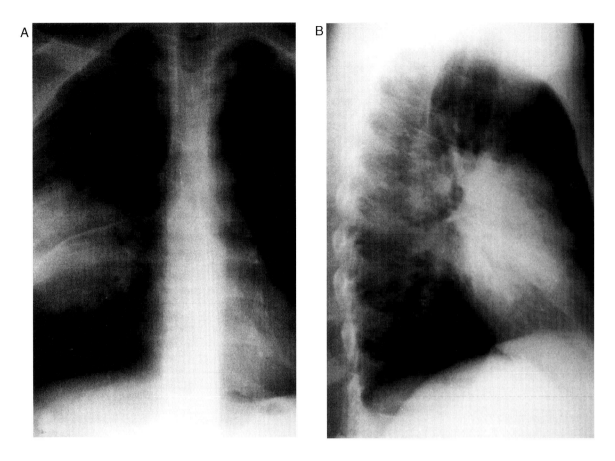

FIGURE 23.11 (**A** and **B**) Right-sided pneumonia due to Legionnaire's disease.

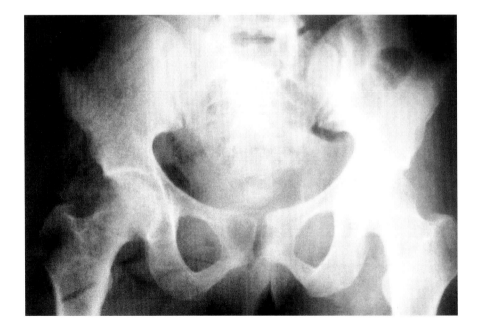

FIGURE 23.12 Gas gangrene in the soft tissues over the right pelvis and buttock. Faint parallel black lines are seen over the right ileum between and along the fibers of the gluteus maximus. Similar linear densities are seen over the proximal right femur. The overall density of the right half of the pelvis is diminished compared to the left because of the abundant gas in the tissues. This is an infection with clostridium.

Section VI

Radiologic Identification and Evaluation

In most jurisdictions under common circumstances, positive identification of the deceased is necessary before a legal certification of death is possible. Once a certification of death is made by authorized agencies, legal matters related to the deceased can progress. Insurance payments can be made and safety deposit boxes can be entered. Death benefits and insurance payment can be made; surviving spouses can remarry; business matters can be resolved; and, when appropriate, criminal and civil proceedings can begin.

Beyond the legal requirements, there are intense personal and emotional reasons for identification of the dead. The need for identity lies deep within the human psyche. Every unidentified body represents to someone a relative, loved one, friend, acquaintance, associate, missing person, fugitive, or even an enemy. Without identification, the search must go on if resolution is to be achieved. Our laws, our emotions, most religions, and common decency require that the dead finally must be laid to rest—in our hearts and minds as well as in more earthly connotations.

Identification of the human, living or deceased, may be accomplished by several different means. Legally valid, positive identification can be made through visual means, genetic information (DNA), fingerprint analysis, comparison of postmortem and antemortem images of anatomic structures, and dental records. Not infrequently, civil litigation associated with the circumstances surrounding the death or injury of an individual will require identification of that individual through radiologic evidence.

Although images of anatomic structures continue to play a key role in the identification process, during the last decade identification through genetic information has become more widely available and more accessible through various individuals and agencies. At the present time, DNA analysis is more time-consuming and expensive than other means of identification. However, it is anticipated that as technology improves, DNA analysis will become equally valuable or more valuable compared to other current means of identification.

Once radiologic evaluation of identity begins, chartings, photographs, and images are made of the remains. The postmortem records are then retained by the appropriate agency. Depending on the jurisdiction, once a positive identification is made, the original records (including the radiographs) may be retained by the agency or returned to the submitting source. In other jurisdictions, copies are made of the original records, which are then returned to the submitting source.

The radiologic comparison begins by establishing the chain of evidence of the pertinent images. Presently, images can be scanned and sent electronically over great distances in a very short period of time. Because there are many potential sources of transmission error, the accuracy of the transmission must be assured by medical, dental, and technical personnel. All transferred images must be identified as to type, source, and date of acquisition. It must be firmly established that the images truly represent the body of the person to whom they are attributed. Establishment of the right and left sides of the image is essential.

Once the antemortem evidence is received, it can be compared to postmortem remains. This can best be accomplished when teams of forensic experts (physicians, dentists, anthropologists, criminalists, etc.) can work together. When sufficient anatomic details are available, a positive identification or exclusion can be made.

Although the principles of identification are the same, special care, organization, and management of the process is required when mass casualties are involved. The availability of the computer has greatly facilitated this work. Present concerns about contaminated blood and body fluids have somewhat complicated and compromised the investigation of the dead in mass casualty situations. This is because the availability of clinical facilities for that purpose is severely restricted or nonexistent in most venues.

The cost and availability of the newer radiologic modalities has limited their use in forensic work. However, applications of those modalities, particularly computed tomography and magnetic resonance imaging, is reported with increasing frequency and holds great promise for the future.

Evaluation is indicated of both the dead and the living for cause of death or injury and for recovery of foreign material. Detection of live ordinance within bodies is important for the safety of other personnel. Religious beliefs or other reasons may preclude postmortem examination and require rapid disposal of the body. In those cases, the radiologic method can often quickly provide useful information.

The final chapter of this section is a report of exciting work being done at one institution through model cooperation between radiologic and forensic experts, which virtually replaces the conventional autopsy or evaluation of cause and manner of death.

B.G.B.

J.D. McD.

24 Dental Identification

John D. McDowell, D.D.S., M.S.

INTRODUCTION

Historically, one of the most efficient means of identification is through evaluation of the dentition, the jaws, or adjacent structures. In February 1896, the month after Röntgen's announcement of his discovery, W. Koenig was taking intraoral films of the teeth (Figure 24.1), leading the way for the science of forensic odontology.[1] Several historical figures, including Lollia Paulina, John Tabot, Charles the Bold, General Joseph Warren, Dr. George Parkman, and Louis Napoleon IV were either identified or ruled out as the decedent based on visual examination of the dentition. Two infamous characters, Adolph Hitler (Figure 24.2)[2] and Lee Harvey Oswald, were identified through comparison of antemortem and postmortem dental records.

Although more sophisticated identification techniques are now available when compared to even 20 years ago, the principles of dental identification remain the same. The principle of comparing features accepted as being unique to an individual remains the cornerstone of the dental identification. If sufficient antemortem and postmortem dental evidence is available, identification of the deceased can be made quickly and accurately. Teeth, the alveolar crest, the jaws, and adjacent structures contain a nearly unlimited number of physical and radiographic features that allow for the comparison process to proceed to a meaningful conclusion. However, this comparison process and conclusions reached are limited by the reliability of the antemortem and postmortem records.

Dental charts (also called odontograms) often present challenges to the identification process. Records forwarded for comparison can be incomplete or inaccurate. Some dentists record only the procedures (extractions, restorations, fixed or removable dentures, etc.) that they have performed. Records can contain errors in charting, or can be misinterpreted when provided by dentists or agencies using different languages or charting systems. In some disasters, fragments of jaws have been recovered in which no dental procedures have been performed, leaving no dental charting other than the presence or absence of individual teeth. These sources of errors in the written record emphasize the value of radiographic images. Properly exposed, labeled, and archived, radiographs provide the most valuable means of comparison.

Whether originals or duplicates, dental chartings are critical to identification processes using computer programs. Several different programs are available to sort the deceased and rank the probability of a positive identification of a given individual using the dental chart. Whenever possible, the dental chart of the putative deceased is then extensively compared to any available radiographic evidence. Radiographic evidence gives much greater detail and precision than does a written dental chart.

The process of radiographic dental identification is an integral part of the postmortem analysis of evidence. In the case of death, the decedent is examined and radiographed in compliance with appropriate infection control and forensic techniques. The American Board of Forensic Odontology and other forensic organizations recommend using a standardized process for the comparison of antemortem and postmortem records. At the beginning of the process, appropriate medical, dental, and anthropologic personnel assign case numbers to the individual decedents. Identification numbers are assigned to antemortem records and the correlation of those two databases begins.

Radiographic dental identifications have repeatedly been shown to be of great value when large numbers of individuals have died during natural or man-made disasters. When persons are crushed, burned, partially or totally decomposed (skeletonized), mutilated, or comingled, dental radiographic identification is especially valuable. Positive identifications can be made from small jaw fragments or in some cases from individual teeth. Dental identifications are frequently performed following disasters resulting in the death of a few or many people. Natural disasters, such as forest fires, floods, hurricanes, tornadoes, earthquakes, and volcanic eruptions, frequently result in human death. Man-made disasters resulting in death and disability can include acts of war, terrorist activities, airplane crashes and other transportation accidents, and hotel fires. Local, regional, and federal governments as well as worldwide agencies have utilized the services of forensic odontologists to identify victims of those disasters. Forensic scientists have also used dental records to identify victims of war crimes and other crimes against humanity.

The technique of dental radiographic identifications is based on the uniqueness of the human child, older child-adolescent mixed dentition, or adult dentition and its associated structures. The human dentition begins to develop at approximately the sixth week of fetal development. There are normally 20 deciduous teeth (also called milk teeth) and 32 permanent teeth. The stage of individual tooth development and dental eruption sequences are especially valuable in determining a person's age. Radiographic records indicating the presence or absence of teeth, anatomic location, and pathologic conditions in the detition's natural state can be used to identify a specific person. Pathologic conditions resulting in variations in growth and development can also be valuable in differentiating between individuals. Dental and jaw abnormalities, dental caries, and periodontal disease can result in medical and dental procedures that more clearly separate individuals. Especially valuable to the identification process are dental procedures, including extractions, orthodontic procedures, and restorations (fillings, crowns, bridges, dentures, etc.). These dental procedures give further variability to the dentition and are used by physicians and dentists in the identification process.

Dental restorations, root canal fillings, dental implants, extractions, and orthodontic and orthognathic procedures are examples of specific items used in the comparison process. Once sufficient individuality and comparison criteria are established, a death certificate can be signed by the medical examiner or other authorized individual.

It is anticipated that for the foreseeable future, radiographic imaging and analysis will continue to be an invaluable part of the dental identification process.

EXAMPLE CASES

Figures 24.3 through 24.10 demonstrate the range of findings that can lead to positive identification on the basis of comparative analysis of antemortem and postmortem dental radiographic images. Label "A" indicates antemortem study, and "P" indicates postmortem study. "R" and "L" refer to the sides of the patient.

REFERENCES

1. Brogdon, B.G., *Forensic Radiology*, CRC Press, Boca Raton, FL, 1998, chap. 2.
2. Petrova, A. and Watson, P., *The Death of Hitler: The Full Story with New Evidence from Secret Russian Archives*, Norton, New York, 1995, p. 118.

CREDIT

From Brogdon, B.G., *Forensic Radiology*, CRC Press, Boca Raton, FL, 1998. With permission. Figures 24.1, 24.2, 24.6, 24.7, 24.10.

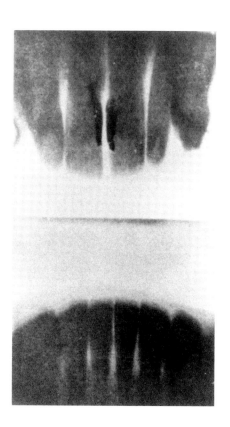

FIGURE 24.1 Dental x-rays by W. Koenig in 1896. Restorations are seen in the maxillary central incisors.

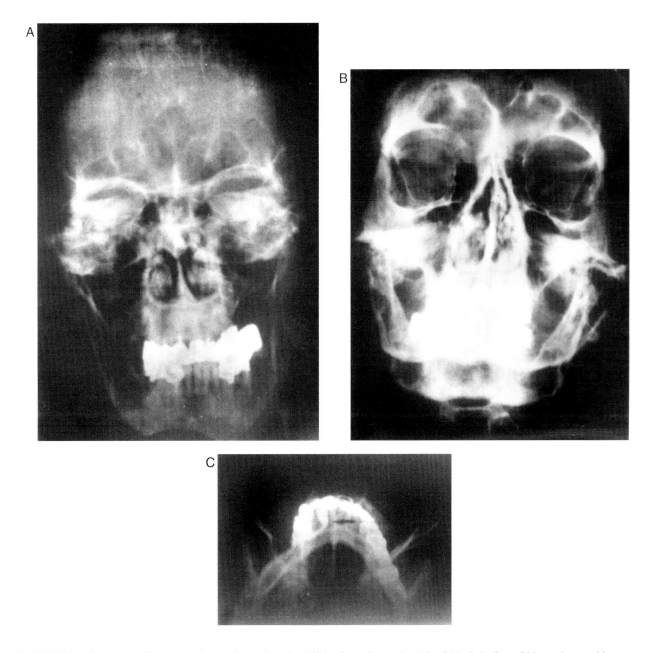

FIGURE 24.2 (A, B, and **C)** Antemortem radiographs of A. Hitler from September 19, 1944. Only five of his teeth were his own, and the extensive and unusual dental work allowed the Russians to identify his remains easily.

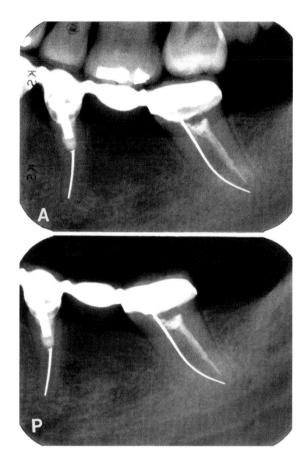

FIGURE 24.3 A human mandible **(P)** found in a wooded area was thought to be that of a 58-year-old Caucasian man who had been missing for over 2 years. **(A)** Antemortem dental radiographs were provided by a local law enforcement agency. Comparison of the antemortem and postmortem radiographs show identical and unique dental work indicating that the discovered mandible is that of the missing individual. A death certificate could be signed by the medical examiner.

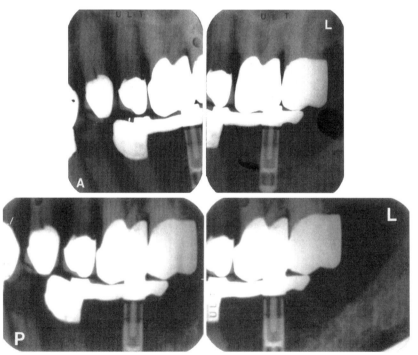

FIGURE 24.4 Extensive dental procedures including crowns and a fixed bridge retained by a dental implant lead to a positive identification in this case. Personal communication with Dr. Jeffrey R. Burkes, Chief Forensic Dentist of the City of New York, indicates that approximately 10% of the victims of the World Trade Center disaster identified through dental records had dental implants. This relatively new dental procedure (dental implants) will undoubtedly have increasing value in dental identification procedures. **(A)** Antemortem study, **(P)** postmortem study.

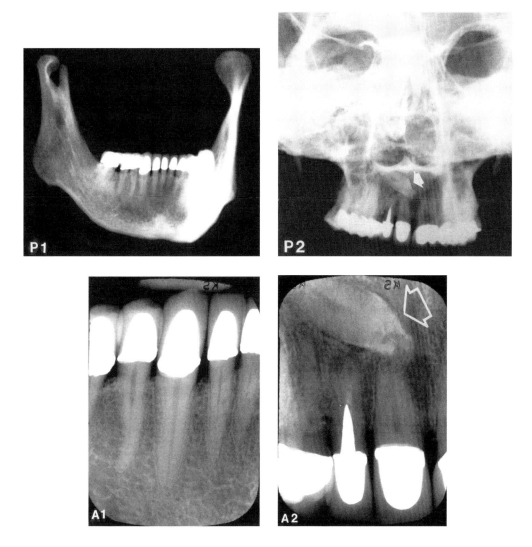

FIGURE 24.5 Skeletonized remains discovered in Central America were thought to be that of a missing American citizen. Postmortem examination showed extensive dental restorative procedures in the mandible **(P1)** and in the maxilla **(P2)**. Comparison of the postmortem radiographs with acquired antemortem studies **(A1 and A2)** allow positive identification of the purported deceased. Note the very uncommon impacted maxillary canine tooth (arrow) clearly visible on both antemortem and postmortem radiographs **(A2** and **P2)**.

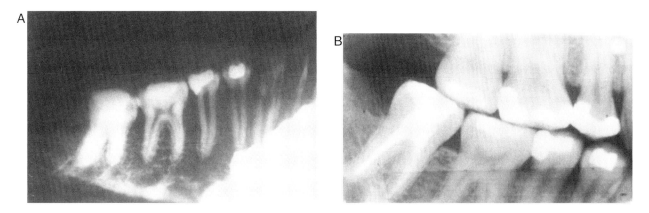

FIGURE 24.6 Only a fragment of the mandible **(A)** was found in scattered skeletal remains in a wooded area. However, the restorations, including the root canal, matched perfectly with an antemortem bite wing radiograph **(B)** of the presumed decedent.

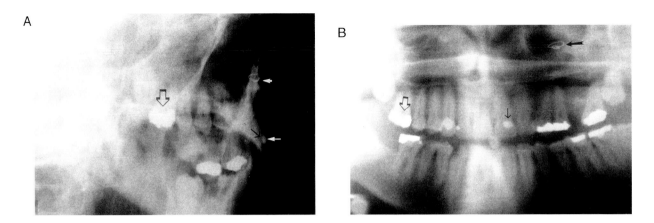

FIGURE 24.7 (**A**) A radiograph taken through a body bag is poorly positioned. Yet, distinctive dental restorations, a cosmetic implant on a central incisor, and a suture left from an orbital floor fracture repair could be seen. These findings helped lead to a presumed decedent. (**B**) The antemortem panoramic dental examination was a perfect match for all three features found on the postmortem study.

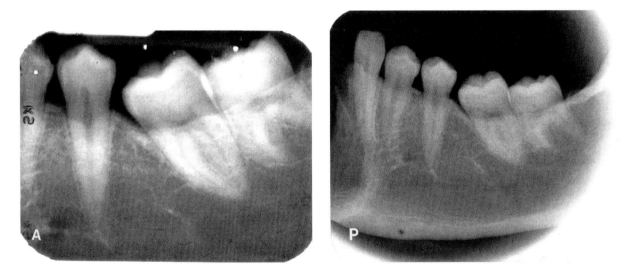

FIGURE 24.8 Recovered remains were thought to be those of a 37-year-old Hispanic male. Personal identification cards recovered with the body assisted law enforcement agents in the collection of dental records. The putative decedent had presented for an emergency dental visit because of pain caused by food impaction associated with the missing mandibular first molar. (**A**) Antemortem dental records were limited to one periapical film of the symptomatic area. A positive identification was possible because of the uniqueness of the dental anatomy perfectly matching on both antemortem and (**P**) postmortem dental radiographs. Although no dental restorations were present, the identification based solely on the perfect match of anatomy features could be made very quickly.

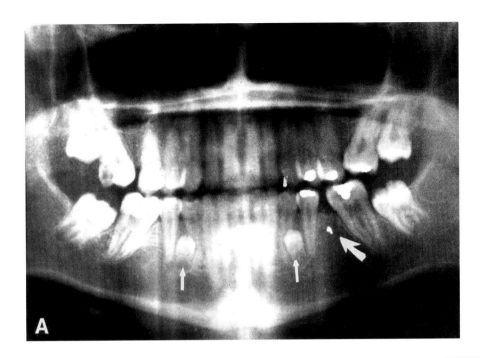

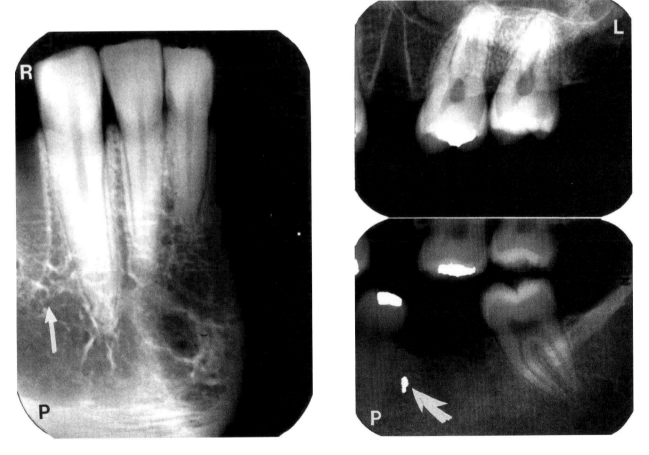

FIGURE 24.9 Partially decomposed remains of a murder victim were examined by the medical examiner. There were no identifying documents found with the body. **(A)** Antemortem and **(P)** postmortem radiographs were compared and a positive identification was made. Note the presence of supernumerary mandibular teeth (arrows) on the antemortem film, which had been extracted between the antemortem study and time of death. The metallic foreign body between the second premolar and the second molar on the left mandible on the antemortem study is still present on the postmortem study, although the second molar has since been extracted. Anatomic comparisons and comparisons of restorations can still be accomplished.

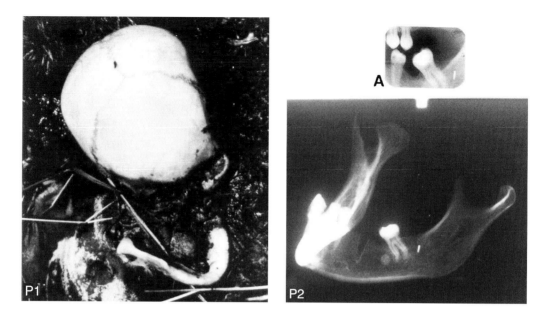

FIGURE 24.10 A few badly decomposed, almost skeletal remains were found in the woods near the neighborhood where a mentally retarded female had disappeared some 3 months earlier. **(P1)** A mandible was included in the remains. **(A)** A single dental x-ray of the missing person was available. It showed a single molar with a restoration and a nearby broken drill bit. **(P2)** The mandible from the retrieved remains had exactly matching features. (Courtesy of Dr. Leroy Riddick.)

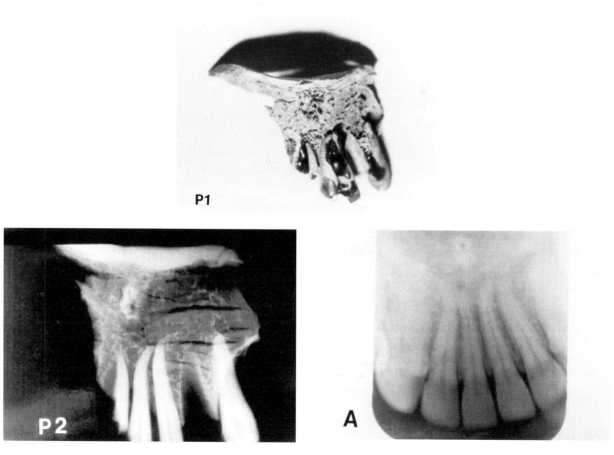

FIGURE 24.11 The only remaining portion of the dentition **(P1)** of a burn victim was sprayed with lacquer thinner for stabilization, then reassembled parts were held together with dental sticky wax. A radiograph **(P2)** of the reassembled fragment could be matched perfectly with **(A)** the antemortem radiograph. Note the configuration of the roots including the root socket of the missing incisor. (Courtesy of Dr. David P. Sipes.)

25 Conventional Radiologic Identification

B.G. Brogdon, M.D. and Hermann Vogel, M.D.

INTRODUCTION

Identification of unknown human remains is one of the substantial contributions of radiology to the forensic sciences. As early as October 1898, Dr. Fovau d' Coumelles wrote, "Knowing the existence of a fracture in a person, who has been burned or mutilated beyond recognition, we can hope to identify him by the x-ray…". It was a prescient prediction. Yet, it was a long time coming to fruition. In the meantime, as we have seen, Koenig found that he could demonstrate identifying features in dental x-rays as early as 1896. Yet, it was not until 1927 when Culbert and Law[1] identified a body by roentgenography of the nasal sinuses and mastoid processes that radiologic identification came into its own. Dental identification really did not take off until after World War II when the identification of Hitler brought some notoriety to the process (see Chapter 24). However, now, the use of radiologic comparison for identification of unknown remains is well established.

There are three levels of contribution that the radiologist can make.[2,3] First, there is the anthropological contribution. That is, the determination whether the discovered remains are animal or human, and if human, to develop a biological profile having to do with age, sex, stature, and race or population ancestry. We share this burden with the physical anthropologists. They are extremely adept and skillful at their work, but require defleshed bones. We can make our contribution by viewing somewhat similar indicators in bones that are still encased in flesh, but rendered visible by the probing x-rays. Of importance, particularly in the next chapter, is the determination of whether one is dealing with one or more bodies. Are there commingled remains? If so, they must be separated by all of the anthropological and radiological parameters available.

Once unidentified human remains are ready for investigation, the radiologic method can provide assistance at two levels. First, there can be a search of the body. This ordinarily would require a full body search using standard radiological positioning whenever possible. This will take between 12 and 14 full-size (14 × 17 inch) x-ray films. The need for conforming to standard clinical radiological positioning of bodies and body parts should be obvious. Sooner or later, the identification will depend upon comparison with clinical x-rays obtained while the assumed decedent was alive and undergoing examination for some medical purpose. Acquiring radiographs of deceased bodies in standard radiologic positions is not an easy task and requires great dedication and skill on the part of the radiographer.

Once the body has been imaged, the first level of contribution comes into play. Any variation from normal is noted and can then be compared with the medical history of the presumed decedent. If there is a healed fracture, or a metallic foreign body (Figure 25.1), then this is a lead for the investigators trying to solve the problem of the unknown. If there is a suspected decedent who has the history of a fracture and of a foreign body, then one has a presumptive or possible identification. If then, upon search, authorities can find an antemortem radiograph of a presumed decedent showing identical abnormalities, a positive identification may be established. Sometimes, antemortem radiographs can be found that do not precisely match the postmortem studies. If so, then one may have a presumed or probable identification which can still not be entirely termed positive (Figure 25.2). Sometimes, one will find an abnormality that cannot be verified on any antemortem studies or there may not be any antemortem studies at all. As a result, one must depend upon historical data to establish a possible diagnosis, which cannot be considered as legally positive unless there is other corroborating information.

The positive identification of unknown remains by the radiologic method depends upon the comparison of antemortem radiographs and postmortem radiographs or other radiologic images, and finding one or more points of absolute matching features. These can lead to the conclusion that, beyond reasonable doubt, the images represent one and the same person as recorded by the radiographic method before and after death. These requirements apply to both dental and conventional radiologic identification. The compared tissues usually are bone or teeth because these are the structures that are most durable, most likely to survive death and the destructive conditions that follow it, and most susceptible to imaging methodology. It is true that on occasion one can make comparative identifications on the basis of other tissues, but this is not a common situation.

REGIONAL CONSIDERATIONS

The various portions of the human body contain structures, particularly bony structures, tending to have normal variations that may be characteristic for the individual examined. These areas then are most helpful in producing positive results from comparative analysis of antemortem and postmortem radiologic studies. We will take these up in a systematic fashion by body region.

THE SKULL

DENTAL ARCHES

The possibilities of identification by dental radiography have already been discussed in Chapter 24 and will not be dealt with further here.

PARANASAL SINUSES

The size, configuration, and septation of the paranasal sinuses are as unique to each individual as are his fingerprints (Figure 25.4). Unless destroyed by fire, tumor, disease, or trauma, the paranasal sinuses do not change after adulthood is attained. Even when the projection and the positioning of the sinuses is somewhat different, one can still compare the septation and the configuration quite successfully most of the time (Figure 25.5).

TEMPORAL BONE

The petrous ridges in frontal projection and the mastoid tips in the lateral projection can frequently be used for matching purposes (Figure 25.6).

OTHER FEATURES

The sella tursica, the configuration of the brow and the inion, and the overall shape of the skull are all matchable features (Figure 25.7).

THE CHEST

The thoracocervical junction is the most useful portion of the chest for purposes of identification since it is often best preserved and has several structures that are prone to individual variation. The clavicle, the cervical and thoracic vertebra, and the upper ribs all contribute to the identification process (Figures 25.8 and 25.9). This area does not change much over time except for calcification or ossification of costal cartilages.

ABDOMEN AND PELVIS

These structures best will stand the insults of decomposition, incineration, scattering, carnivorous activities, and other hazards that befall unattended traumatized bodies. The thick musculature of the back and buttock help protect the bony structures of the lumbar spine and pelvis. The lumbar spine is particularly prone to individual variation and anomaly. In fact, a study has shown that 44% of healthy young males have some identifiable anomaly in their lumbar spine (Figures 25.10 and 25.11).[4]

EXTREMITIES

Extremities can have very useful features. A study of the hand and wrist shows, for instance, that even in identical twins there are distinctive features.[5] However, extremities often do not survive catastrophe or prolonged exposure to the elements.

SINGLE BONE IDENTIFICATION

Features that can be definitive when identifications are attempted on a single bone include:

1. Anomalous or unusual development
2. Disease or degeneration
3. Tumor
4. Trauma
5. Iatrogenic interference
6. Vascular grooves and trabecular patterns

Examples are shown (Figures 25.12 to 25.18).

REFERENCES

1. Culbert, W.L. and Law, F.M., Identification by comparison of nasal accessory sinuses and mastoid processes, *JAMA*, 98, 1634, 1927.
2. Brogdon, B.G., *Forensic Radiology*, CRC Press, Boca Raton, FL, 1998, chap. 3.
3. Vogel, H., *Gewalt in Röntgenbild*, ecomed verlagsgesellschaft mbH, Landsberg/Lech, 1997, chap. 9.
4. Crow, N.E. and Brogdon, B.G., The "normal" lumbosacral spine, *Radiology*, 72, 97, 1959.
5. Greulick, W.W., Skeletal features visible on the roentgenogram of the hand and wrist which can be used for establishing individual identification, *Am. J. Roentgenol.*, 83, 756, 1960.

CREDITS

From Brogdon, B.G., *Forensic Radiology*, CRC Press, Boca Raton, FL, 1998. With permission. Figures 25.2, 25.4, 25.6, 25.7, 25.9, 25.10, 25.11, 25.13, 25.14, 25.15, 25.18.

From Vogel, H., *Gewalt in Röntgenbild*, ecomed verlagsgesellschaft mbH, Landsberg/Lech, 1997. With permission. Figures 25.1, 25.3, 25.5, 25.8, 25.16.

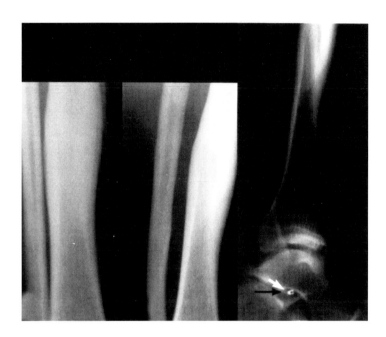

FIGURE 25.1 Recovered remains show evidence of an old healed fracture of the midshaft of the tibia and a tiny metallic foreign body in the subtalar joint. These are good leads for the investigator to follow.

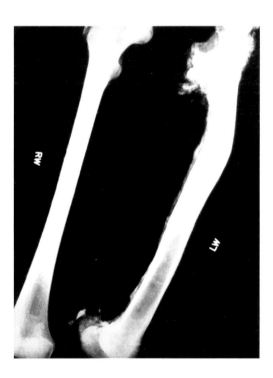

FIGURE 25.2 Skeletanized remains show an old healed fracture of the left proximal femoral shaft with the residual bowing and shortening. This was consistent with the history of a suspected decedent, but no previous films were available for positive comparison and identification.

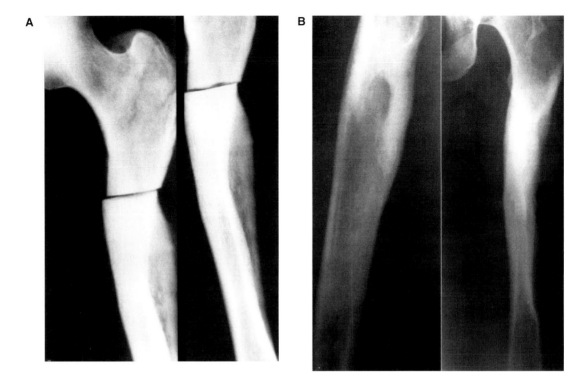

FIGURE 25.3 **(A)** Postmortem views of the proximal femur show evidence of an old healed fracture with deformity. **(B)** Some antemortem views of the same area show a similar entity, but they cannot be precisely matched because of differences in positioning.

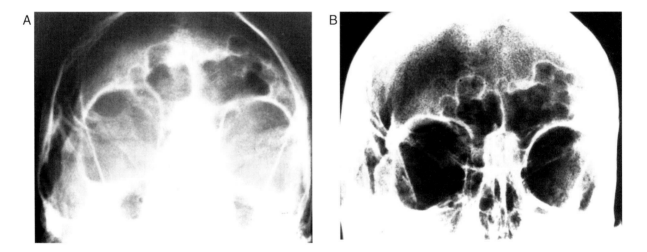

FIGURE 25.4 **(A)** The antemortem view has a different projection than **(B)** the postmortem view. Still, there is no doubt that the sinuses are exactly the same in terms of configuration and the shape of the central septum.

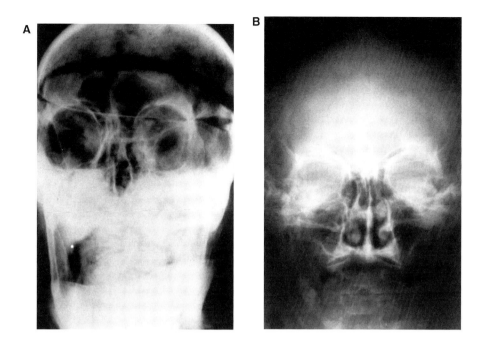

FIGURE 25.5 (A) The postmortem, postautopsy film of the skull is not well positioned. Furthermore, the right to left orientation is reversed from that of the antemortem film shown as (B) Still, one can be certain that these are mirror images and that the identification is positive.

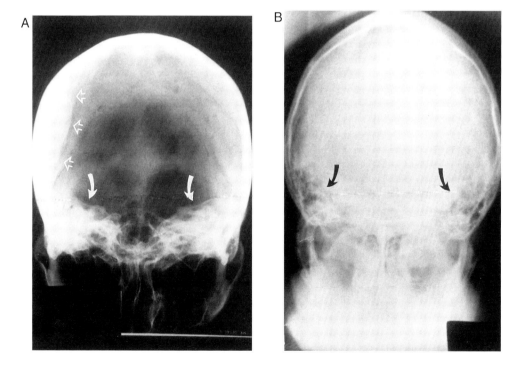

FIGURE 25.6 (A) Postmortem and (B) antemortem frontal views of the skull were submitted for possible identification. The configuration of the petrous ridges (curved arrows) clearly is different. This is a nonmatch. (The skull on the left also has a calcified subdural hematoma.)

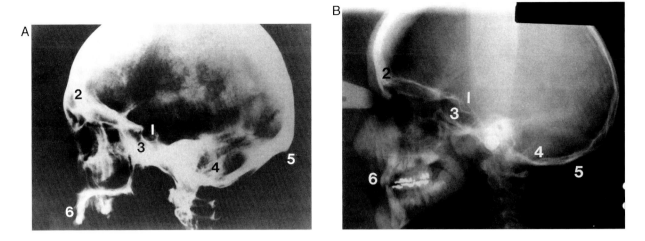

FIGURE 25.7 **(A)** Skull thought to be that of a 16-year-old girl who had disappeared from her home. She had had an orthometric skull examination a year earlier. **(B)** Skull found some 2 years later sent for comparison. There is no match. Note the differences in the sella tursica (1), frontal sinuses (2), and sphenoid sinuses (3). Also note the general configuration of the skull, brow slope, and posterial fossa (4) does not match. The inion (5) and angles of the maxillary incisors (6) are all different.

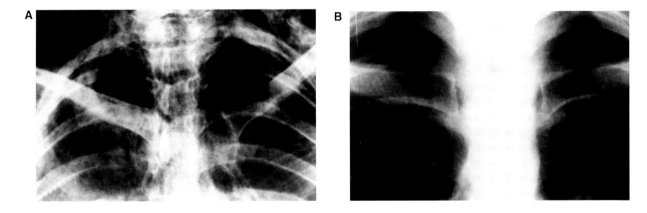

FIGURE 25.8 **(A)** Postmortem view of the thoracic inlet can be compared to **(B)** a tomographic study of the sternoclavicular joint. The ends of the clavicles are identical.

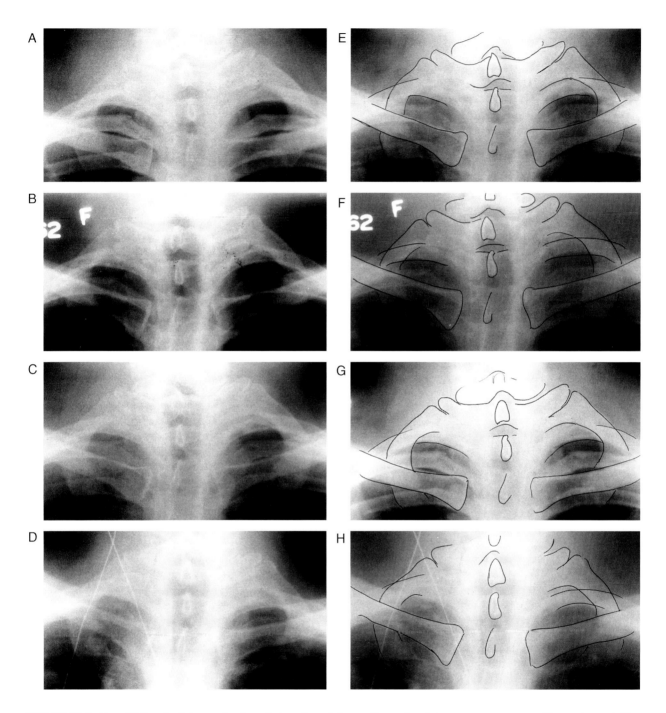

FIGURE 25.9 (A to D) Detail of the cervicothoracic junction of chest radiographs of the same person over a 50-year interval. Note the identical configuration of the bony landmarks. The first costochondral cartilage became ossified during this period of observation. **(E to H)** The same studies are shown on the right with anatomic details outlined to assist the inexperienced viewer in seeing the similarities.

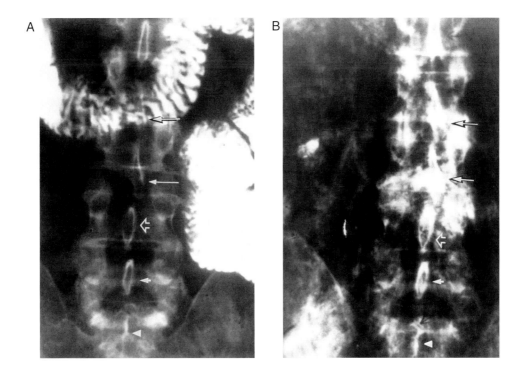

FIGURE 25.10 Good police work brought up this view of the lumbar spine obtained during the course of a gastrointestinal series. It could be matched with the presumed decedent's spine even though there had been a lot of decomposition in the interval period. Matching features of the spinous processes are marked with arrows.

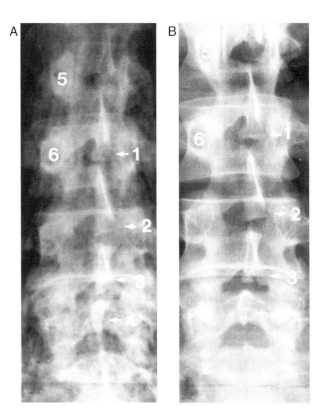

FIGURE 25.11 (A) Postmortem and **(B)** antemortem frontal views of the lumbar spine show highly individualistic configurations of spinous processes and other features that are numerically matched on the two films.

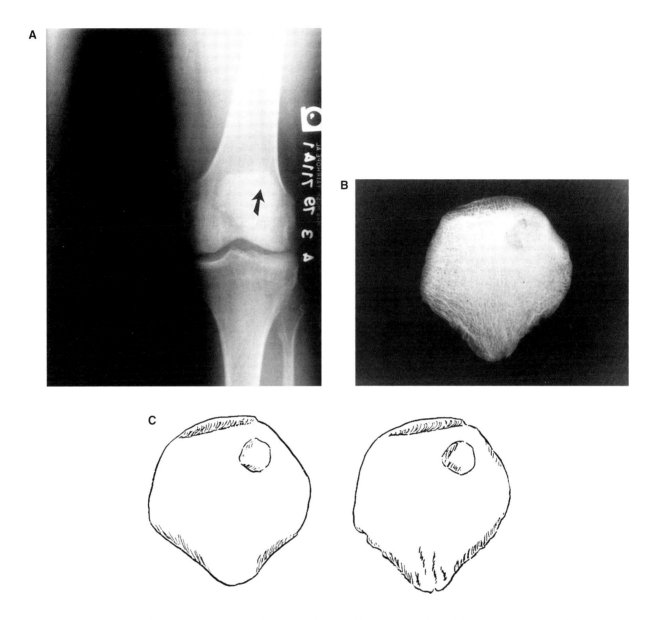

FIGURE 25.12 Example of an anomalous or developmental change. (**A**) An examination of the knee taken 5 years before the death of the individual. It shows a defect of the upper outer quadrant of the patella. An identical lesion was found in a patella recovered from incinerated remains in the trunk of a burnt-out car. (**B**) A radiograph of the recovered patella. (**C**) A tracing of the knee film and the isolated patellar film corrected for magnification. The features are identical. This is a positive match based on a lesion called a "dorsal defect of the patella." (From Riddick, L., Brogdon, B.G., Laswell-Hoff, J., and Delmar, B., *J. Forensic. Sci.*, 28, 263, 1983. With permission.) (Copyright ASTM International. With permission.)

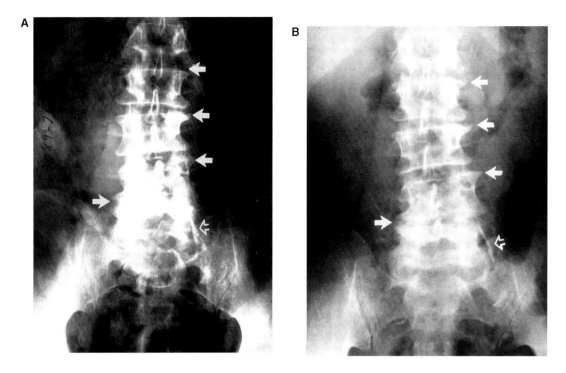

FIGURE 25.13 Degenerative disease. **(A)** Postmortem and **(B)** antemortem films of the abdomen show highly distinctive degenerative changes in the lumbar spine marked by arrows. Also arterial calcification is shown on both studies (open arrow).

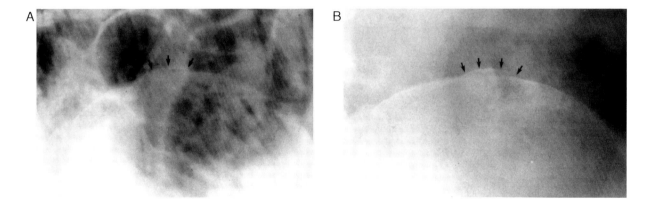

FIGURE 25.14 (A) Postmortem and **(B)** antemortem pelvic radiographs were matched by an unusual bony excrescence or tumor on the left iliac crest (arrows).

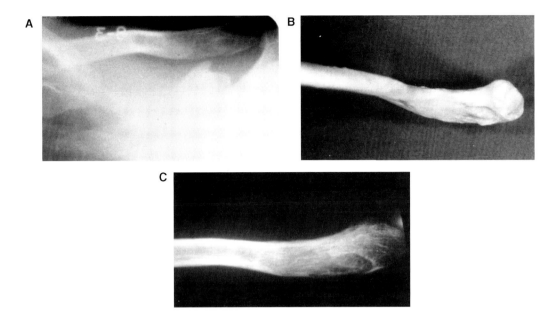

FIGURE 25.15 Example of a match on the basis of early trauma. Skeletonized remains were all normal except for an old healed fracture of the left clavicle. Presumed decedent had broken his clavicle at age 14. That film was available but would not match. Two years later, a chest film on the suspected decedent was found. A perfect match was made between the clavicle on the chest film and a radiograph of the isolated clavicle, after trial and error positioning to exactly match the projection on the antemortem study.

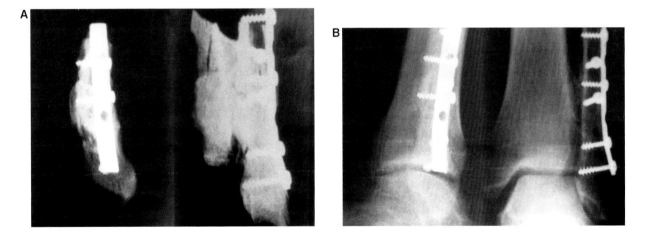

FIGURE 25.16 A fragment of the tibia was found with orthopedic plate and screws. These eventually could be matched with discovered antemortem films showing the identical fixation device.

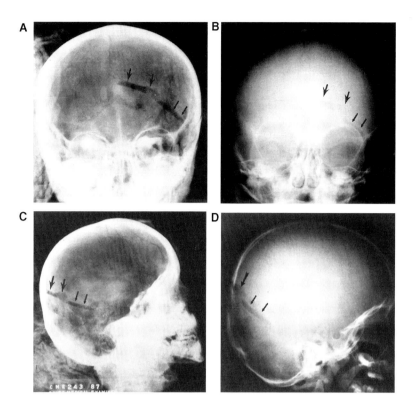

FIGURE 25.17 Identification of decomposed postmortem remains (**A** and **C**) by comparison with antemortem skull examination (**B** and **D**) showing surgical defects from a lambdoid synostectomy. (From Hogge, J.P., Messmer, J.M., and Fierro, M.F., *J. Forensic Sci.*, 40, 688, 1995. With permission.) (Copyright ASTM International. With permission.)

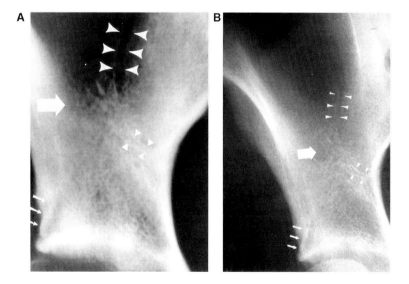

FIGURE 25.18 (**A**) Slightly enlarged detail of postmortem x-ray study of the innominate bone. (**B**) Detail from antemortem pelvic radiograph. There are many matching features: general configuration, large vascular or nutrient groove (arrowheads), linear trabecular pattern (triangles), coarse trabecular pattern (large arrows), and focal contour feature (small arrows).

26 Mass Casualty Situations

B.G. Brogdon, M.D., Gary S. Silverstein, M.D., and Joel E. Lichtenstein, M.D.

INTRODUCTION

Mass casualty situations by their very nature tend to be stressful situations, involving unexpected emergencies in which even those with little prior interest or experience might be called upon to help.[1-3] Although the same principles of radiological identification apply as in the identification of a single set of human remains, the task is enormously complicated by the sheer numbers involved; the logistics of an unexpected operation in a usually uncomfortable or unfamiliar setting; and often there is makeshift, portable, jury-rigged equipment. The problems of handling a mass casualty situation from the standpoint of the pathologist, the radiologist, the dentist, and other paramedical personnel have to do with the current fear of blood and body fluid. When Air India Flight 162 disintegrated at 3100 ft off the South Coast of Ireland as a result of a bomb explosion, the 131 bodies recovered were all brought directly to the Cork Regional Hospital, a modern university teaching facility, where postmortem identification procedures could be carried out under almost ideal situations. Attitudes have so changed that by the time of the bombing of the Federal Building in Oklahoma City, all of the processing of bodies was handled in makeshift additions to the medical examiner's office despite the many hospitals within a very short radius of the explosion.

Despite the field operation character of most disaster scenes, there are well-established organizational patterns, and there are trained disaster teams scattered about the country ready to respond on very short notice to any disaster location in the country and most of the world. Identification of bodies in mass disaster situations is a team effort. A few of the bodies can be identified by visual inspection. If this is impossible, the forensic odontologist usually is responsible for the highest percentage of identifications. The fingerprint experts usually follow. The radiologists rank somewhat high, usually in third place. Undoubtedly, in the near future, DNA identification will take over the lion's share of the work. However, it is expensive and takes a long time, and there is a great pressure to get the job done sooner by other means.

The bodies or parts are usually collected in body bags and the initial imaging examination may be obtained through the bag. Mobile x-ray equipment ordinarily will be utilized (Figure 26.1); portable or movable lead-lined x-ray shielding must be used for protection of personnel (Figure 26.2A). Conveyors may be used to transport heavy remains (Figure 26.2B). The ubiquitous linescan low-dose baggage scanning fluoroscope (Figure 26.3) can be extremely useful in the quick evaluation of bodies for obviously significant findings; foreign bodies; and, in the case of military or terrorist operations, live ordinance.

Computerized record keeping of findings is imperative. The comparison matches of images may not always be at an absolute level of confidence sufficient to establish a positive identification. However, the exclusionary benefits of a large matrix of findings helps narrow the identification field and makes more meaningful what would ordinarily be a presumed identification. Examples of the spectrum of radiologic identification in mass disaster situations follow. In every instance, the postmortem findings will be presented on the reader's left.

REFERENCES

1. Lichtenstein, J.E., Radiology in mass casualty situations, in *Forensic Radiology*, Brogdon, B.G., CRC Press, Boca Raton, FL, 1998, chap. 9.
2. Silverstein, G.S., personal communication, 2002.
3. Brogdon, B.G., Forensic aspects of radiology, in *Medicolegal Investigation of Death*, 4th ed., Spitz, W.U., Ed., C.C. Thomas, Springfield, IL, chap. XXI.

CREDIT

From Brogdon, B.G., *Forensic Radiology*, CRC Press, Boca Raton, FL, 1998. With permission. Figures 26.1B, 26.2B, 26.3.

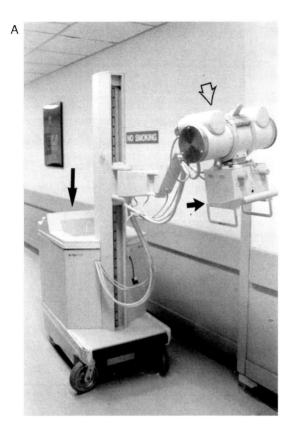

FIGURE 26.1 **(A)** Mobile x-ray unit of the type frequently used in mass casualty and disaster situations. The long black arrow points at the generator and controls. The open arrow points at the x-ray tube housing. The short black arrow points at the beam collimator. **(B)** Digital C–arm fluoroscope of the type used in the Gulf War. Its television monitor display is useful for initial screening, and images can be stored on a hard disc for later analysis or printout.

FIGURE 26.2 **(A)** Portable lead-lined x-ray shield being assembled. This protects the individuals who are working in the area from scattered radiation. (From Lichtenstein, J.E., Madewell, J.E., McKeekin, R.R., Feigin, D.S., and Wolcott, J.H., *Aviat. Environ. Med.*, 51, 1004, 1980. With permission.) **(B)** Roller-bearing conveyor is set up to assist in transporting heavy remains. Note the use of several individual x-ray shields for protection of personnel in the area.

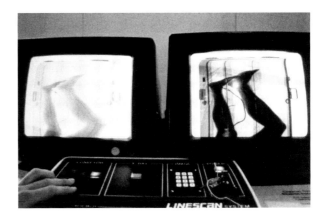

FIGURE 26.3 Linescan fluoroscope used for baggage inspection is useful for preliminary inspection through body bags or caskets. Pertinent anatomic lesions, foreign bodies, and ordinance can be found.

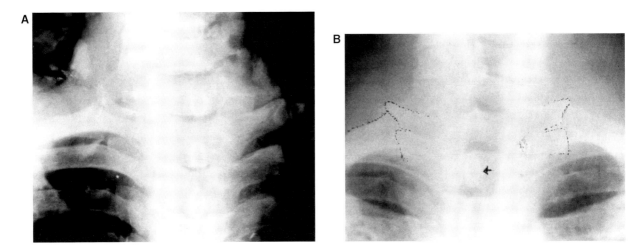

FIGURE 26.4 Badly burned and partially dismembered crewmen were extracted from the engine of a train that left the tracks and plunged into a swamp. Portions of the thoracocervical junction were intact to allow identification. (A) The postmortem fragment. (B) An earlier radiograph. The differences in the exposure techniques are a problem. The bony structures have been highlighted to assist the reader (Brogdon).

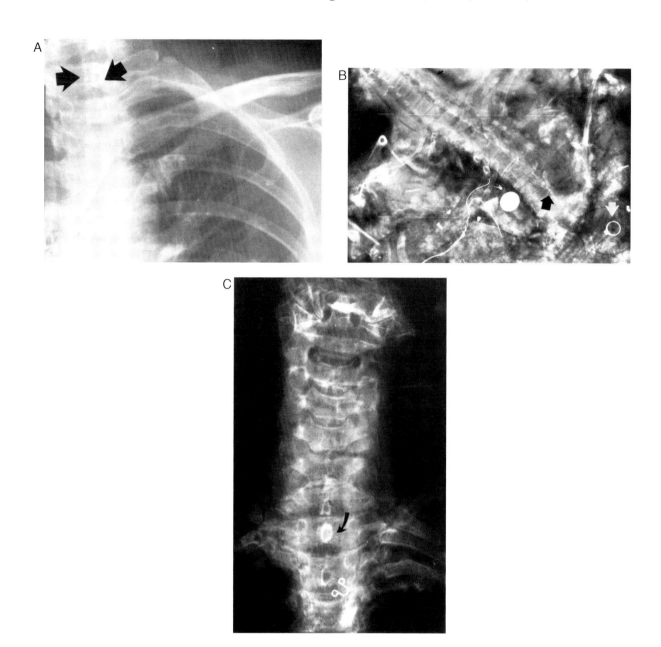

FIGURE 26.5 (**A**) An antemortem film from an aircraft accident. Tracheal calcification and a dense cortical change in the T-1 spinous process (arrows) are seen. (**B**) Postmortem radiograph with the remains in a body bag show severe dismemberment of the skeleton and multiple foreign bodies including aircraft parts. The black arrow points to calcified tracheal cartilages similar to those seen in (**A**). (**C**) The thoracocervical portion of the skeleton was cleaned and photographed in standard position. This reproduces the appearance of the spinous process of T-1 vertabra as demonstrated on the antemortem study. (From Lichtenstein, J.E. et al., *Am J. Roentgenol.*, 150, 751, 1998. With permission.)

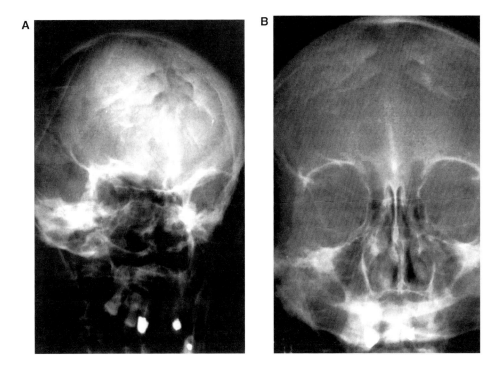

FIGURE 26.6 (**A**) The skull of the victim of an aircraft explosion over the ocean shows a condition called hyperostosis interna frontalis. (**B**) Among the radiographs collected of all the victims was another skull that showed a similar condition. The hyperostotic changes cannot be exactly superimposed. However, there are additional crowns and filling in the teeth, which permitted a presumptive diagnosis later held up by exclusion (Silverstein).

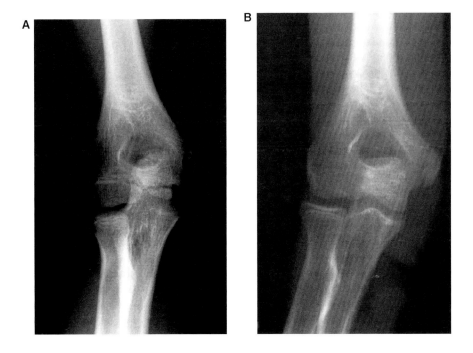

FIGURE 26.7 (**A** and **B**) Antemortem and postmortem examination of an adolescent elbow shows precisely identical tribecular patterns above the olecranon fossa of the humerus, which also is identical on the two studies. There has been some aging since the antemortem film; note closure of some of the epiphyses. Nevertheless, identification is positive (Silverstein).

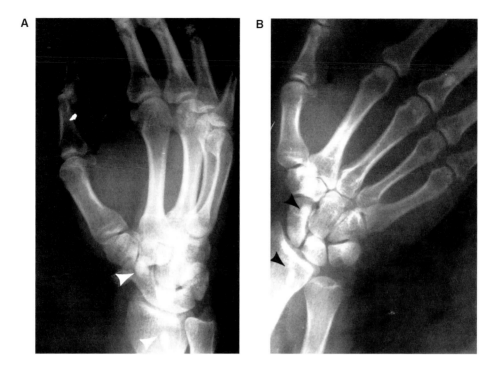

FIGURE 26.8 (**A** and **B**) Antemortem and postmortem views of the hand and wrist show several small dense bone islands, a normal variation (arrows). These allowed the positive identifications (Silverstein).

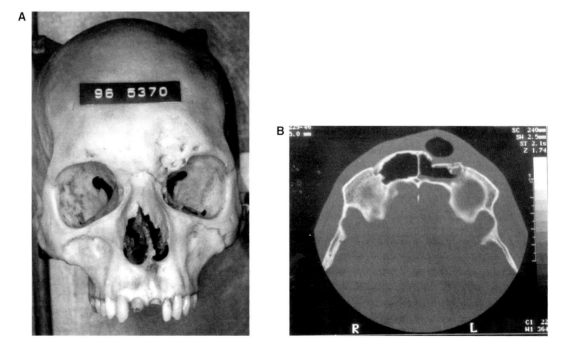

FIGURE 26.9 (**A**) Skull of this aircraft explosion victim showed a remarkable healed depressed fracture of the left frontal sinus and orbital roof. (**B**) An antemortem computed tomography was found showing the fresh depressed fracture of the frontal bone with air escaping from the sinus into the soft tissues of the forehead (Silverstein).

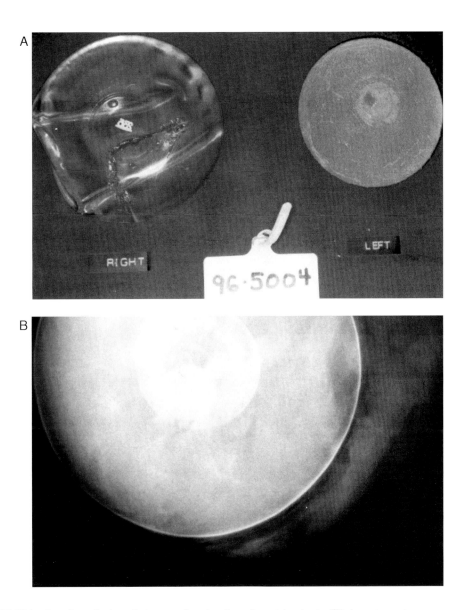

FIGURE 26.10 **(A)** This aircraft explosion victim was found to have breast implants. **(B)** An antemortem mammogram of the left breast completely matches, and is of exactly the same type, as the postmortem specimen (Silverstein).

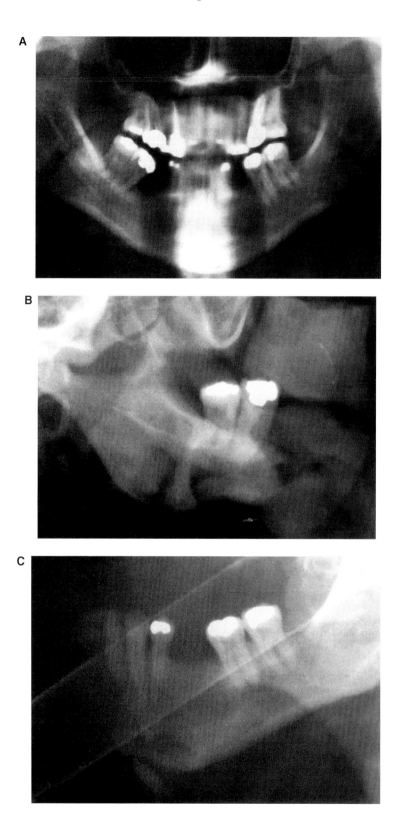

FIGURE 26.11 (**A**) An antemortem panoramic view of the mandible and the maxilla showed mandibular restorations which could be exactly matched with postmortem oblique views (**B** and **C**) of mandibular fragments (Silverstein).

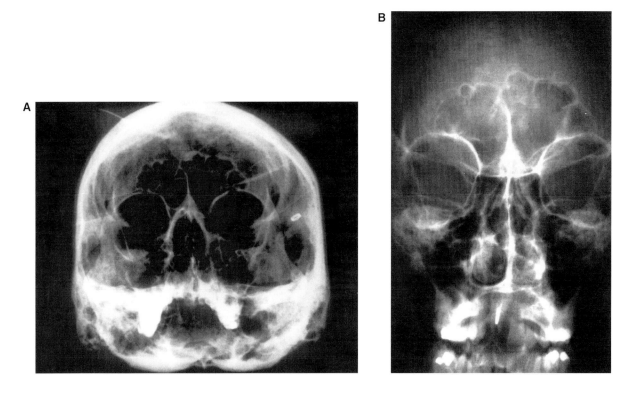

FIGURE 26.12 (A) Postmortem frontal sinus configuration can be exactly matched with **(B)** an antemortem study (Silverstein).

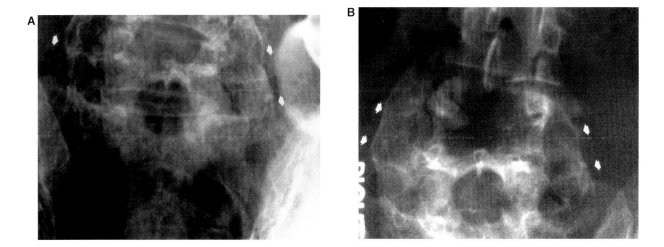

FIGURE 26.13 (A) Postmortem view of the lumbo-sacral junctions shows evidence of a spinal fusion and configurational changes in the posterior elements of L-5, which could be exactly matched with **(B)** the antemortem study (Silverstein).

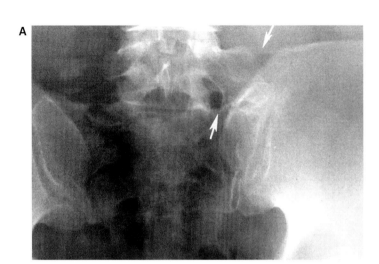

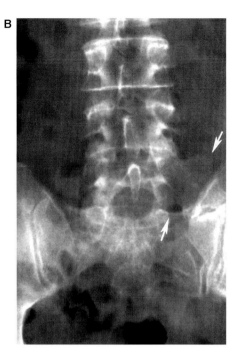

FIGURE 26.14 **(A)** Aircraft accident victim whose postmortem examination showed a unilateral sacralization of L-5 on the left (arrow). This was matched with **(B)** an antemortem study. Note also the identical shape of the visualized spinous processes (Silverstein).

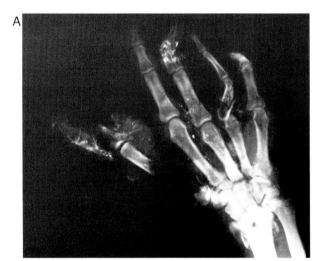

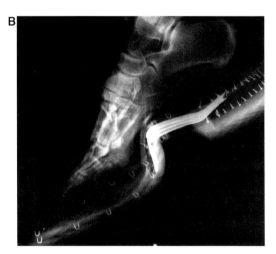

FIGURE 26.15 Sometimes the postaccident radiographic study can provide valuable information about the crew members. **(A)** The shattered hand with, especially, the fracture and separation of the thumb suggests this pilot was holding the control yoke at the time of the crash. **(B)** The deformity of this heavy flying boot indicates that its wearer was putting great force on the rudder pedal at the time of the crash. The heavy boot saved him from what has been recognized for many years as an *"aviator's foot"*—a fracture dislocation of the midfoot from the rudder bar (Lichtenstein).

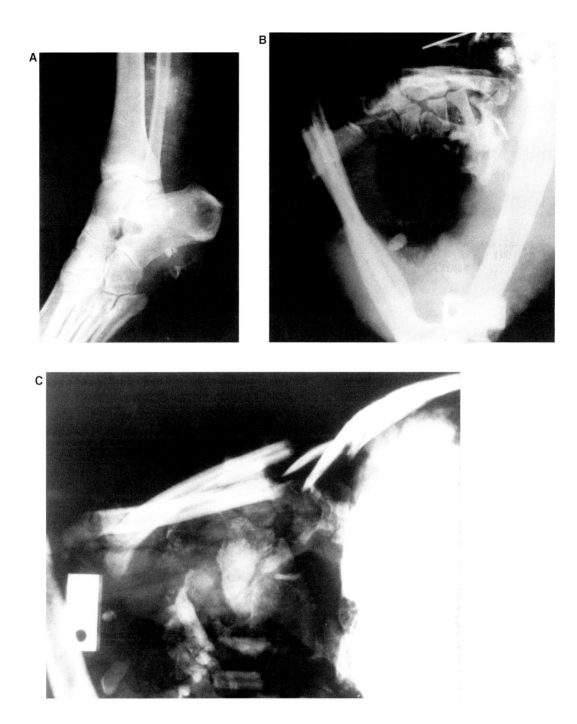

FIGURE 26.16 Bodies that have been burned severely show a degree of tissue destruction, which is a function of temperature and time. Distortions of body position by shrinkage of flexor muscle groups produce the pugilistic attitude, which may complicate radiologic evaluation. The bones and teeth are most likely to survive thermal destruction. The bones burned through the flesh tend to shrink as temperatures increase to 1100°C. Bones at high temperatures may develop multiple perpendicular fractures to the long axis of the bone. The long bones may show warping or bowing as they cool. Defleshed dry bones tend to develop longitudinal fractures or striae. Although it may be difficult, one must try to differentiate thermal fractures from impact fractures in crash and burn situations or where the fire may be intended to hide other evidence. **(A)** Mild flexion deformity as a result of flexor group shrinkage during the fire. **(B)** Transverse fracturing and marked pugilistic position of the upper extremity after a high intensity fire in an aircraft accident. **(C)** Transverse fracturing and bowing of upper extremity bones from a high temperature fire (Brogdon).

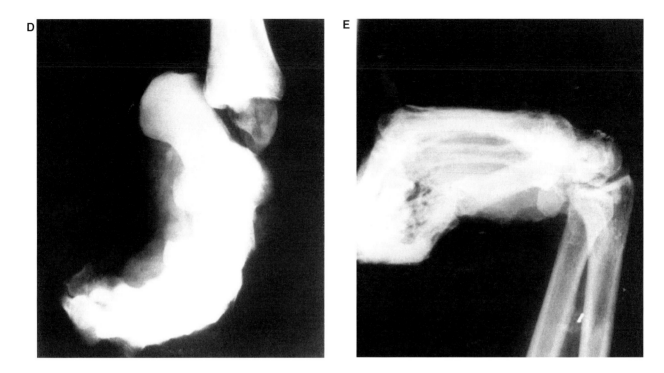

FIGURE 26.16 (Continued) Bodies that have been burned severely show a degree of tissue destruction, which is a function of temperature and time. Distortions of body position by shrinkage of flexor muscle groups produce the pugilistic attitude, which may complicate radiologic evaluation. The bones and teeth are most likely to survive thermal destruction. The bones burned through the flesh tend to shrink as temperatures increase to 1100°C. Bones at high temperatures may develop multiple perpendicular fractures to the long axis of the bone. The long bones may show warping or bowing as they cool. Defleshed dry bones tend to develop longitudinal fractures or striae. Although it may be difficult, one must try to differentiate thermal fractures from impact fractures in crash and burn situations or where the fire may be intended to hide other evidence. **(D)** Extreme flexion deformity of the foot from high temperature. **(E)** Typical pugilistic fist (Brogdon).

27 Other Modalities, Other Reasons

B.G. Brogdon, M.D. and Hermann Vogel, M.D.

Although great progress has been made in the development of new techniques and new modalities in the field of diagnostic radiology since the 1950s, the application of the radiologic method in the forensic identification process has changed little since that time in most jurisdictions. Problems of cost, accessibility, maintenance, and operation of the newer modalities have restricted their use in the forensic sciences. This is gradually changing and opens up areas of great progress or promise in the field. There are other ethical, religious, and social reasons for increasing utilization of the radiologic analysis of the dead, particularly with the newer modalities.[1]

NEWER MODALITIES

Riepert and co-workers[2] published one of the first reports of the use of computed tomography (CT) in identifying unknown human remains (Figure 27.1). Since then, there has been a gradual increase in the use of CT for these purposes. In addition, the topogram or scout image acquired before most CT studies to position slice levels can be quite successfully employed to match with conventional radiographs (Figure 27.2). The ability to reconstruct three-dimensional images, which can be manipulated, creates a possibility of comparing the skulls of formerly living patients with the actual skulls of deceased patients or with postmortem images of them (Figure 27.3).

Magnetic resonance (MR) images can be compared to postmortem x-rays with some degree of success on occasion (Figure 27.4). However, there are pitfalls in trying to match these two disparate images (Figure 27.5).[3]

OTHER USES, OTHER REASONS

Other uses have been found for the new modalities in forensic science beyond identification of unknown remains. Clinically prompted sectional images by CT and by MR can make powerful exhibits to jurors. The 3-D capability of CT also permits the construction of striking courtroom exhibits[4] (Figure 27.6).

A team at the University of New Mexico was perhaps the first to demonstrate the usefulness of MRI in determining the extent of injury or cause of death.[5,6] Examining cases of unexplained death or suspected child abuse in children up to 8 years of age or younger within 24 hours of death provided extremely useful information that could later be verified at autopsy (Figures 27.7 to 27.9). Conventional radiographs and CT can give good evidence concerning gunshot wounds and other injuries.

The retrieval of foreign bodies from decedents who have been involved in explosions or other accidents can be useful in determining the source of the foreign body, serial numbers or part numbers, or trace evidence such as chemicals or explosives (Figure 27.10).

In a study at Hadassah University Hospital in Jerusalem, postmortem CT was later compared with the conventional postmortem studies. The victims were investigated radiologically up until 6 hours after death. All were victims of accidents. The impetus for this study was the fact that large parts of the population are opposed to autopsy of family members or themselves. There is also pressure for the early release of the body and burial. The findings were encouraging. From 127 pathologic findings, 45% were found by CT and autopsy. The CT discovered more bone lesions, the autopsy more soft tissue lesions. Obviously, the combinations of both methods produced the best results.[1] Examples of some of the preautopsy CT findings are shown in Figures 27.11 to 27.15.

REFERENCES

1. Vogel, H., *Gewalt in Röntgenbild*, ecomed verlagsgesellschaft mbH, Landsberg/Lech, 1997.
2. Riepert, T., Rittner, C., Ulmcke, D., Oghuihi, S., and Scheveden, F., Identification of an unknown corpse by means of computed tomography (CT) of the lumbar spine, *J. Forensic Sci.*, 40, 126, 1995.
3. Brogdon, B.G., *Forensic Radiology*, CRC Press, Boca Raton, FL, 1998.
4. Oliver, W.R., Chancellor, A.S., Soltys, M., Symon, J., Cullip, T., Rosensman, J., Hellman, R., Boxwala, A., and Gormley, W., Three-dimensional reconstruction of a bullet path: validation by computed radiography, *J. Forensic Sci.*, 40, 321, 1995.
5. Hart, B.L., Dudley, M.H., and Zumwalt, R.E., Post-mortem cranial MRI and autopsy correlation in suspected child abuse, *Am. J. Forensic Med. Pathol.*, 17, 217, 1996.
6. Hart, B.L., Dudley, M.E., and Zumwalt, R.E., Post-mortem MR imaging in suspected child abuse: radiologic and pathologic correlation, RSNA 1994 Selected Award-Winning Scientific Exhibits, CD-ROM, 1995.

CREDITS

From Brogdon, B.G., *Forensic Radiology*, CRC Press, Boca Raton, FL, 1998. With permission. Figures 27.2A, 27.3, 27.4, 27.5.

From Vogel, H., *Gewalt in Röntgenbild*, ecomed verlagsgesellschaft mbH, Landsberg/Lech, 1997. With permission. Figures 27.11, 27.12, 27.13, 27.14, 27.15.

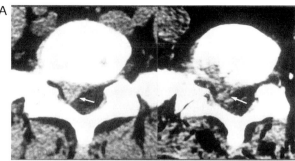
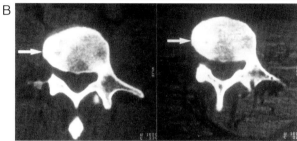
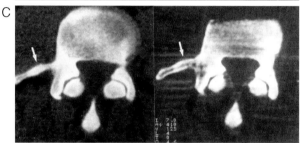
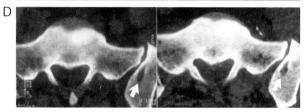

FIGURE 27.1 Identification by comparison of antemortem and postmortem CT. The antemortem study is on the viewer's left in every instance. (**A**) Posterolateral disc herniation at L5-S1. (**B**) Small Schmorl's node in the inferior end-plate of L4. (**C**) Peculiar thickening of the right transverse process of L4. (**D**) Shows identical lucencies in the left ilium at the sacroiliac joint. (Original images courtesy of the authors. Copyright ASTM International. Reprinted with permission.)

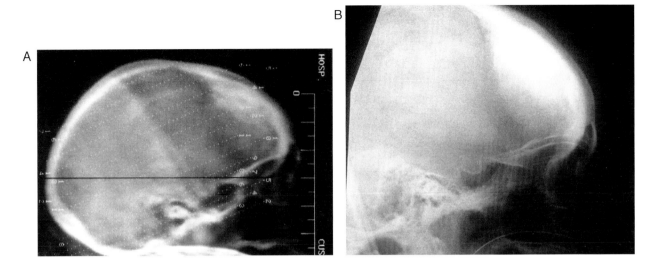

FIGURE 27.2 (A) Topogram, or scout film, of an antemortem CT study of an elderly female with hyperostosis interna frontalis is easily matched with (B) a routine skull film showing the same condition and an identical configuration of the sella and other anatomy of the skull.

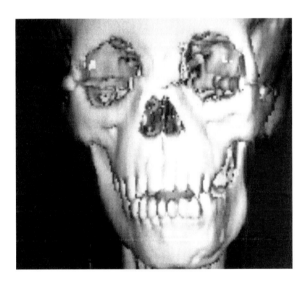

FIGURE 27.3 Example of a reconstructed 3-D image of the skull from a CT study. This image can be manipulated upon any axis to match postmortem x-rays or the defleshed skull.

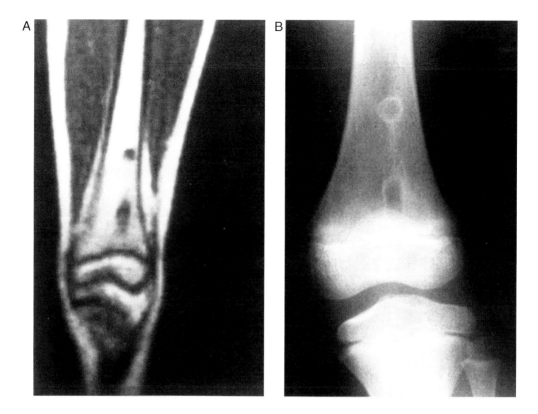

FIGURE 27.4 Pictures of (**A**) an MR and (**B**) radiographic images of an adolescent distal femur containing two fibrous cortical defects.

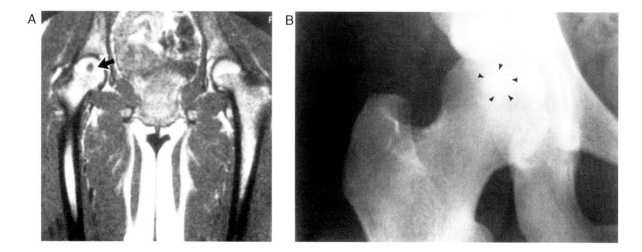

FIGURE 27.5 (**A**) T1-weighted MRI of the pelvis shows a dense calcification registering as a signal void in the right femoral head. (**B**) Radiograph of the right hip showing a round density consistent with a bone island. It is very attractive to match these two different studies for an identification. However, the lesion is common and no additional matching points are available for a positive identification.

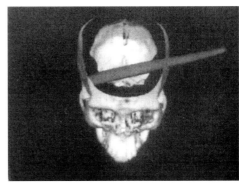

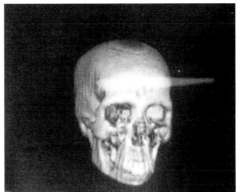

FIGURE 27.6 Three-dimensional reconstructions of an ante-mortem CT examination utilizing advanced computer techniques and stock CT data allows construction of a very convincing courtroom exhibit, showing the path of a bullet as indicated by a light beam that narrows from the entrance to the exit due to modeling of the radiation attenuation. (Copyright ASTM International. Reprinted with permission.) (From Oliver, W.R., Chancellor, A.S., Soltys, M., Symon, J., Cullip, T., Rosensman, J., Hellman, R., Boxwala, A., and Gormley, W., *J. Forensic Sci.*, 40, 321, 1995. With permission.)

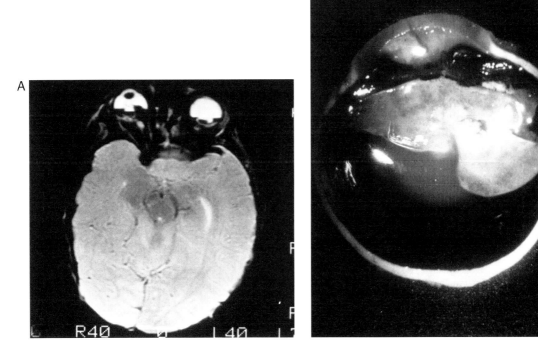

FIGURE 27.7 A 7-month-old girl had reportedly been dropped. Postmortem cranial MRI showed diffuse, severe swelling of the brain. Bilateral retinal detachments and vitreous hemorrhage were visible on MRI. (**A**) Axial T2-weighted image. (**B**) Autopsy. (From Hart, B.L., Dudley, M.H., and Zumwalt, R.F., Post-Mortem Cranial MRI Autopsy Correlation in Suspected Child Abuse, poster presentation at 1994 RSNA Conference. With permission of the Radiological Society of North America.)

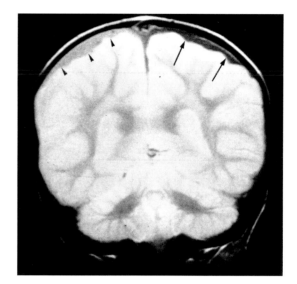

FIGURE 27.8 Bilateral subdural hematomas were identified on the postmortem MRI of a 14-month-old girl who died following a seizure. On this coronal intermediate-weighted image, the subdural hematomas (arrowheads) on the right and on the left (arrows) display different signal intensities consistent with blood of different ages. (From Hart, B.L., Dudley, M.H., and Zumwalt, R.F., Post-Mortem Cranial MRI Autopsy Correlation in Suspected Child Abuse, poster presentation at 1994 RSNA Conference. With permission of the Radiological Society of North America.)

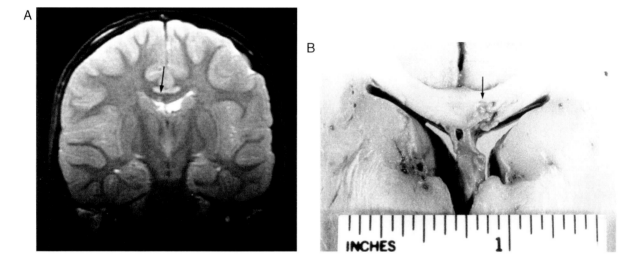

FIGURE 27.9 This 19-month-old boy had suffered cardiopulmonary arrest during the trip to the hospital after reportedly having been beaten. (**A**) A coronal T2-weighted image from the postmortem MRI shows a small focus of increased signal intensity in the body of the corpus collosum (arrow). (**B**) Careful sectioning of the brain at the corresponding location disclosed a tear of the corpus collosum (arrow). (From Hart, B.L., Dudley, M.H., and Zumwalt, R.F., Post-Mortem Cranial MRI Autopsy Correlation in Suspected Child Abuse, poster presentation at 1994 RSNA Conference. With permission of the Radiological Society of North America.)

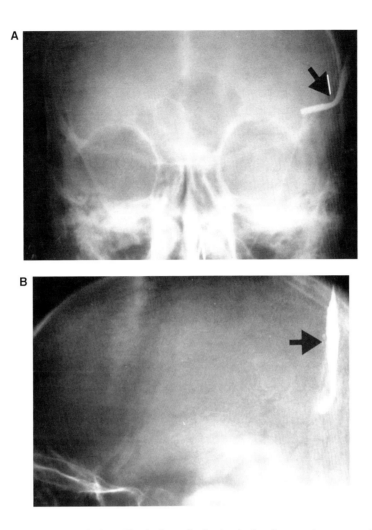

FIGURE 27.10 **(A)** Frontal view. **(B)** Lateral view. The finding of a foreign body after a major catastrophe such as an explosion or aircraft accident calls for identification and retrieval of the foreign body in an attempt to gain valuable information from serial or part numbers, source of origin, or trace evidence of explosives or chemicals.

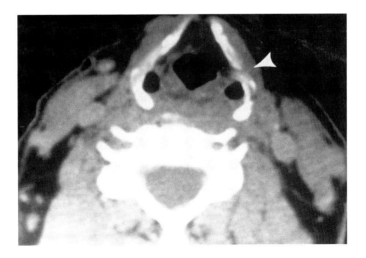

FIGURE 27.11 Fractured larynx due to strangulation. (CT examination.)

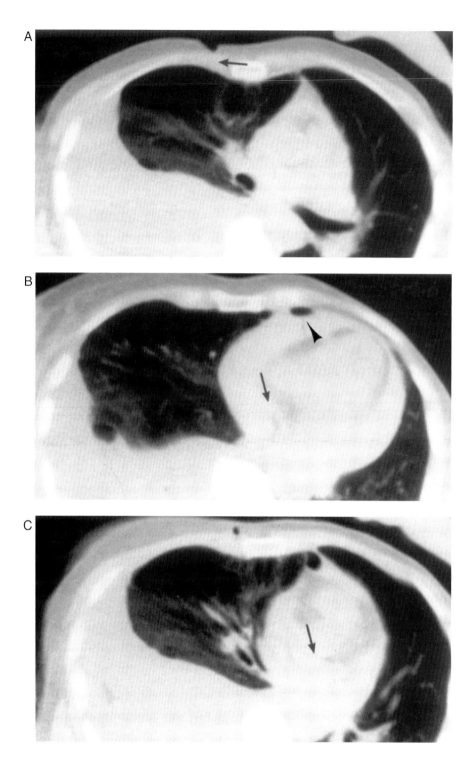

FIGURE 27.12 (**A**) A stab wound in the chest is indicated by the defect in the anterior thoracic wall (arrow). (**B**) A pneumothorax developed along with a pleural effusion; consequently the heart is displaced to the left. There is an air bubble (arrowhead) and blood (arrow) in the pericardium. (**C**) Massive collection of blood and fluid in the right pleural space is evident along with the defect in the chest wall, the pneumopericardium, and the hemopericardium (arrow). (CT images.)

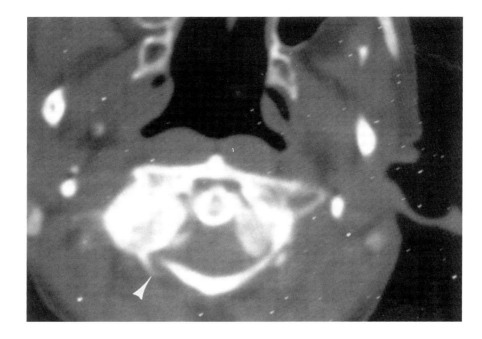

FIGURE 27.13 Fracture of the posterior elements of C1, not found or looked for in the postmortem examination. (CT examination.)

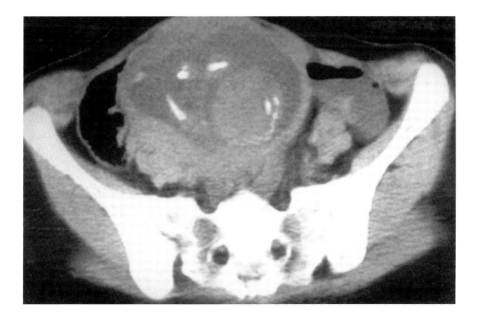

FIGURE 27.14 This woman was killed by a gunshot. She was found to be pregnant. Calcified fetal parts can be seen in utero on CT examination.

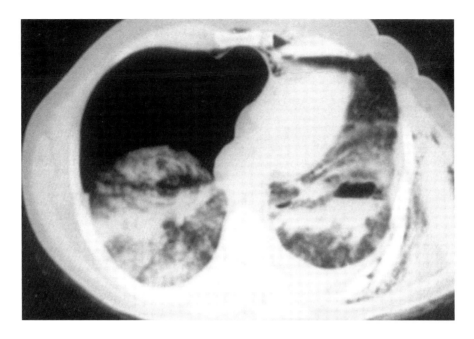

FIGURE 27.15 Examination of this victim shows multiple fractures of the left rib cage with internal displacement. There is massive swelling and hematoma of the left chest wall. There is soft tissue emphysema, interstitial and pulmonary emphysema, and pneumothorax with mediastinal shift to the left. This is massive fatal trauma. (CT examination.)

28 Virtual Autopsy with Radiological Cross-Sectional Modalities: Multislice Computed Tomography and Magnetic Resonance Imaging

Michael J. Thali, M.D., Peter Vock, M.D., and Richard Dirnhofer, M.D.

Classical radiography, based on the projection technique, reduces three-dimensional information of the body due to superposition to a plane. Exact 3-D localization of the structures or foreign bodies *in situ* is lost using the modality of classical radiography.

In contrast, modern cross-sectional imaging techniques, such as multislice computed tomography (MSCT) and magnetic resonance imaging (MRI) can provide a full-body documentation with excellent spatial resolution in all three dimensions.

We agree with Brogdon's statement made in his textbook, *Forensic Radiology*, that to date, there is no general appreciation in the forensic sciences of the potential of modern, noninvasive sectional imaging.[1]

The Institutes of Forensic Medicine and of Diagnostic Radiology of the University of Berne, Switzerland, started a feasibility study in 2000, hypothesizing that noninvasive imaging might predict autopsy findings and maybe give additional information.[2] Until July 2002, 60 forensic cases have since received a full body examination by MSCT and MRI before autopsy. After the cross-section examination, the results of virtual autopsy by MSCT and MRI were correlated with the findings of real autopsy.

In this project called Virtopsy, we used the newest generation of multidetector row CT (MSCT) and a 1.5 Tesla MR scanner. Spiral CT allows for continuous volumetric data collection within one scan. MSCT, its newest generation, was introduced in 1998 and scans complete anatomical regions within a few seconds. The acquisition of volume data also makes it possible to create new 2-D and 3-D depictions based on mathematical postprocessing of digital sectional images (e.g., 2-D multiplanar reformations [MPR], 3-D shaded surface display [SSD], and 3-D volume rendering [VR]). Using the MSCT technique, any new 2-D or 3-D views can easily be reconstructed from the native data set and used for visualization. MPR creates coronal, sagittal, and any other oblique views from the axial data set. Furthermore, it is possible to reconstruct 3-D views to visualize both soft tissues and bones.

In our preliminary experience, MRI—as compared to CT—has had a higher sensitivity, specificity, and accuracy in demonstrating soft tissue injury and organ trauma or pathology, whereas CT has evolved as a superior tool for imaging most types of skeletal trauma.

Radiological documentation offers some advantages in comparison to the standard forensic autopsy. It is rapid, objective, noninvasive, and nondestructive. We are aware that it still has to be developed and its value to be proven for the many specific forensic requests. However, we are optimistic that postmortem imaging by MSCT and MRI will become a recognized forensic examination tool in the near future, with a great potential for both documentation and visualization.

The following pictorial overview of unpublished material is intended to demonstrate some of this potential.

REFERENCES

1. Brogdon, B.G., *Forensic Radiology*, CRC Press, Boca Raton, FL, 1998.
2. Thali, M.J., Yen, K., Schweitzer, W., Vock, P., Boesch, C., Ozdoba, C., Schroth, G., Ith, M., Sonnenschein, M., Doernhofer, T., Scheurer, E., Plattner, T., and Dirnhofer, R., Virtopsy, a new imaging horizon in forensic pathology: virtual autopsy by postmortem multislice computed tomography (MSCT) and magnetic resonance imaging (MRI): a feasibility study, *J. Forensic Sci.*, in press.

FIGURE 28.1 (A) Photograph of suicidal gunshot injury through the face. Entrance wound at the mouth and exit wound at the neurocranium. **(B)** Detailed photograph of the face showing the injury of the mouth, nose, right eye, and the neurocranium. **(C)** Classical CT scout view of the head. This projectional overview is obtained in the CT scanner for planning the range of cross-sectional scanning. Like a classical radiograph, the scout view shows this massive head injury with fractures (arrow) in a predominantly anterior-posterior direction. Note the bright dental work in the mouth area. **(D)** Classical CT scout view of the trunk. This projection again gives an overview, for example, to detect or exclude foreign bodies, such as bullets, orthopaedic implants, etc. This method of digital documentation takes only a few seconds during MSCT planning.

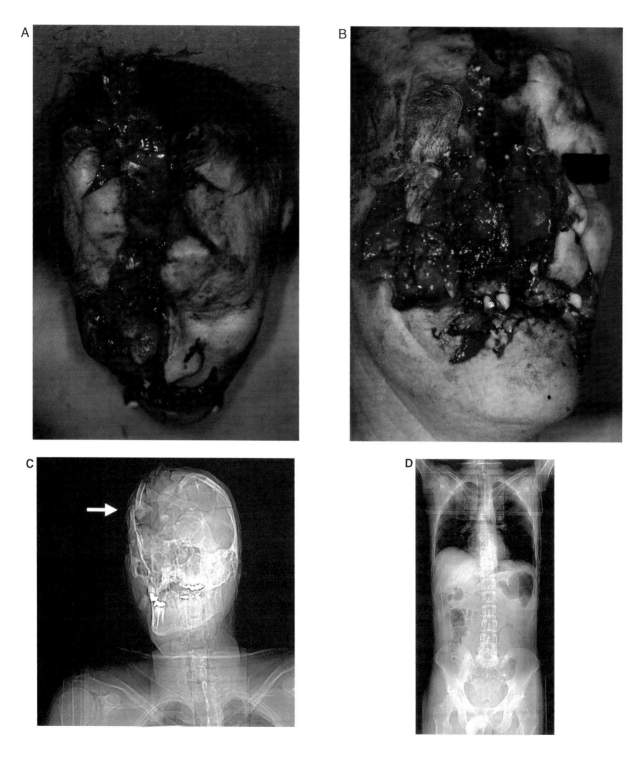

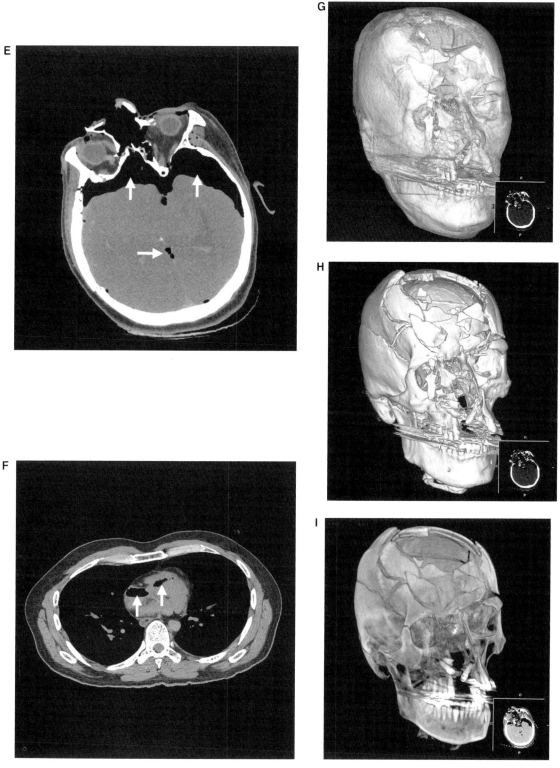

FIGURE 28.1 (Continued) (**E**) Axial CT shows the fractures in the face area; the bones supporting the nose, the orbits, and the skull base are broken. A huge intracranial air collection in the subarachnoid space and some air in cerebral vessels are additional findings caused by the gunshot injury (arrows). (**F**) The CT cross-section through the heart proves the presence of intracardiac gas embolism (arrows), which was not visible on the radiograph (scout view, Figure 28.1D). Intracardiac air embolism is a common finding after head trauma when the vessel system is injured. (**G**) 3-D reconstruction based on the MSCT data set. By using the VR technique the face is visualized in 3-D. Artefacts in the area of the mouth are caused by the dental work. (**H**) 3-D CT reconstruction of the skull using SSD. This 3-D reconstruction technique affords a better overview of the extent of the bone trauma. (**I**) Using transparent VR as visualization method, the 3-D extent of the skull injury is demonstrated even more impressively than in (**G**) and (**H**).

FIGURE 28.2 **(A)** Large entrance wound on the right temporal scalp. **(B)** Autopsy finding. Brain stem laceration with hemorrhage (arrow) above the cerebellum due to the gunshot injury. **(C)** Sagittal MR cross-section showing the brain stem avulsion (arrow) as well as other lesions to the skull and the brain. There is no damage to the cerebellum visible on this section. Note that the brain has collapsed and been replaced by air anteriorly.

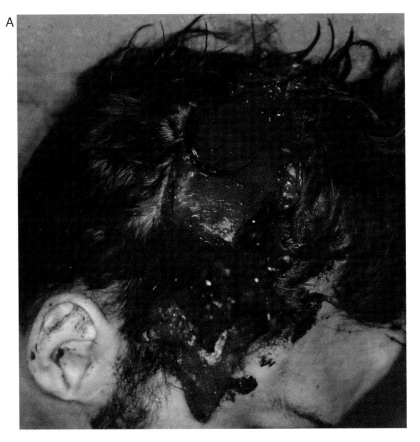

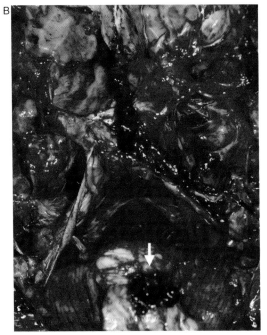

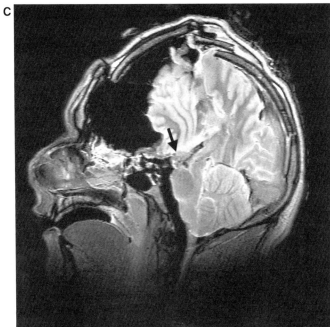

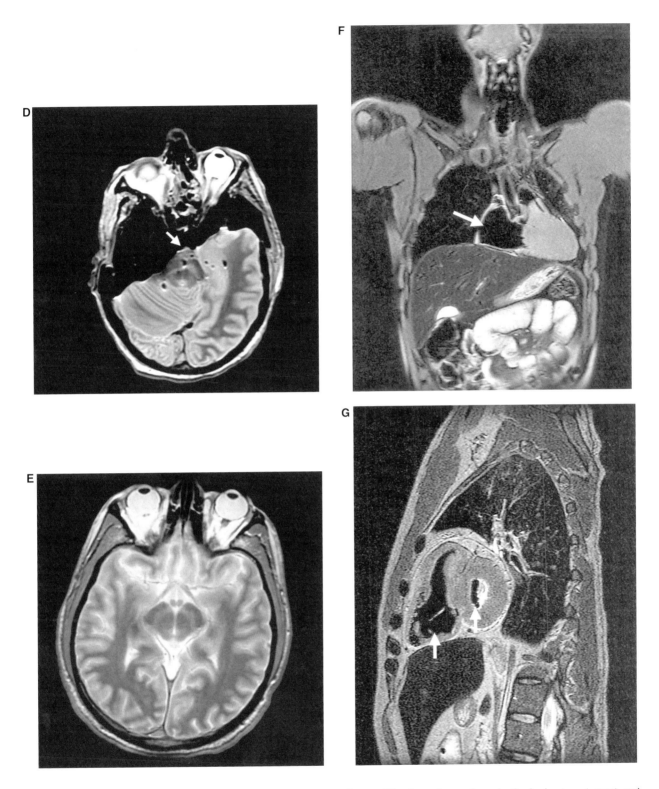

FIGURE 28.2 (Continued) (**D**) Axial MR cross-section, corresponding to (**B**), shows hemorrhage in the brain stem (arrow) and pathological air in cerebral vessels. (**E**) Normal postmortem axial MRI section of the brain some hours after death (for comparison purposes). Note the excellent visibility of anatomy including intact layers of the brain. (**F**) Coronal MRI cross-section of the above-mentioned gunshot victim, proving the presence of air in the right heart (arrow) and the pulmonary trunk. Tiny black areas of signal void in hepatic vessels represent intrahepatic gas as well. (**G**) This sagittal MRI section of the heart shows gas in the right and left ventricles (arrows).

FIGURE 28.3 Autopsy, CT, and MRI data of motor vehicle accident victim. **(A)** At autopsy, blunt force injury to the head had caused several impact abrasions of the face. **(B)** 3-D CT reconstruction of the skull, showing the underlying complex fracture system through the orbits, the midface, and the mandible. **(C)** Lateral autoptic view: the bony impaction of the face due to blunt force injury can easily be estimated from the contour of the face.

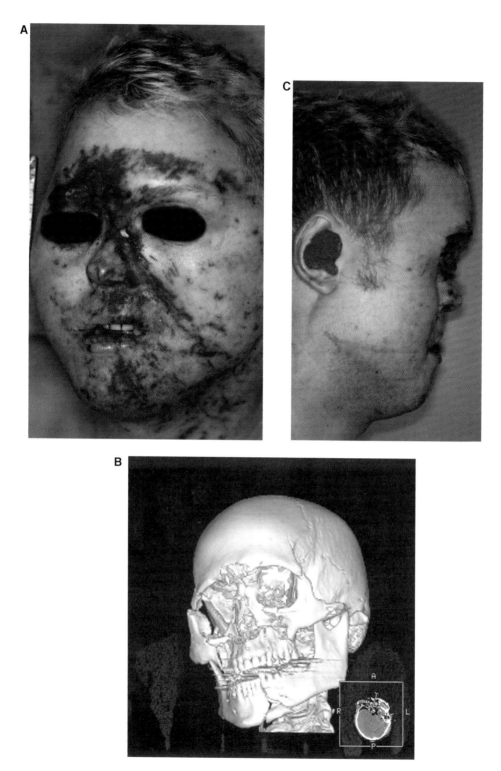

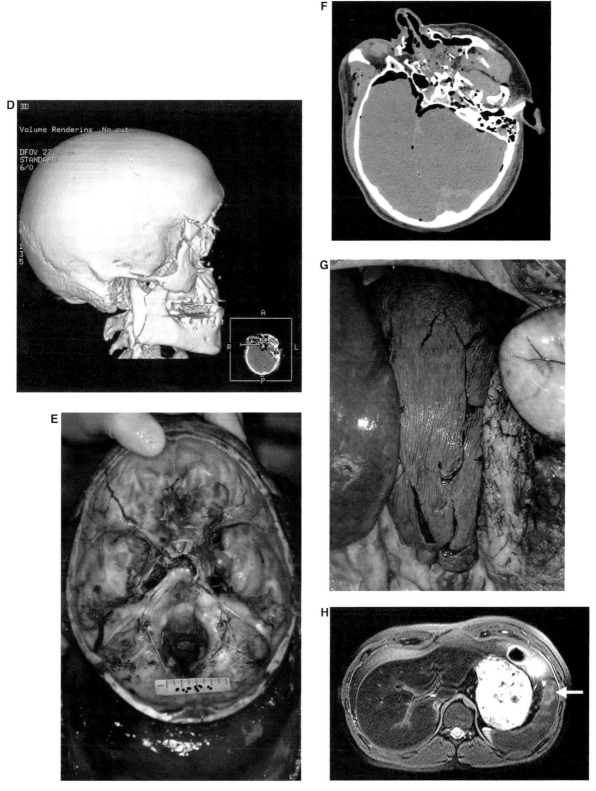

FIGURE 28.3 (Continued) Autopsy, CT, and MRI data of motor vehicle accident victim. (**D**) 3-D bony surface reconstruction of CT data, corresponding to (**C**) and showing the fracture system. (**E**) Superior view of the skull base at autopsy, showing bilateral supraorbital fractures. (**F**) This CT cross-section demonstrates a complex fronto-ethmoido-orbito-sphenoid fracture system with deformation of both the neurocranium and the viscerocranium. Intracranial air around the frontal lobes and intracranial vessels is also present. (**G**) An autopsy view of multiple lacerations of the spleen due to blunt force. (**H**) Corresponding axial MRI section, showing laceration to the spleen noninvasively (arrow).

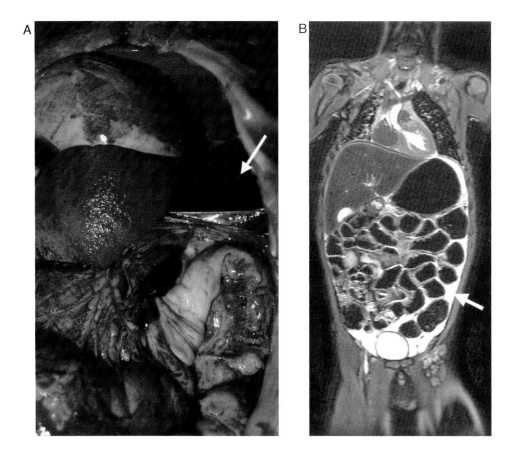

FIGURE 28.4 **(A)** Autopsy shows free blood (arrow) in the abdominal cavity due to liver trauma in a victim who was run over by a car. **(B)** This coronal MR section easily demonstrates the volume and distribution of blood in the peritoneal cavity (arrow). Note that in this T2-weighted type of MR image all types of fluid have high signal intensity and appear bright, such as blood in the heart and the peritoneal cavity, urine in the bladder, and bile in the gallbladder.

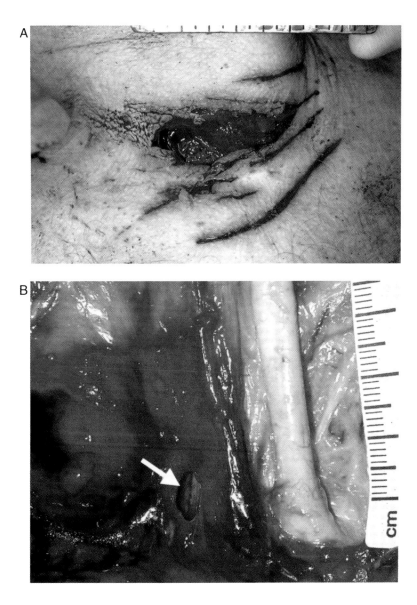

FIGURE 28.5 Autopsy and CT data of a victim with suicidal incised wound of the neck (sharp force injury). (**A**) Autopsy picture showing incised wounds of the right neck with several hesitation marks. (**B**) Close-up view of wound incision. There is partial severing of the internal jugular vein (arrow), whereas the common carotid artery (to the right of the vein on this image) is intact.

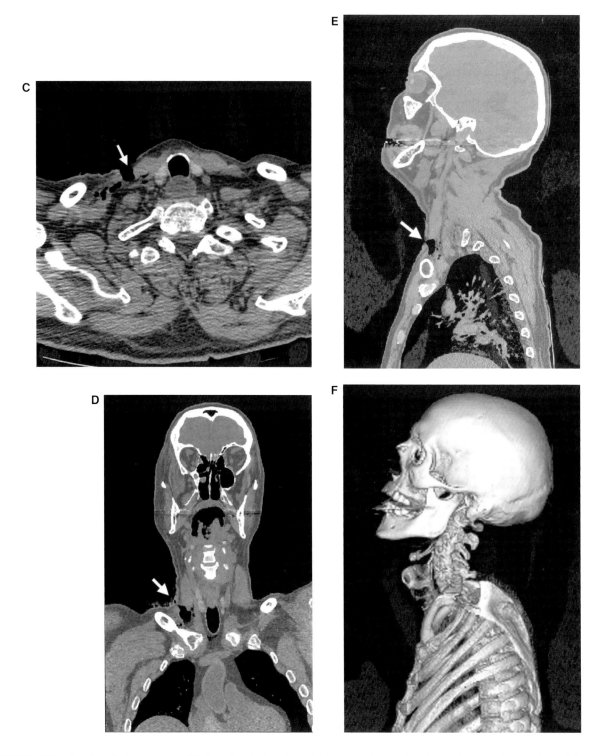

FIGURE 28.5 (Continued) Autopsy and CT data of a victim with suicidal incised wound of the neck (sharp force injury). (**C**) Axial CT cross-section. The gap in the skin lateral to the right sternocleidomastoid muscle and the depth of the incision are shown. Pathological air in and around the internal jugular vein is an indirect sign of the injury to the vein. (**D**) This reformatted coronal 2-D view of the MSCT data shows the extent of the sharp injury (arrow) and its relation to the right clavicle. Note that there is no intracardiac air in this case; the cause of death was exsanguination rather than air embolism. (**E**) This reformatted sagittal 2-D view of the MSCT data adds to the 3-D understanding of wound topography (arrow). (**F**) 3-D surface-shaded display, reconstructed from the same CT data set as (**C**) to (**E**) and visualizing the underlying bony structures and the relation of the sharp injury to the clavicle below and the laryngeal structures above.

Section VII

Border Control and Internal Security

Early in 1896 Dr. T. Bordas of the Faculty of Medicine of Paris suggested that x-rays be used on suspicious packages suggestive of being infernal machines.[1] A logical extension of that concept was the use of x-ray devices in customs houses. The Bureaux de Douanes began using fluoroscopy to examine the luggage, purses, hats, and hair of travelers for contraband in 1897 (Figure VII.I). Customs officers were looking for a wide range of smuggled items from jewels to cigarettes and matches (which were monopolies of the French government).

Today, radiologic investigation of travelers, their effects, luggage, vehicles, and unattended shipment continues to an extent never imagined a century ago, or even a decade ago.

Radiation by x-rays or gamma rays is used in a variety of ways to control borders and to provide internal security. Common targets for these radiation searches include:

1. Drugs
2. Explosives
3. Weapons
4. Cigarettes
5. Alcohol
6. Stolen vehicles
7. Jewels
8. Books
9. Tapes
10. Videos
11. Protected animals
12. Proscribed plants
13. Undocumented humans

The use of diagnostic imaging in age determination in the criminal justice system has a history of several decades. Now this technique is important in the evaluation of asylum seekers or political refugees and the determination of eligibility for military service, pensions, or other social entitlements.

The technology of radiologic applications in security operations of all types is progressing rapidly and, in some instances, with considerable secrecy. This section will attempt to illustrate some of the current uses to the extent that such information is in the public domain.

B.G.B.

H.V.

REFERENCES

1. Collins, V.P., Origins of medico-legal and forensic roent-
   genology, in *Classic Descriptions in Diagnostic Radiology*, Vol. 2, Bruwer, A.J., Ed., C.C. Thomas,
   Springfield, IL, 1964, p. 1578.

FIGURE VII.1 The French customs officer on the right uses a handheld fluoroscope to examine a piece of luggage held between the fluoroscope and a naked x-ray tube (arrow). (From Angus, W.M., *RadioGraphics*, 9, 1225, 1989. With permission.)

29 Search of the Person

B.G. Brogdon, M.D. and Hermann Vogel, M.D.

INTERNAL SEARCH

Early in the 1970s, a new breed of smuggler began to be recognized and apprehended by the radiological method.[1] This was the body packer or mule, who smuggles contraband drugs across borders in specially constructed packages to be carried hidden inside the body in the rectum, vagina, or alimentary canal. The rectum and vagina are too easily accessible for search and discovery by manual means, so the alimentary canal has become the favored internal receptacle. The early drug packages were fairly primitive, using one or more layers of latex in the form of condoms, the fingers of surgical gloves, or even toy balloons. Almost inevitably air was trapped between the layers of the latex, and these telltale crescentic shadows were easily detected by routine radiography or fluoroscopy. Those early packages were also susceptible to rupture or leakage with sometimes fatal results (Figure 4.8).

Packaging methods became more sophisticated but did not keep pace with the rapid developments in diagnostic imaging, and computed tomography (CT) examinations disclosed the internal packages with great efficiency (Figure 29.1). Obstruction has also been an occupational hazard for the body packer; consequently, the configuration of the package has been improved for more easy transport through the gut. Modern packaging is shown in Figure 29.2 as exemplified by the "bolitas" in a body packer traveling from Aruba to The Netherlands. The containers are roughly egg-shaped or oblate spheroids. There is no air entrapment, but the wall of the individual packets have become more dense to radiologic examination. They are constructed of alternating layers of latex, electric tape, and candle wax with as many as four of these compound layers per package.[2] Recently, magnetic resonance imaging (MRI) has shown a superiority over even CT in the detection of drug packets in the body (Figure 29.3).[2]

Other items can be transported in body cavities or the gastrointestinal tract including jewels. Earlier studies have shown that diamonds are virtually invisible once swallowed.[3] Other stones having higher atomic numbers become more visible. Some of the newer imaging techniques may be more effective in discovering precious stones (Figure 29.4). Small items can be transported beneath the skin.

EXTERNAL SEARCH

Smuggling of contraband materials on the body rather than inside has required a pat-down, strip search, or body search. The recent development of back-scatter imaging provides an excellent method of hands-off body search for external contraband (Figure 29.5). This system is capable of detecting metals (inorganic) materials, such as wires of a bomb, gun, blades, etc., and can also detect plastics (organic) materials such as explosives and drugs. The radiation dose is very low, comparable to a few minutes flight at 30,000 ft in a commercial aircraft. In the United States, individuals are given a choice of simply standing in front of the imaging device fully clothed, or undergoing a pat-down (in either case conducted by a member of the same sex). The suspect must consent to the search by radiation. It is said never to be used in secret in the United States. In other countries, there are reports that similar devices are used on unsuspecting travelers.

Of course fluoroscopy, using penetrating radiation, is also used to search the person and shows the object of search in superimposition on anatomic structures, whereas the back-scatter imaging system does not penetrate the skin. Although radiation dosage is higher with the fluoroscopy method (Figure 29.6), it is also used on unsuspecting persons in some parts of the world.

AGE DETERMINATION

Internal search of the human body by radiologic methods in order to determine the age of an individual has several indications that can be important both to the individual and the state. Age determination at time of death may be an important step toward identification of unknown remains. It may modify both trial and punishment in criminal cases. In civil matters, age is an important determinant in terms of eligibility for military service, retirement benefits, health care, or other entitlements. Of particular significance to this chapter is the radiologic investigation of age in asylum seekers, political refugees, or illegal immigrants.

There are many methods of radiologic age determination based on skeletal maturation of certain body parts or cumulative analysis of several body areas. Standards for these determinations are readily available from both primary and secondary sources.[4–12] Other systems of radiologic investigation, sonography, scintigraphy, CT, and MRI are less commonly employed.[13,14]

The sequence of dental eruption also is a useful guide to age determination (see Chapter 24).

Age determination based on skeletal and dental maturation is useful and accurate only into early adulthood. These are variations from published standards attributed to race, nutrition, disease, metabolism, and intoxication (i.e., lead or fluoride). One must allow a range of approximately two standard deviations from the norm.

The sternal end of the clavicle has been utilized for evaluation of the late second to the middle third decade of life. Four stages have been suggested:

1. No medial ossification center on the clavicle (16 years or less)
2. Separate but ossified medial epiphysis (age 13 to 22 years)
3. Partial union of the medial epiphysis (16 to 26 years)
4. Complete union of epiphysis from age 22 to age 27 when 100% are fused[16,17]

Estimates of aging past early adulthood by radiologic evaluation of cortical thickness, demineralization of bone, degenerative changes, and laryngeal and costal cartilage calcification or ossification are fraught with error and inaccuracy.[18]

There are ethical problems with radiologic age determination. In some countries, there is great resistance from both the public and physicians to radiation exposure without a *medical* indication. This problem comes to ultimate resolution in the courts.

REFERENCES

1. Brogdon, B.G., *Forensic Radiology*, CRC Press, Boca Raton, FL, 1998, chap. 12.
2. Marugg, R.C., personal communication, 2002.
3. Brogdon, B.G., *Forensic Radiology*, CRC Press, Boca Raton, FL, 1998, chap. 13.
4. Graham, C.B., Assessment of bone maturation: methods and pitfalls, *Radiol. Clin. N. Am.*, 10, 185, 1972.
5. Girdany, B.R. and Golden, R., Centers of ossification of the skeleton, *Am. J. Roentgenol.*, 68, 922, 1952.
6. Keats, T.E., *Atlas of Roentgenographic Measurement*, 6th ed., Mosby Year Book, St. Louis, 1990, chap. 4B.
7. Meschan, I., *Roentgen Signs in Clinical Practice*, Vol. I, W.B. Saunders, Philadelphia, 1966, chap. 4.
8. Sontag, I.W., Snell, D., and Anderson, M., Rate of appearance of ossification centers from birth to the age of five years, *Am. J. Dis. Child.*, 58, 949, 1939.
9. Pyle, S.I. and Hoerr, N.L., *Atlas of Skeletal Development of the Knee*, C.C. Thomas, Springfield, IL, 1955.
10. Hoerr, N.L., Pyle, S.I., and Francis, C.C., *Radiologic Atlas of the Foot and Ankle*, C.C. Thomas, Springfield, IL, 1962.
11. Greulich, W.W. and Pyle, S.I., *Radiographic Atlas of Skeletal Development of the Hand and Wrist*, 2nd ed., Stanford University Press, Palo Alto, CA, 1959.
12. Ontell, F.K., Ivanovic, M., Ablin, D.S., and Barlow, T.W., Bone age in children in diverse ethnicity, *Am. J. Roentgenol.*, 167, 1395, 1996.
13. Brossmann, J., Stabler, A., Preidler, K.W., Trudell, D., and Resnick, D., Sternoclavicular joint: MR imaging-anatomic correlation, *Radiology*, 198, 193, 1996.
14. Guillet, J., Guillet, C., and Blanauet, P., Evaluation radio-isotopique de la croissance et de la maturation osseues, *Sem. Hop. Paris.*, 38, 2199, 1982.
15. Kreitner, K.F., Schweden, F., Piepert, T., Nafe, B., and Thelen, M., Bone age determination of the clavicle: review article, *Europ. Radiol.*, 8, 1116, 1998.
16. Kreitman, K.F., Schweden, F., Schild, H.H., Ripert, T., and Nafe, B., Die computerotomographisch bestimmte Ausreifung der medialen Klaikularepiphyse- eine Additive Methode zur Alterbstimmung im Adoleszentalter und in der dritten Lebensdekade?, *Fortschr. Rontgenstr.*, 166, 481, 1997.
17. Brogdon, B.G., *Forensic Radiology*, CRC Press, Boca Raton, FL, 1998, chap. 5.
18. Butting, H., Die computertomographisch ermittelte Ausreifung der medialen Calvicularepiphyse als Untersuchungsmethode der Lebenslaterbestimmung, Inaug. Diss., Unwersität Hamburg, 2002.

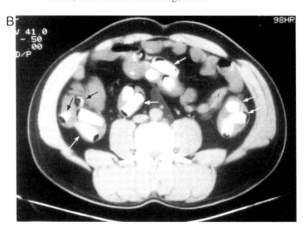

FIGURE 29.1 CT images of a body packer. The drug packets are easily discerned by density and configuration as well as by the entrapped air. (Courtesy of Dr. Richard N. Aizpuru.)

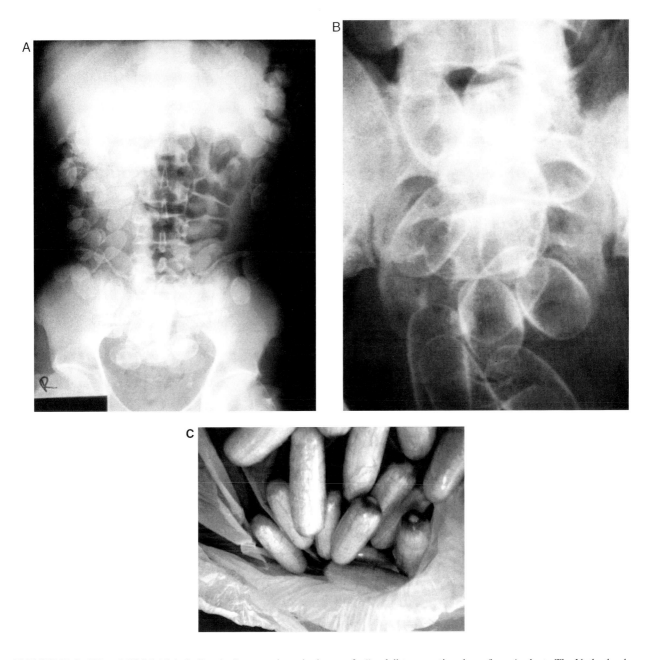

FIGURE 29.2 (A) and (B) Multiple bolitas in the gastrointestinal tract of a "mule" transporting drugs from Aruba to The Netherlands. (Courtesy of Dr. Paul R. Algra, Alkmaar, The Netherlands.) (C) Photograph of the retrived bolitas. (Courtesy of Dr. R.C. Marugg.)

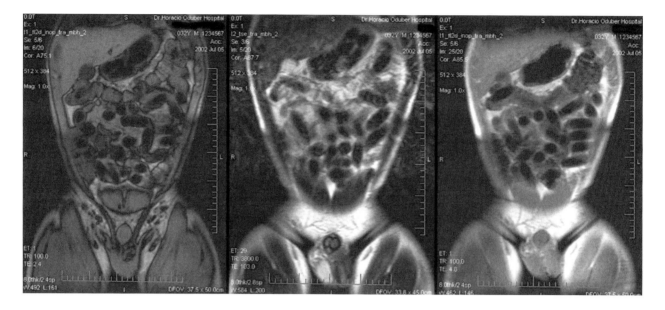

FIGURE 29.3 MR images using three different protocols, all of which show the drug packets with superb clarity. These are provided by Dr. R.C. Marugg, radiologist at the Dr. Horacio E. Oduber Hospital in Aruba. He reports that he finds more drug packets with MR than with CT examination of the same subject.

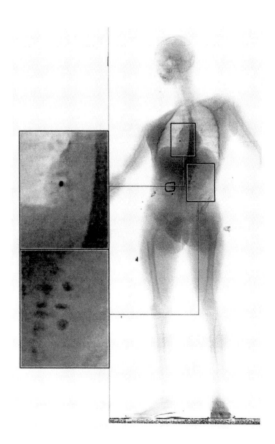

FIGURE 29.4 Full body fluoroscopy scan showing precious stones in the esophagus and gastrointestinal tract (Hamburg).

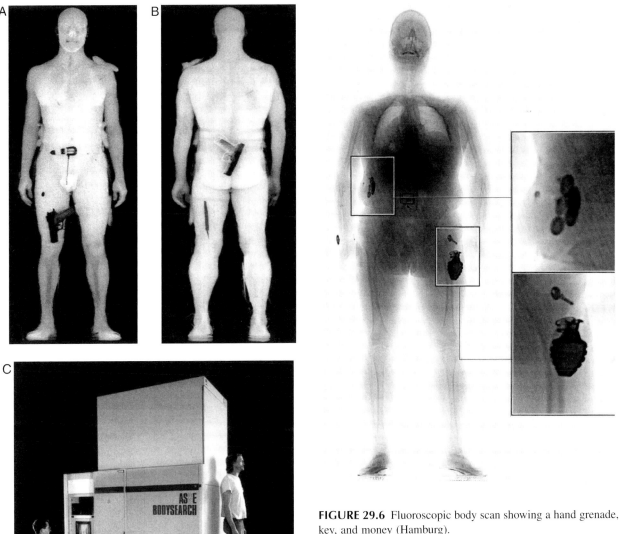

FIGURE 29.6 Fluoroscopic body scan showing a hand grenade, key, and money (Hamburg).

FIGURE 29.5 Frontal and rear images of a model with hidden contraband obtained with the BodySearch™ device made by American Science and Engineering Incorporated of Billerica, MA. **(A)** In the frontal view, a gun and other metal objects, as well as several organic packets of explosives or drugs are visible. **(B)** In the rear view, a plastic Glock 17 hand gun, Plexiglas knife, and simulated drug packets, as well as a metal file and a stainless steel scalpel blade are seen. **(C)** BodySearch imaging device with operator and model suspect. (Courtesy of A.S.&E., Inc. With permission.)

FIGURE 29.7 Examples of age determination by evaluation of the ossification of the medial end of the clavicle. **(A)** Stage I—no ossification of the medial epiphysis, up to 16 years of age. This patient was aged 10 years, 10 months. **(B)** Stage II—a separate identifiable ossification center, not united with the medial metaphysis of the clavicle, consistent with age 13 to 22 years. This patient is 17 years, 1 month of age. **(C)** Stage III—observed from age 16 to age 26. There is partial union of the epiphysis. This patient is 20 years, 6 months of age. **(D)** Stage IV—complete union of the epiphysis with the metaphysis at the medial end of the clavicle, observed not before age 22 and in 100% at age 27. **(E and F)** It may be difficult or even impossible to differentiate between stages I and IV by CT alone since the appearance is much the same. **(E)** is a child 11 years, 5 months of age with no appearance of the medial epiphysis. **(F)** is of an adult age 27 years, 3 months with total union of the medial epiphysis of the clavicle. (Courtesy of H. Butting, University of Hamburg.) (From Butting, H., Die computertomographisch ermittelte Ausreifung der medialan Calvicularepiphyse als Unterschungsmethode der Lebenslaterbestimmung, Inaug. Diss., Unwersität Hamburg, 2002. With permission.)

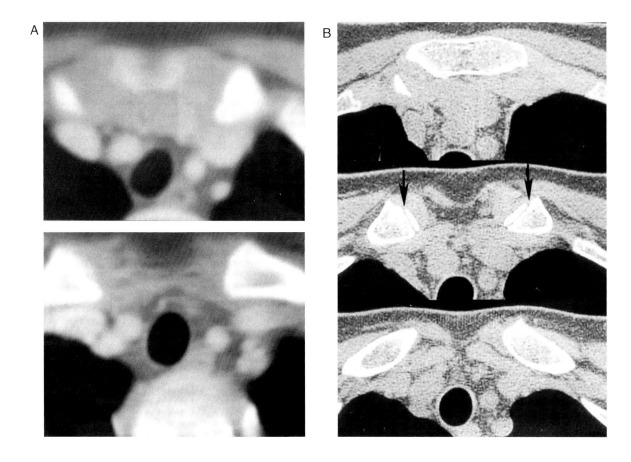

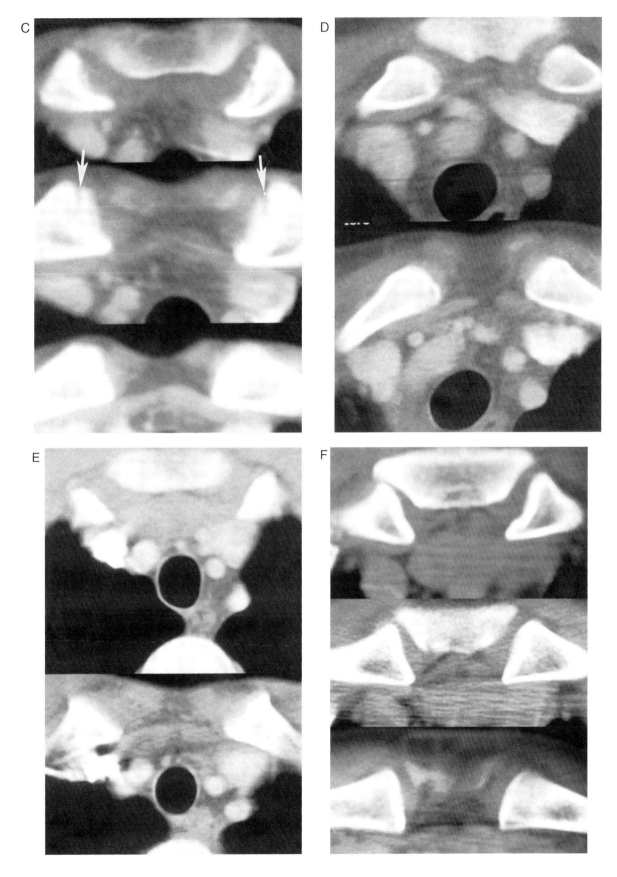

FIGURE 29.7 (Continued) (C to F).

30 Search of Luggage, Cargo, and Transport

Hermann Vogel, M.D. and B.G. Brogdon, M.D.

At international borders and at internal control points, governmental control agencies are using x-rays and gamma rays to inspect and control not only persons (as described in Chapter 29), but also goods and the systems that transport them. Radiation systems employed range from conventional industrial x-rays through accelerators with 5 to 10 MeV energy through gamma ray units using sealed sources of cesium 137 or cobalt 60. Transparency (fluoroscopic) images and analysis of forward and backward radiation scatter are used. Transparency or fluoroscopy images show the object in question in superimposition upon its container and other contents. Computed tomography used for luggage inspection produces a digital image without superimposition. The identification of chemical components is possible by means of analysis of scatter radiation.[1-4] The addition of a color palette by computer manipulation aids in identification of specific substances.

Explosives, transported in luggage or other carriers, can only be identified indirectly or suspected on transparency images. Double imaging or scatter systems, particularly if color can be added, can provide direct identification (Figure 30.1). Illegal transport of protected species can be detected by similar methods (Figure 30.2). Narcotics can be detected by radiologic inspection of luggage where even a visual inspection might fail (Figure 30.3).

For some years the Israeli National Police used a simple industrial x-ray machine to identify auto theft and auto forgery. Often, a new identity is created for a stolen vehicle by transferring the vehicle identification number (VIN) and key parts from a wrecked vehicle to a stolen vehicle. Properly positioned radiographs readily display the telltale welding seams of the forged VIN on the stolen auto (Figure 30.4). Since then, very sophisticated integrated systems for examining vehicles and their contents have been developed. For instance, SAIC, a U.S.-based, employee-owned company, pioneered gamma-ray-based inspection systems to develop a vehicle and cargo inspection system (VACIS). This system uses highly penetrative gamma rays, sensitive image receptors, and video monitors in a variety of configurations which can scan large containers with a track driven system; rail cars as they pass through port entry points; mobile platforms, which can be set up quickly; and systems for imaging pallets or pallet-size containers. This system can inspect moving vehicles as well as stationary ones and still produce high detailed images. Examples of images generated by SAIC's VACIS system are shown (Figure 30.5).

Other imaging systems for large vehicles and their contents have been developed elsewhere. Even China is producing a fluoroscopic system with a fixed detector and a movable source.

There are special restrictions and uses in some locations. In Germany, for instance, exposure of food by x-rays or gamma rays is not allowed. The unit in the Port of Hamburg is operated so as to prevent the direct radiation exposure of people. Pamphlets and Internet information available from some manufacturers suggest they do not bother to prevent direct radiation exposure of human beings, such as truck drivers or passengers (Figure 30.6). Furthermore, the exposure of the equipment operator often is not discussed. Operators of these detection devices look for:

1. Densities where there should be voids (Figure 30.7)
2. Motion where there should be stillness (Figure 30.8)
3. Symmetry where there should be symmetry (Figure 30.9)
4. Ominous silhouettes, particularly of weapons (Figure 30.10)

REFERENCES

1. Lotz, P., Durchleuchtung an Grenzen Die Container-durchleuchtungsanlage am Hanburger Hafen, Inaugural Diss., Hamburg, 2002.
2. Seche, A., Das Rontgenauge der Zoufahnder, Peter Moosleitners Magazine, *P.M. Diemoderne Welt des Wissens*, Mai 2002, 38.
3. Halter, H., Es gibt Entrinnen-uber die radioaktiven Grenzkontrollen der DDr, Der Spiegel, 51, 1994, p. 176.
4. Eisenfeld, H. et al., Einsatz von Röntgenstrahler und radioaktiven Stoffen durch das Ministerium fur Staatssicherheit gegen Opositionelle-Fiktion der Realitat? De Bundesbeauftragte fur die Unterlagen des Staatssicherheitsdienstes der ehemaligen DDR, Projektgruppe Strahlen, 2000, Berlin.

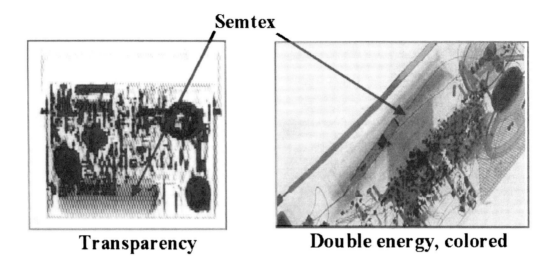

FIGURE 30.1 Semtex plastic explosive can only be suspected inside a radio with ordinary transparency or fluoroscopic imagery. The addition of double energy analysis and color palette makes detection much easier.

FIGURE 30.2 Smuggled protected species (salamanders) in a suitcase.

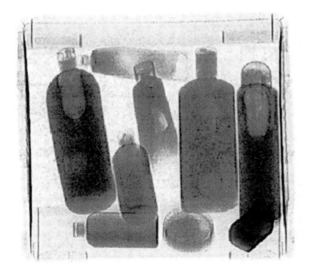

FIGURE 30.3 Perfume bottles in a box. Some of them have a condom fitted in the neck of the bottle, with drugs inside the condom.

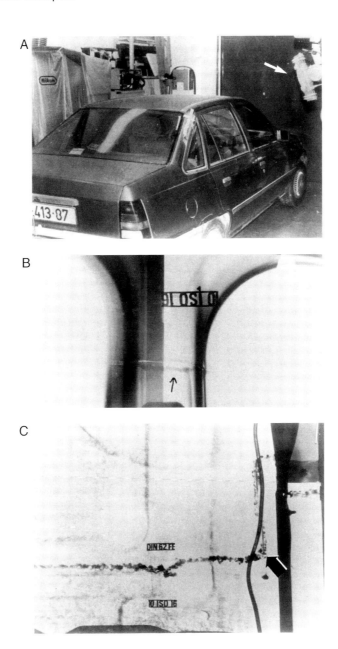

FIGURE 30.4 (**A**) An industrial x-ray tube in the upper right-hand corner of the photo (arrow) is positioned to radiograph the door post of a suspected stolen and re-identified automobile. (**B**) Radiograph (positive print) shows a nonoriginal welding seam (arrow) on the door post below the number from a wrecked car. (**C**) Radiograph (positive print) of the flooring in the front passenger compartment showing nonoriginal welding. (From Springer, E. and Bergman, P., Applications of non-destructive testing (NDT) in vehicle forgery examinations, *J. Forensic Sci.*, 39, 751, 1994. With permission.) (Copyright ASTM International. Reprinted with permission.)

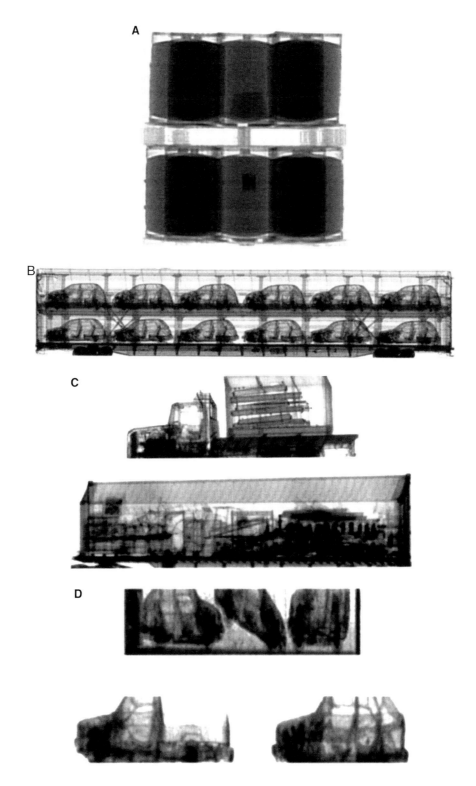

FIGURE 30.5 (**A**) Pallet image obtained in a self-shielded dedicated unit that can become operational in a matter of minutes. (**B**) Image of a railroad car hauling new automobiles as it passes through the gamma-ray beam at speeds up to 10 mph. Even at those speeds a high resolution image is produced, yet the gamma-ray radiation is at a low enough level to pose no risk to stowaways who may be inadvertently scanned. (**C**) Truck-mounted mobile gamma-ray imaging systems can inspect both stationary and moving vehicles. The beam source is not opened until the driver of the vehicle is clear, keeping radiation exposure to no more than normal background. (**D**) A high throughput system for port gates and roadways to scan the contents as the vehicles pass through can be configured to meet special needs, such as the detection of stolen automobiles. (Images courtesy of SAIC, 16701 West Bernardo Drive, San Diego, CA, 92127).

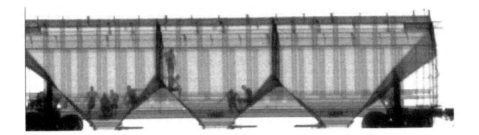

FIGURE 30.6 Stowaways imaged in a railway hopper car (Mexico).

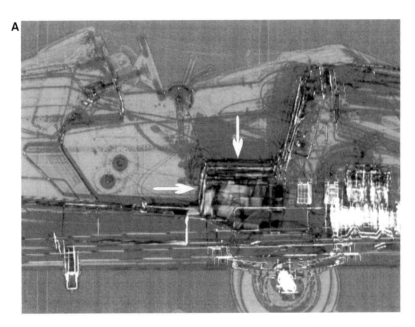

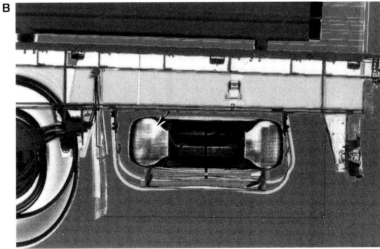

FIGURE 30.7 (A) Densities (drug packages) under the front seat of an automobile where there should be a clear space (Hamburg). **(B)** Cigarette cartons in the spare tire under a truck. Notice how clear the air-filled tire on the ground just in front of the tire is, as compared to the spare carrying drugs (Hamburg).

FIGURE 30.8 Liquid in containers inside a truck makes a wavy pattern as it sloshes around. This is illegal alcohol being hauled in a truck supposedly loaded with solid freight.

A

FIGURE 30.9 (**A**) This is a truck full of lemons.

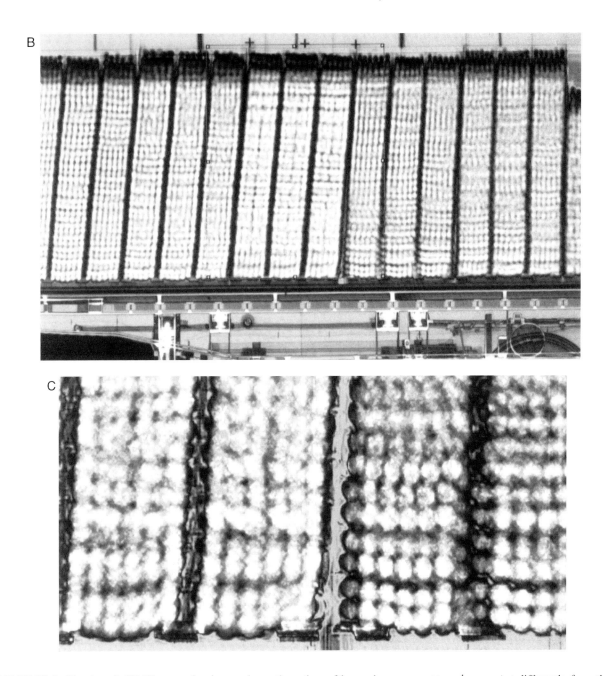

FIGURE 30.9 (Continued) **(B)** The scanning image shows three tiers of lemon boxes are patterned somewhat differently from the rest. **(C)** Close-up showing the "funny lemons" on viewer's left. These actually were packages of cocaine shaped and wrapped like real lemons.

FIGURE 30.10 This truck is loaded with household items, but clearly visible in one of the cartons is the profile of a military weapon standing on its muzzle (arrowheads) (Hamburg).

Index